JANE AUSTEN
AND HER ART

BY

MARY LASCELLES

OXFORD UNIVERSITY PRESS

OXFORD LONDON NEW YORK

Oxford University Press, Walton Street, Oxford OX2 6DP

OXFORD LONDON GLASGOW
NEW YORK TORONTO MELBOURNE WELLINGTON
KUALA LUMPUR SINGAPORE JAKARTA HONG KONG TOKYO
DELHI BOMBAY CALCUTTA MADRAS KARACHI
NAIROBI DAR ES SALAAM CAPE TOWN

ISBN 0 19 881061 X

© *Mary Lascelles 1939*

First published by the Clarendon Press 1939
First issued as an Oxford University Press paperback 1963
This reprint 1979

*Printed in Great Britain
at the University Press, Oxford
by Eric Buckley
Printer to the University*

PREFACE

I SUPPOSE that it must happen to writers on every one of the most generally interesting subjects of literary criticism to be told very often in the course of their writing that everything worth saying on that subject has been said already. And it is likely that they may all feel (as I do), as they wind themselves into it, that all who have written before them have stopped short as they were arriving at the most interesting point. In Jane Austen's case there is at least this particular justification for such an impression, that the most part of Dr. Chapman's work has taken the direction of biographical investigation in which criticism is incidental, and the professed critics—such as A. C. Bradley, Saintsbury, Walter Raleigh, John Bailey, and Dr. Chapman himself in his few critical papers—have all chosen to work on a small scale—so small that the reader does not see how they have reached their conclusions until he has patiently found his own way to them. Is this perhaps a characteristic of that generation of critics, that they exclaim with Jonson 'By God, 'tis good, and if you like't, you may', and carry entire conviction—but leave us at the beginning of the exciting 'how?' and 'why?' of analysis? At least I am sure that while quotations from Bradley's essay might well head most parts of this book I should not have realized all that they meant if I had not written it.

There may, then, still be something to say about Jane Austen; there is certainly much to be said about narrative art. When so important a critic as Professor Stoll tells us that 'all narrative art seems . . . to aspire towards the condition of drama',[1] and the most illuminating writer on the art of the novel tries to drive a wedge between the 'art of narrative' and the 'art of fiction'[2]—then it is surely time to look into the story-teller's peculiar problems.

But, it may be objected, is it at this time worth while to study narrative art in so simple a form as that which it

[1] E. E. Stoll, *Art and Artifice in Shakespeare*, 1933, p. 60.
[2] P. Lubbock, *The Craft of Fiction*, 1921, p. 62.

assumes in Jane Austen's novels? Without as yet accepting
or denying the implications of such an objection, I am content to answer that the simplicity of Jane Austen's work is
the simplicity of a thing made with simple tools; and
although we cannot go back on our (sometimes troublesome) benefactors, the inventors, we must value, may love,
and should examine, what was well made before they got to
work. But this answer may itself provoke objection from
those who, with Mr. Read, think admirers of this sort of
simplicity disagreeably eccentric;[1] and to them I can only
say that I am satisfied with the company in which I find
myself. To the more common charge—that my subject
was herself disagreeable—I can offer no answer, unless one
should be found implicit in this book, because I understand
it less as I become more familiar with her writings. It is
based on one coarse and ill-natured passage, two or three
ill-humoured and two or three sharply satirical passages, in
her letters—or so I must assume from the invariable quotation of these passages every time it is renewed. The censor
who has never suffered the shame of recollecting equivalent
words of his own is much to be envied, whether for the
goodness of his disposition or the badness of his memory.

I hope, then, in this book to give some account first of
Jane Austen—approaching her by way of a brief narrative
of her life and an inquiry into the scope, the quality, and
the outcome of her reading—and then of her art, approached
through her use of language and studied most fully in
relation to the narrator's peculiar problems.

I have to thank the English Association for permission
to reproduce much of the substance of an essay which
appeared in a recent volume of *Essays and Studies*.

To the chief sources of information about Jane Austen—
to her brother's *Biographical Notice*, her nephew's *Memoir*,
and the delightful *Life and Letters* of William Austen-Leigh
and Mr. R. A. Austen-Leigh—I am, of course, deeply
indebted. And I hope that my notes will make clear the
extent of my debt to other informants. But it must be
evident from the first that to none can I owe so much as to

[1] H. Read, *English Prose Style*, 1928, p. 120 n.

Dr. Chapman, not only for all that his invaluable editions contain but for suggestions, encouragement, and kindness. To other friends also, and in particular to Mrs. Geoffrey Tillotson, I am obliged for stimulating talk and a patient hearing.

To Miss Spens I owe all that is customarily implied in a Dedication.

1938 M. M. L.

A NOTE ON REFERENCES

IN referring to Jane Austen's six novels, I give the number of the page as it appears in Dr. Chapman's edition, followed by the number of the chapter as it would appear in any other modern edition. For her letters and other unpublished writings, I refer likewise to his editions. References to the letters are simple; those to the other writings require a little explanation. When I completed my book, Dr. Chapman had already edited (in separate volumes) practically all of Jane Austen's unpublished work other than those three note-books of juvenilia entitled *Volume the First*, *Second*, and *Third*; but of these we had only the *First* from his hand. *Volume the Second* had appeared (with a preface by G. K. Chesterton) under the title of its principal content, *Love and Freindship*, and it was by this name, therefore, that I referred to it, and to all that it contained. *Volume the Third* had not been printed, nor was it accessible to me in manuscript; it had therefore to be left out of my account. This latter note-book has since been edited by Dr. Chapman, who has moreover now gathered all these and some smaller pieces into a single volume of *Minor Works*. Thus, for Jane Austen's tales, fragments, and drafts, except the contents of *Volume the Second*, we have two editions from his hand; differing in that the earlier records the traces of revision discernible in her manuscripts. Mindful of the diverse needs of readers possessing these different editions, I have retained my original page-reference for every passage quoted, but added another, to the *Minor Works*—*except* where the subject under discussion was Jane Austen's practice in revision.[1]

For her brother's *Biographical Notice* and her nephew's *Memoir* also I refer to Dr. Chapman's editions, except in those instances where it was necessary to use the first edition of the *Memoir*, or a passage from that part of the second which his edition does not reproduce.

For other books I have, of course, referred to the first editions, except where an authoritative collected edition of the author's works seemed preferable. In references to novels, mindful of the difficulty of getting access to a first edition of many of those I cited, I have given the number not of the page but of the chapter.

In my necessarily brief account of Jane Austen's life (intended only as a foundation to the critical part of this book) I have, I hope methodically, preferred the earliest source of information, except where a later source of equal authority gave fuller detail—for example, where the *Life* was fuller than the *Memoir*.

[1] Since this was written, the second note-book, formerly known as *Love and Freindship* has joined the other two, under its proper title *Volume the Second* (ed. B. C. Southam, Oxford, 1963). [M.M.L.]

CONTENTS

PART I

PART II

FULL TITLES OF WORKS TO WHICH FREQUENT REFERENCE IS MADE

H. AUSTEN, *A Biographical Notice of the Author* prefixed to *Northanger Abbey and Persuasion*, 1818 (reprinted with slight alteration in Bentley's collected edition of J. A.'s novels; the version of 1818 reprinted in R. W. C.'s edition of *Northanger Abbey and Persuasion*).

J. E. AUSTEN-LEIGH, *A Memoir of Jane Austen*, 1870 (reprinted with parts of J. A.'s unfinished works, 1871; the second edition, with some of the additions, reprinted, R. W. C., 1926).

M. A. AUSTEN-LEIGH, *Personal Aspects of Jane Austen*, 1920.

R. A. AUSTEN-LEIGH and W. AUSTEN-LEIGH, *Jane Austen: Her Life and Letters*, 1913.

A. C. BRADLEY, 'Jane Austen', in *Essays and Studies by Members of the English Association*, 1911.

E. M. FORSTER, *Aspects of the Novel*, 1927.

H. W. GARROD, 'Jane Austen: A Depreciation', in *Essays by Divers Hands* (*Transactions of the Royal Society of Literature*), 1928.

C. HILL, *Jane Austen: Her Homes and Friends*, 1902.

P. LUBBOCK, *The Craft of Fiction*, 1921.

W. SCOTT, review of *Emma* in the *Quarterly Review*, vol. xiv (for 1815; appeared 1816).

VIRGINIA WOOLF, *The Common Reader*, 1925.

PART I
JANE AUSTEN

She was ful mesurable, as wommen be.
CHAUCER, Squire's Tale

CHAPTER I

BIOGRAPHY

JANE AUSTEN was born on the 16th of December 1775 at Steventon rectory in the county of Hampshire, and there spent her years of childhood and youth. Steventon lies in fresh upland country, which holds copses tucked into folds of the ground and lanes sunk in the chalk and overhung by yews. Above, Steventon warren with its close texture of herbage and its junipers looks as though it had never been very different and would not easily be changed; below, the taller elms mark the courses of the valleys. All still keeps some air of privacy and retirement.

Of landscape Jane Austen says little in her novels; but that little is to the point. She gives, as a countrywoman would, the county and the season, and expects the *mind's eye* of the reader, supported by memory and imagination, to form the visible background of her stories for itself. Her family have recorded her 'love of the country and delight in natural scenery';[1] and some part of her range of observation is reflected in Fanny Price's mind on the way from Mansfield to Sotherton, when 'in observing the appearance of the country, the bearings of the roads, the difference of soil, the state of the harvest, the cottages, the cattle, the children, she found entertainment . . .'—while Mary Crawford, on the other hand, wanting 'Fanny's delicacy of taste, of mind, of feeling . . . saw inanimate nature with little observation'.[2] There is indeed little, if any, landscape in her novels, hardly a field or hedgerow, but is presented through the eyes of a character. Each is coloured, and so differentiated from the rest, by the mind and mood of the imagined observer. But all alike show cognizance of man's handiwork, the outcome of his draining and felling and planting. So much of herself their author imparts to each.

For Jane Austen, humankind was of first importance; and in her human world her own family stood foremost.

[1] Constance Hill, *Jane Austen: Her Homes and Friends*, 1902, pp. 91, 92 (quoting 'Family MSS.').   [2] *Mansfield Park*, pp. 80, 81, ch. viii.

She was by no means confined to its society,[1] but she was never, unless in short visits to her intimate friends, quite separated from it. When she left her own home it might be to travel in company with her parents or her sister, to stay for a while in the home of some of her connexions, or (so soon as they had homes of their own) of one or another of her brothers. From the beginning she was accustomed to the pressure of close quarters on a large family whose notions of hospitality were liberal, pressure under which an individualist would lose spirit or else rebel. She learnt how to lead her life unperturbed in a throng—and so eventually to lead, besides, that other, subterranean life which the novelist must pass in the company of his fictitious creatures if he is to persuade the reader of their authenticity. Jane Austen's family was indeed so important in her life that it may be as well to say something, here, of the two genera-tions that made up the Steventon household, and—later—of the youngest generation which knew her after she had left Steventon.

Her father, George Austen, was gentle and strongly attached to his family; he occupied himself with the cares of his parish, his farm, and his pupils, and left a reputation for scholarship and literary taste which was supported in his day by his having prepared two of his sons, with other pupils, for Oxford, and rests more firmly now on his quick perception of his daughter's gifts. Mrs. Austen[2] was a countrywoman and busy gardener, with vital energy enough to carry her through long stretches of ill health. She was mistress of that terse, forcible mode of expression that is neighbour to wit,[3] and keenly enjoyed comedy—the broad comedy of Lady Catherine and Mr. Collins;[4] and she liked, when she was old, the ungenteel vantage-point of a window

---

[1] The author of the *Memoir* gives—perhaps not deliberately—such an impression, which the authors of the *Life* show to be misleading.

[2] She had been Miss Cassandra Leigh.

[3] *Memoir*, p. 11. Jane speaks appreciatively of her mother's letter-writing (*Letters*, p. 367).

[4] *Life*, p. 328. All the opinions of the Austens and their friends to which no particular reference is given are cited from the collection quoted in the *Life* (pp. 328–331); since this was made in J. A.'s lifetime it does not, of course, take *Northanger Abbey* nor *Persuasion* into account.

overlooking a village street.[1] In Jane's own generation, the
eldest was James, whose career—at Oxford, in his first
curacy, and, when he succeeded his father, at Steventon—
never carried him far from his sisters, and who played a
constant if unobtrusive part in their lives. He dabbled
modestly in letters. Edward was adopted, while a boy, by
his distant cousins—Thomas and Catherine Knight of Godmersham in Kent—who brought him up to be their heir.[2]
His share in the family life became larger when he married
and settled in a home of his own, to be visited often by his
brothers and sisters. Henry, next in age after Edward, was
thought by the rest to have been closest of all the brothers
to Jane herself in sympathy and understanding; his reputation among them for brilliance and unfulfilled promise
puzzled even the succeeding generation[3] and is now little
more than a ghostly echo of wit, for it depends, not on any
fragment of his writing that survives, but on his sister's
response—'he cannot help being amusing . . .'.[4] He was
certainly of a sanguine,[5] probably of a happy disposition,
with its peculiar charm. Cassandra, most important of them
all in Jane's life, yet remains the most shadowy. A strong
and subtle sympathy bound these two together. 'They were
everything to each other', wrote the one of their nieces who
had known them longest. 'They seemed to lead a life to
themselves within the general family life which was shared
only by each other. I will not say their true, but their *full*,
feelings and opinions were known only to themselves. They
alone fully understood what each had suffered and felt and
thought.'[6] Outside this charmed circle Cassandra left a reputation for sterling sense—*Mansfield Park* was her favourite
among the novels—and, in Jane's letters, as faint an echo
of raillery as Henry's—'You are indeed the finest comic
writer of the present age.'[7] If a hoard of lost letters were
still to come to light, I could wish that they might be

---

[1] M. A. Austen-Leigh, *Personal Aspects of Jane Austen* (1920), p. 141.
[2] He took the name of Knight in 1812.
[3] *Life*, p. 49.   [4] *Letters*, p. 152.
[5] He was successively, and apparently with equal enthusiasm, militia officer,
banker, and clergyman.
[6] *Personal Aspects*, pp. 147, 148 (quoting Anna Lefroy).
[7] *Letters*, p. 8.

Cassandra's to Jane rather than Jane's to Cassandra. Francis was next of the family, and nearest to Cassandra in steady good sense. Last of all came Charles; like Frank, his father's pupil until he became a sailor, and, like Frank, still tenacious when at sea of his share in family affections. Frank, as an officer, left a reputation for sound discipline and just consideration of others' claims; Charles, for the power of engaging affection.

Jane had always been, the rest of them recollected, a particular favourite in her own family; and there is independent evidence that she never wanted for appreciation and encouragement there. It was her father who, as soon as her first novel was completed, wrote to inquire of a publisher 'what would be the expense of publishing it at the author's risk'[1]—meaning, presumably, at his own. And the dedications of the early burlesque pieces, besides the circumstances of their survival, show not only that parents and brothers enjoyed these first sports of wit when they were freshly written, but that they still valued them long afterwards— after the writer was grown up and before she was famous. The manuscript of her first venture outside burlesque was read aloud at home, and this custom of reading aloud persisted, at first to Cassandra as sole auditor,[2] later, when publication had given confidence, to a little company of nieces.[3] Henry seems to have succeeded his father as Jane's adviser in practical affairs, and it is clear that his lively and active enthusiasm encouraged her to further ventures— though she may not have relied on his literary taste. Cassandra was the most soberly and resolutely careful of her fame, then and afterwards; but they were none of them behindhand in bringing her news of it—Frank and Charles writing eagerly of praise overheard, her mother and James concerned and pleased with every symptom of growing recognition. It is perhaps the air of gay confederacy which hangs about their letters and messages when Jane's reputation is the subject that has aroused vague and irrational

[1] *Life*, pp. 97, 98.
[2] *Homes and Friends*, p. 86 (quoting from 'Family MSS.').
[3] Ibid., p. 202 (quoting from the talk of Marianne Knight).

suspicions of the trustworthiness of the whole family as
witnesses.

This group of people was the focus of Jane Austen's
early life. If its members regarded themselves, as a family,
with some complacency, it was not to be wondered at.
Their powers of pleasing were considerable: they had between them a more than average share of good looks and
good humour, lively minds and spirits.[1] And with even
more excuse they might pique themselves on their family
relationships. They were not quarrelsome among themselves—that was the impression which Jane's own generation left on her nephews and nieces;[2] and they preserved,
besides easiness of temper, a careful delicacy in their dealings
with one another. This proved itself in the nature of the
arrangement by which the sons, after their father's death,
shared the responsibility of providing for their mother and
sisters;[3] in the relations of the Knights with their adopted
heir[4] and his own family;[5] and it carried them through the
difficulties of a shared household—a feat twice accomplished
(though Mrs. Elton 'knew a family near Maple Grove who
had tried it, and been obliged to separate before the end of
the first quarter')[6]. It gave to the youngest generation an
assurance that, unreserved as Jane and Cassandra were with
one another, nothing confided to one would ever be disclosed to the other.[7] It was indeed apparent in numberless
little ways, down to Jane's last courteous stratagem devised
for her mother's comfort.[8] With this, they might pride
themselves on a steady tenacity in their family relationships:
Edward, on picking up the threads of shared interests and affection in spite of separation in youth; Francis and Charles, on
never having let them drop, in spite of their long absences

---

[1] Agnes Leigh, 'An Old Family History', *National Review*, April 1907, p. 286.
[2] *Personal Aspects*, p. 132.
[3] Ibid., p. 131.   [4] *Life*, pp. 75, 76.
[5] When Jane, after telling Cassandra that Mrs. Knight's generosity to Edward
still leaves her something to live upon, gravely concludes: '. . . this ought to be
known, that her conduct may not be overrated' (*Letters*, p. 51), no one who is
familiar with the other references to Mrs. Knight in her letters can fail to recognize
the ironical tone, or the glow of feeling which it conveys.
[6] *Emma*, p. 469, ch. liii.
[7] *Personal Aspects*, p. 148 (quoting Anna Lefroy).
[8] *Memoir*, pp. 165, 166.

at sea. Sisters-in-law were accepted—critically, it might be, and with occasional asperities in judgement: Cassandra and Jane, pushed by circumstances into responsibility for the bringing up of some of their brothers' children,[1] may have come to look upon themselves as censors of all; but the family tie easily survived such friction. It had, in a greater degree, the toughness and elasticity of the tie which bound country society; there was room for differences of opinion, and a breach, an alienation, was unlikely.

The years at Steventon seem to stand apart from the latter half of Jane Austen's life; perhaps one may even perceive a difference between the first sixteen of them and the rest.

The first recorded happening is her visit, with Cassandra, in 1782, to a connexion of their mother's, followed shortly by a stay of a year or two at a school in Reading. Perhaps they were 'sent to be out of the way and scramble themselves into a little education', like Mrs. Goddard's pupils,[2] for the rectory was full to overflowing, Cassandra was now ten years old, and where she went Jane must go because she would not endure separation. By 1784 or 1785 they were at home again, ready to scramble themselves into a little more education, much as Fanny Price did after the departure of Miss Lee—dependent on father or brothers to encourage and direct their reading, and on themselves for any development of taste in music and drawing—the two accomplishments proper to young ladies.[3] James, while still at Oxford, would probably spend his vacations with them; Henry and Francis were both at home until 1788; they may have read seriously together, the sisters drawing up admirable lists, like Emma's; they must besides have joined in hilarious mockery of much of what they read. Their father may have formed their taste in poetry, if only by his custom of reading aloud his favourites. The arrangement of the Steventon household must have given opportunity for more leisurely, sociable reading and talk than Fanny and Susan Price could contrive at Portsmouth: Anna, the one niece[4] who could

[1] At one time or another they were in charge of some of the children of James, Edward, and Charles.   [2] *Emma*, p. 22.

[3] R. W. C., notes to *Emma*, p. 508.

[4] Daughter of James Austen by his first wife.

BIOGRAPHY 7

remember that household, recalls the small, plainly furnished
'dressing-room' that served as sitting-room for her aunts
when she was living at Steventon (after her mother's death
in 1795), and suggests that they may have been in possession of it since their return from school.[1] The Miss Austens
would probably get less teaching but more stimulus and
encouragement than the Miss Bennets. There was a neighbour, Mrs. Lefroy of Ashe, who—herself a lady of more
than usual culture—was fond and proud of Jane and took
particular pains to foster her natural gifts.[2] There was,
besides, a cousin, an occasional visitor, who could not fail
to leave some mark on their lives: their father's sister, Mrs.
Hancock, was, by the time of Jane's birth, a widow with an
only daughter, Elizabeth, both welcome in the Steventon
family. Before Cassandra and Jane had left home for school,
their cousin had 'finished her studies' in Paris and was
married to a Frenchman, the Comte de Feuillide; but her
friendship with the Austens, loss of her mother, the troubles
in France, all strengthened her association with Steventon.
By 1794 she was a widow,[3] and settled in England. In 1797
she was to marry her cousin, Henry Austen. Jane must
have been often in her company during these years; certainly
she found this gay and pretty cousin very entertaining—
the most ambitious of the early burlesques[4] is dedicated to
her; and it is probable that Eliza talked of the world outside
Steventon—sometimes, perhaps, with the effect of confirm-
ing Jane in her half-humorous insularity—and read French,
and perhaps Italian, with her and with Cassandra.

Of Jane's reading under these various influences there is
no explicit record; but she must have been young when
she made the acquaintance of the eighteenth-century prose
writers who so strongly influenced her style, and of Johnson,
whose thought coloured her view of life—of Cowper, too,
whose phrases lingered in her memory. Goldsmith was a
favourite of those years; and perhaps she already enjoyed
Crabbe; her liking for books of travel may have developed

[1] Quoted in *Life*, p. 15.
[2] *Memoir*, pp. 56, 57.
[3] The Comte de Feuillide was condemned and executed by the Republican
government on 22 February 1794.
[4] *Love and Freindship*.

later; Scott was not yet above the horizon. For one kind of writing she seems always to have had an insatiable appetite: novels, good and bad, were all grist to her mill. Her enjoyment of what was absurd in current fiction must have begun to develop early; *Sanditon* shows how long it lasted.

Perhaps it was the possession of a room of Cassandra's and her own that prompted Jane Austen to scribble her first mimicries of her fellow novelists. Some of them were pieces of serious, direct imitation;[1] others, of outrageous burlesque. The author of the *Memoir* implies[2] that there was a period of simple, nonsensical writing, followed by another of mocking mimicry. The authors of the *Life* notice a 'second stage in her literary education: when she was hesitating between burlesque and immature story-telling'.[3] The order is of small importance; very likely these phases were not distinct; and what we have of this childish writing survives only in copies made several years afterwards.[4] One thing is clear; there was a great deal of scribbling done before the end of those first sixteen years. 'There are copybooks extant', the author of the *Memoir* says, 'containing tales some of which must have been composed while she was a young girl, as they had amounted to a considerable number by the time she was sixteen.'[5] And his sister Caroline remembers her aunt's warning to her when she was less than twelve: '. . . if I would take her advice I should cease writing till I was sixteen; . . . she had herself often wished she had read more, and written less in the corresponding years of her own life.'[6]

All of Jane Austen's juvenilia known to survive have now been published: three note-books full of tales and fragments which she herself collected and transcribed, calling them

---

[1] See *Life*, pp. 31, 32—a passage from an 'early unpublished sketch', which formed part of *Volume the Third*.

[2] pp. 44, and 47–48. James Edward Austen-Leigh (he took this name in 1837 after succeeding to some property in the Leigh family) was son of James Austen by his second wife, half-brother to Anna and brother to Caroline.

[3] p. 57.

[4] R. W. C., Introduction to *Volume the First*, p. viii; cf. *Lady Susan*.

[5] p. 44.

[6] *Memoir*, p. 47.

(with playful pretentiousness) *Volume the First, Second*, and *Third*.[1]

Volume the First is made up of many small burlesque pieces, most of them introduced with the flourish of a mock dedication to one or another of Jane's family. Dr. Chapman shows how two of these dedications indicate dates before 1793,[2] while 'June 3d 1793' is written at the end of the collection. He goes on to say: 'The handwriting, which in most of the book is large and not completely formed, becomes smaller and more mature towards the end, and in the concluding pages is not unlike the hand which wrote *The Watsons* not earlier than 1803.' This was a time at which Jane would hardly have been making fair copies of her childish squibs unless they should still preserve some value for her family. The note-book called *Volume the First* seems to have been given or left to Charles.[3]

Love and Freindship (which may be called the second volume of this set of three) is made up of four parts; there are: two fairly ambitious tales told in letters—the hilarious burlesque (dated 13 June 1790) which has lent its name to the published collection, and the more ambiguous experiment *Lesley Castle*; there is a rowdy mock-history of the reigns of the kings of England from Henry IV to Charles I (dated Saturday, Nov. 26th, 1791); and there is a group of odds and ends. Like the pieces in *Volume the First*, these are dedicated to various residents and migrants of the Steventon household. In fact, the two collections carry throughout the stamp of a family joke—probably as spontaneous as the 'charades' in verse which every member of the family wrote. They are evidently allusive, sprinkled with references to which a list of the books that were then

---

[1] See A Note on References, p. vii, above.
[2] The 'dedication to "Miss Cooper", who became Jane Williams December 1792', and the 'dedication to Francis Austen, "Midshipman on board his Majesty's ship the Perseverance"; for Francis left the *Perseverance* in November 1791'. *Volume the First*, Introduction, pp. vi, vii.
[3] See R. W. C., Introduction to *Volume the First*, p. vii, for the inscription inside the cover.

in Steventon rectory would be a key; but the general intention of the satire is so clear as to leave little excuse for
curiosity about these books. If such an excuse *should* ever
be found, it would, I think, be among the pieces dedicated to
Cassandra and Eliza de Feuillide, which have, more markedly
than the rest, the air of a joke shared between people who
are reading a particular book together. For the most part,
however, it may be wiser to rest content with understanding
the main purpose of these burlesque pieces, their criticism
of the false conventions which governed mood and expression in the fiction current during Jane Austen's early youth.
Two among their more ambitious ventures draw a little
apart from the rest: in *Lesley Castle*, burlesque is not the
sole aim; in *The Three Sisters* it is not even predominant.
This, the least-exuberant sketch in *Volume the First*, has
been further flattened by the erasure of gay, nonsensical
passages here and there,[1] and might, so corrected, pass for
the rough draft of an episode in much later work; it is
cruder but not more extravagant than the introduction of
Lady Middleton's children into the drawing-room at Barton
Park. I suspect that there was no very arduous transition
from these two pieces to *Elinor and Marianne*.

During Jane Austen's last years at Steventon the bounds
of her human world were steadily widening: her mother's
relations—the Leigh Perrots and Coopers in particular[2]—
her father's, too, and her own friends—especially the Lloyds[3]
and the Biggs[4]—became more important in her life. She
paid visits among them: it is likely that she spent some time
with both the Leigh Perrots and the Coopers in Bath—
which Mrs. Thrale had called 'a good place for the initia-
tion of a young lady'[5]—and with connexions in Gloucester-

[1] pp. 114 and 119.
[2] James Leigh Perrot, Mrs. Austen's brother, and Jane (Mrs. Edward Cooper),
her sister.
[3] Martha and Mary Lloyd were to be more closely associated with the Austen
family. Mary became James Austen's second wife (in January 1797); Martha, after
her mother's death, shared the home of Mrs. Austen and her daughters; she was
to become Frank's second wife.
[4] Elizabeth (who became Mrs. Heathcote), Catherine (who became Mrs. Hill),
and Alethea were constant friends of Cassandra and Jane. (Their parents and brother
took the name of Bigg Wither.)
[5] *Letters to and from the late Samuel Johnson*, 1788. Letter CCXXXVII.

shire. She stayed with Edward in his new home[1] at Rowling
in 1794; and in 1798, when he had succeeded Thomas
Knight at Godmersham,[2] paid the first of many visits to
him there; in the following year Jane and her mother,
Edward, and his wife, Elizabeth, forgathered in Bath. Such
expeditions as these, and the local dances, must have furnished her with a considerable variety of acquaintance; but
among them there would be no very striking variation in
circumstances, no greater social range than that between the
Basingstoke assemblies and the private balls in big houses.
It was within this range that she taught herself to discriminate
exquisitely, and to enjoy, as an artist, the minute differences
which she had learnt to perceive; so that even when she
should become acquainted with a more varied society—
with the French *émigrés*, for example, who were her cousin's
friends—she would still prefer, as Macaulay says, to give 'us
a multitude of characters, all, in a certain sense, commonplace, all such as we meet every day. Yet they are all as
perfectly discriminated from each other as if they were the
most eccentric of human beings.'[3] She had, indeed, no
inclination to play with social contrasts of the broad kind
that had pleased Fanny Burney—no more than to add
personally eccentric characters, such as her neighbours the
Chutes,[4] to her store of artistic material. At this period she
must also have been enlarging her acquaintance with the
world by hearsay, through Eliza de Feuillide; I think that
she always found entertainment in knowledge of this sort,
but she was never to make use of it for any but burlesque
writing.

From 1796 onwards we have Jane's own letters to give us
a direct impression (though at first very slight) of her and
her life. Their mood seems to reflect 'plenty of the miscellaneous, unsettled sort of happiness'[5] that she was to notice

---

[1] He married in 1791.
[2] Thomas Knight had died in 1794, leaving his estates to his widow for her life;
in 1798 she gave them to Edward, who was to have inherited them after her death.
[3] Review of the 1842 edition of *Diary and Letters of Madame d'Arblay* (*Edinburgh
Review*, January 1843, article ix). By 'commonplace' he would seem to intend a
contrast with Fanny Burney's sensational variety of social types.
[4] See James Edward Austen-Leigh, *Recollections of the Early Days of the Vine Hunt*,
1865.
[5] *Letters*, p. 289.

in Anna's youth. Miss Mitford thought that she had heard
her mother speak of the young Jane Austen as 'the prettiest,
silliest, most affected, husband-hunting butterfly she ever
remembers'.[1] The story as it stands will not do; Mrs.
Mitford left the Austens' neighbourhood before Jane was
ten years old;[2] but gossip of this kind may have been carried
to her—may even have been, though malicious, not quite
groundless. A clever girl may pass through the phase of
foolish miss on the way to sensible woman. The early
letters do not forbid this supposition; they ring with that
kind of heedless gaiety which the milder of Mrs. Mitford's
epithets imply. Like her own favourite heroines, Jane knew
'how *to be particular*'.[3] She knew, too, how to make the
most of her indiscretions in her letters to Cassandra, for there
she could count on being understood. Cassandra might
well have responded to any of these early letters in Lady
Sarah Lennox's words: 'I will answer your delightful silly
letter, for silly it is to be sure but you know 'tis not the
worse but the better for that, in my opinion'[4]—and might
still find some to agree with her. These early letters are
written for one particular reader; they are elliptical, allusive,
interspersed with references to shared reading and talk,
with burlesque of local gossip[5] and of the style of the letter-
writer who means to publish.[6] There is, besides, more sheer
nonsense in them than one would expect of the cool, observant author of *Love and Freindship*; but they cease for a
time after September of 1796,[7] and so there is no reflection
of the mood of those years which brought a train of sober-
ing events. In 1795 James's wife had died, leaving him with
a child of two years old; Anna was sent to Steventon rectory
to be cared for, and remembered afterwards how her aunt,
then busy with the first draft of a novel,[8] had amused her
with stories of another kind, appropriate to her age and

[1] *Life of Mary Russell Mitford Related in a Selection from her Letters to her Friends*,
ed. A. G. L'Estrange, 1870, vol. i, pp. 305, 306. Letter of 3 April 1815.
[2] *Memoir*, p. 210; *Life*, p. 84.
[3] *Letters*, p. 1.
[4] *Letters*, ed. the Countess of Ilchester and Lord Stavordale, 1901, p. 126.
[5] e.g. *Letters*, p. 98.
[6] Ibid., p. 112.
[7] There is none between 18 September 1796 and 8 April 1798.
[8] *First Impressions*.

taste, and had written down for her those that she invented in busy imitation.[1] Sad experience came nearer in 1797: Thomas Fowle, whom Cassandra was to have married, died in February. Jane seems to have spoken proudly to Eliza de Feuillide of her sister's fortitude under this blow,[2] and I believe that if she ever allows the substance of actual experience, imperfectly transmuted, to enter a novel it is in her defence of Elinor Dashwood and her explicit protest, there, that fortitude has nothing to do with insensibility. Indeed, I think that this experience may divide a light-hearted *Elinor and Marianne* from the grave *Sense and Sensibility* we know. It is vexatious that *Elinor and Marianne* should be lost, and that we must be content with what we are told about it: that it was written before 1796; that it was cast in the form which Richardson had made popular—a fictitious correspondence—and was to be recast in direct narrative as *Sense and Sensibility*.[3] We know, too, that it was read aloud;[4] and we can assume that, however much it pleased the family, Mr. Austen did not take it seriously enough to think of publication.

It may have been about this time that *Lady Susan*, too, was written,[5] although it survives only in a fair copy made not earlier than 1805.[6] Like *Elinor and Marianne*, it is a tale told in a series of letters; but, though it is carried through resolutely in a mood of straightforward comedy to the end of the last letter, the plot is wound up in a Conclusion which allows the author to make fun of the very device she has been employing: 'This Correspondence, by a meeting between some of the Parties & a separation between the others, could not, to the great detriment of the Post office Revenue, be continued longer.'[7] It is not, I suppose, impossible that the series of letters was written at Steventon[8] and left incomplete—there is a great deal of winding-up to be done in the Conclusion—and that this Conclusion was added at

[1] See *Life*, p. 73.
[2] Ibid., p. 105.
[3] Ibid., p. 80.
[4] Ibid.
[5] Ibid.
[6] R. W. C., Introduction.
[7] *Lady Susan*, p. 166; *Minor Works*, p. 311.
[8] For all its sharp wit, I do not think it very different, in ability or temper, from the corrected version of *The Three Sisters*.

some time nearer to the date of the fair copy, when Jane
Austen had lost patience with the device of the novel-in-
letters. This is, of course, mere guess-work; but she certainly never used the device again.

At this point, Cassandra's Memorandum[1] of dates begins
to help. *First Impressions*,[2] she records, was begun in
October 1796, and finished in August 1797. Cassandra had
heard—and Anna overheard—it read aloud, but the writing
of it was a secret from the rest, perhaps because it was a
more serious, ambitious venture than any that had gone
before. Soon after it was finished, however, Mr. Austen
(at least) must have shared the secret, for, in the following
November, he was offering it to the London publisher,
Cadell.[3] He describes it as being 'about the length of Miss
Burney's *Evelina*', and asks whether Cadell will 'choose to
be concerned in it, what will be the expense of publishing it
at the author's risk, and what you will venture to advance
for the property of it, if on persual it is approved of'.
Cadell declined to be concerned in it. The Austens, however, continued to think well of *First Impressions*; there are
references to readings and re-readings of it in Jane's letters,[4] and in its later form it remained a favourite among
them. She was particularly attached to it herself, and seems
to have recovered her confidence in it without waiting for
encouragement.[5]

Perhaps this piece of direct narrative writing showed her
what was her own proper mode of expression; at all events,
she began in this same month (November 1797[6]) to recast
Elinor and Marianne in this form. The change must have
been drastic; *Sense and Sensibility* shows hardly a trace of its
origin. One can only guess which of the characters were
the principal correspondents—indeed, there is none of them,
as they now stand, who could want to hear by letter about
the happenings in Devonshire which make up the first and
last parts of the story. The author of the *Memoir* calls this

---

[1] *Life*, p. 96. For the full evidence as to dates see R. W. Chapman, *Jane Austen:
Facts and Problems* (1948)—especially Chapters III, IV, and VI.
[2] To be rewritten as *Pride and Prejudice*.
[3] *Life*, pp. 97, 98.   [4] *Letters*, pp. 52, 67.
[5] See p. 30.   [6] Cassandra's Memorandum.

version 'Sense and Sensibility . . . in its present form'.[1]
Substantially, it may well be, even though he speaks of
another revision in 1809–10[2]—one which, though it may
not have changed the structure, has left curious traces on
the surface. Bradley pointed out[3] that the mention of Scott
as a popular poet belongs not to 1798, but to 1809. His
name is introduced twice with this connotation:[4] Elinor
and Edward both count him among Marianne's favourites,
along with Thomson and Cowper.[5] If this is all, it implies no
more revision of the 1798 manuscript than the insertion of
an additional name into two passages apt to receive it. But
I think it is not all—that there is another allusion to Scott,
indirect and of more significance, as Jane Austen's indirect
allusions often are. There is nothing very remarkable in
Edward Ferrars's mild pleasantries on 'picturesque' taste in
landscape; they are no more than the enthusiastic Gilpin
might expect to provoke in matter-of-fact readers—or
Marianne in Elinor's lover; but when the attack on picturesque jargon with which they open gives place to a
defence of *anti-picturesque* taste in landscape I think I hear a
faintly distinguishable verbal echo of a provocative passage
in *Marmion*, a mocking retort to its challenge. Edward is
bent on justifying his own tranquil enjoyment of the comfortable Devonshire landscape in which Barton is set:

'I do not like crooked, twisted, blasted trees. I admire them much
more if they are tall, straight and flourishing. I do not like ruined,
tattered cottages. I am not fond of nettles, or thistles, or heath blos-
soms. I have more pleasure in a snug farm-house than a watch-tower—
and a troop of tidy, happy villagers please me better than the finest
banditti in the world.'[6]

Now Scott, in the Introduction to Canto Third of *Marmion*,
had set over against his moving and lovely description of
his own country the ungracious fancy of a Scottish drover

---

[1] p. 49.   [2] p. 101.
[3] *Essays and Studies by Members of the English Association*, ii. 8, note.
[4] p. 47, ch. x, and p. 92, ch. xvii.
[5] The association of these three would seem to suggest lapse of time between the
first draft and final version, as though a landscape painter should begin work in a
morning light and finish in the evening—if it were not for the implied revaluation
of Cowper. See pp. 16, 17.
[6] p. 98, ch. xviii.

trudging the length of England, even to Devonshire, that he may compare it unfavourably with his native hills, their proper flowers, and the 'shatt'red tower' which had been the stronghold of border forayers (whom Gilpin persists in calling banditti):

> Ask, if it would content him well,
> At ease in these gay plains to dwell,
> Where hedge-rows spread a verdant screen,
> And spires and forests intervene,
> And the neat cottage peeps between?
> No! not for these will he exchange
> His dark Lochaber's boundless range,
> Not for fair Devon's meads forsake
> Bennevis grey, and Garry's lake.[1]

Jane Austen had called upon Scott by name to represent the romantic spirit of the day; I think this passage shows that it amused her, besides, to record her own whispered challenge to his romanticism. And if this is a true reading of the passage, then it is clear that the manuscripts she kept by her were liable to undergo various kinds of revision, according as she received fresh impressions.[2] One more trace of this kind I seem to see, faint and uncertain though it is, in Marianne's emotional response to Cowper's poetry —to 'those beautiful lines which had frequently almost driven her wild'.[3] Now, our apprehension of the poignancy of many passages in Cowper's poetry—those allusions to his own state, made in his usual quiet, well-bred voice—is dependent on our knowledge of his story; and therefore it may be significant that in 1803 two biographies of Cowper appeared (Cory's and Hayley's), of very different scope, but alike in this: that both contain hitherto unpublished poems—and among these, passages of such dreadful candour as the *Lines written on a Window-shutter at Weston,*[4] *The Castaway*, and the stanzas (so mildly named and opened) to Newton on his return from Ramsgate;[5] and both relate

[1] ll. 143–151. (Gilpin praises these scenes with equal ardour and distinguishes the thistle as a picturesque flower—but he does not trail his coat.)
[2] Compare the reference to Belinda in *Northanger Abbey* (see p. 48).
[3] *Sense and Sensibility*, p. 18, ch. iii.
[4] In *The Life of Willian Cowper, Esq.*, by John Cory, p. 31.
[5] In *The Life and Posthumous Writings of William Cowper, Esq.*, by William Hayley, ii. 214 and 292.

these poems to Cowper's sad history in such a way as to make the reader aware of the poignancy in all Cowper's references to himself. And so the vehemence of Marianne's expressions would be much more natural and intelligible after the appearance of these two biographies—especially Hayley's, with its lavish display of sensibility; and there is encouragement for supposing that this one was known to Jane Austen;[1] for, as Dr. Chapman points out, *Northanger Abbey*[2] and *Emma* agree with it in a misquotation from Gray's *Elegy*[3]—and misquotations are notoriously infectious. Moreover, Cowper's poetry read afresh, with an ear attentive to its emotional implications, makes a vital link between the romantic moods of Thomson and Scott, and justifies the association of these three in Marianne's mind.[4] If *Sense and Sensibility* had been laid aside for yet another revision, perhaps some other traces of Jane Austen's reading might have appeared in it.

In 1798 and 1799[5] she had, also, a new undertaking on her hands: she was at work, according to Cassandra's memorandum, on the first version of the story which (though originally called *Susan*) was eventually to be published as *Northanger Abbey*—a version which probably differed a good deal from *Northanger Abbey* as we know it.

The last two and a half years at Steventon seem to have yielded nothing; they were interrupted by several visits, and, towards the end, by the prospect of change. Mr. and Mrs. Austen had, in 1800, resolved to retire to Bath. Jane is said to have been distressed at leaving Steventon,[6] and certainly she was not to find her life in Bath satisfying; but by January of 1801 she was already writing cheerfully of the plan, hoping that they would be freer than before to travel, and offering mock consolation for the loss of Cassandra's own particular country pleasures:

'I get more & more reconciled to the idea of our removal. We have lived long enough in this Neighbourhood, the Basingstoke Balls are

[1] J. A. possessed Hayley's *Poems and Plays*, 1785; see R. W. Chapman, 'Jane Austen's Library' in *The Book Collector's Quarterly*, number xi, p. 30.

[2] Revised in 1803.

[3] *Northanger Abbey*, p. 15, ch. i; *Emma*, p. 282, ch. xxxiii; Hayley's *Cowper*, i. 39.

[4] The landscape has been painted afresh in an afternoon light.

[5] I owe these dates to Mr. B. C. Southam.

[6] *Memoir*, p. 59.

certainly on the decline, there is something interesting in the bustle of going away, & the prospect of spending future summers by the Sea or in Wales is very delightful.—For a time we shall now possess many of the advantages which I have often thought of with Envy in the wives of Sailors or Soldiers.—It must not be generally known however that I am not sacrificing a great deal in quitting the Country—or I can expect to inspire no tenderness, no interest in those we leave behind . . . In what part of Bath do you mean to place your *Bees*?—We are afraid of the South Parade's being too hot.'[1]

The hoped-for travel took the form of 'rambles', the family—that is, the parents and daughters—visiting Sidmouth in 1801, Dawlish in 1802, Ramsgate (probably) in 1803, and Lyme Regis in the winter of 1803–4.[2] One of these may have led to unhappiness. It was in Devonshire[3] —so Caroline gathered, after Jane's death, from Cassandra— that Jane became acquainted with a gentleman who loved her and to whose love she responded; he died soon afterwards.[4]

Bath was meanwhile the settled home of the family, and to Bath, as a home, Jane Austen never became reconciled; the years spent there were unprosperous, and it must afterwards have been associated in her memory with some vexations, as well as real sorrows. In 1803 she revised her draft of *Northanger Abbey*,[5] and the question arises—how thorough was this revision? Dr. Chapman suggests that the chronology of the story accords well enough with the almanac for 1798,[6] and this would leave little scope for alterations to have been made (since that year) in the *plot*. On the other hand, the allusion which he cites[7] as evidence of an alteration made after the completion of the first draft—that to *Belinda*, which was published in 1801—may possibly in-

---

[1] *Letters*, p. 103.
[2] *Life*, pp. 172–176; R. W. C., note to *Letters*, p. 216   [3] 'not Lyme'.
[4] For the several family traditions concerning this and related events—at variance as to names and particulars, but agreeing in general tenor—see R. W. Chapman, *Facts and Problems*, Chapter V.
[5] Then called *Susan*. The argument in the *Life* (pp. 229–233) for the identity of *Susan* (later called *Catherine*, see p. 38) with *Northanger Abbey* seems to me conclusive. It has been argued that the choise of 'Susan' as title proves that *Lady Susan* could not have been meant for publication. (I have suggested that *Lady Susan* may at this time have been unfinished.)
[6] *Northanger Abbey*, Appendix, pp. 275–278.   [7] Introduction, p. xiii.

dicate something more than a mere additional title inserted into the passage defending novels and novel-readers.[1] If C. L. Thomson was right in supposing that this passage as a whole is a retort to Miss Edgeworth's condemnation of the novel in the 'Advertisement' to *Belinda*,[2] then it must, as a whole, have been added after 1801. And this may be the kind of revision that Jane Austen had in mind when she afterwards spoke of the work as having been 'finished in the year 1803'.[3] At all events, it was prepared for the press in that year and sold to the London publisher, Crosby. Henry must have acted for his sister in this transaction, for it was carried through in the name of his man of business, Seymour. Crosby went so far as to announce the book as already in the press;[4] but there the matter, surprisingly, ended; nothing more was heard of *Susan*.

Such an anti-climax cannot but have discouraged the author, but it did not immediately silence her. The fragment which we know as *The Watsons*[5] was begun not earlier than 1803;[6] it was, however, to be left unfinished. It may be that the setting she had chosen for it failed to satisfy her, though perhaps not quite in the way her nephew suggests;[7] but this supposition is not necessary. There was enough in the circumstances of her life to account for the silence which began when she had settled Emma Watson in her 'low' situation, and which lasted until 1809. She had to suffer two grievous losses in the death of her friend Mrs. Lefroy in December of 1804, and of her father in the following month. She may, moreover, have felt the loss of his encouragement; certainly, with *First Impressions* refused unread and *Susan* buried, she wanted the encouragement of recognition outside her own family. And I am convinced

---

[1] *Northanger Abbey*, p. 38, ch. v.

[2] C. L. Thomson, *Jane Austen*, 1929, pp. 45, 46; see p. 48.

[3] In the note published as 'Advertisement by the Authoress to Northanger Abbey'. [4] R. W. C., Introduction, p. xi.

[5] The title given to it when it was first published in the second edition of the *Memoir*.

[6] See R. W. C. (Introduction to his edition, on the watermarks which, since it is a first draft, give the earliest possible date for composition).

[7] He supposes her to have realized '. . . the evil of having placed her heroine too low, in a position of poverty and obscurity, which, though not necessarily connected with vulgarity, has a sad tendency to degenerate into it' (*Memoir*, 2nd edit., p. 296).

that silence—whether caused by depression or no—in its turn reacted on her spirits in a peculiarly depressing way. Her mood, in those years, seems to be coloured by something more than immediate circumstances. Already, before Steventon is left behind, the letters begin to reflect some sort of irritability. She seems to fear the pressure of new friendships, human contacts of every kind, on an irritably sensitive consciousness; she acknowledges something capricious in her reserve, and tries to laugh it away. 'I do not want people to be very agreeable, as it saves me the trouble of liking them a great deal.'[1] But the impulse will not be subdued; and at Bath it grows in strength, for all her self-mockery. 'I spent friday evening with the Mapletons, & was obliged to submit to being pleased in spite of my inclination.'[2] 'I do not see the Miss Mapletons very often, but just as often as I like; we are always very glad to meet, & I do not wish to wear out our satisfaction.'[3] Her stubborn resistance to this mood is characteristic; there was war within because of her strong natural bent towards acceptance of life as she found it. She might have said of herself what she says of her Elizabeth: '. . . it was her business to be satisfied—and certainly her temper to be happy.'[4] She could indeed say: 'I had a very pleasant evening . . . though you will probably find out that there was no particular reason for it; but I do not think it worth while to wait for enjoyment until there is some real opportunity for it.'[5] But it was not her way to shut her eyes while she swallowed something disagreeable; to herself, and therefore to Cassandra, she would admit, lightly, that there was an unresolved discord such as she might have described in the words which she was to use, later, of stage illusion: 'I fancy I want something more than can be'[6]—and did indeed suggest in the talk between Elizabeth and Jane Bennet. To Elizabeth's dissatisfaction her sister can only reply: 'My dear Lizzy, do not give way to such feelings as these. They will ruin your happiness.'[7] It would have been surprising if there had been

[1] *Letters*, p. 43.   [2] Ibid., p. 64.
[3] Ibid., p. 71; see also letter XXXVII.
[4] *Pride and Prejudice*, p. 239, ch. xlii.   [5] *Letters*, p. 56.
[6] Ibid., p. 415.   [7] *Pride and Prejudice*, p. 135, ch. xxiv.

nothing amiss. The artist (I suppose) usually pays for his privilege by some sort of partial insomnia, by the possession of one faculty that will not be controlled nor put to sleep. In a poet this must often be the visual imagination, bringing before his eyes a succession of images which *he* never summoned, and of which some (it is only too likely) will be ugly or pitiful. In Jane Austen it was the critical faculty that would not be quieted; and that faculty, in her, played on men and women. This war within her, and its outcome, have been exactly described: 'In her there are united, in rare combination, a sense of disillusionment and gaiety of temperament—it is the perception of the comic . . . which reconciles the two.'[1] And further: 'A rational woman, exceptional in intellect, unique in wit, found herself in circumstances which were always meagre, and at times irrational; and endowed with fastidiousness on the one hand and enjoyment on the other, she employed her experience creatively in the service of Comedy. The novels are a vent . . .'[2] But the method of reconciliation had to be learnt. It was not enough—after the high spirits of youth had ebbed—to admit, with her own Elizabeth, 'Follies and nonsense, whims and inconsistencies, *do* divert me, I own, and I laugh at them whenever I can';[3] not enough, even, by finding witty and apt expression for her own perceptions, to share her diversion with Cassandra. She can, and does, scatter throughout her letters to her sister sharply defined sketches of actual people: 'Miss Holder & I adjourned after tea into the inner Drawingroom to look over Prints & talk pathetically. She is very unreserved & very fond of talking of her deceased brother & sister, whose memories she cherishes with an enthusiasm which tho' perhaps a little affected, is not unpleasing.'[4] Here is the gift for observation and expression that the novels show, but something still is wanting. Her critical faculty finds outlet here, but not relief. Jane Austen had to teach herself how to translate these critical perceptions of actual people into more general terms, to smelt the ore of her impressions and fit it for use in the

---

[1] K. Metcalfe, Introduction to *Pride and Prejudice* (1912), p. xiii.
[2] Ibid., p. xv.   [3] *Pride and Prejudice*, p. 57, ch. xi.   [4] *Letters*, p. 135.

mint which issued her fictitious people. She did not learn
this all at once: from the surface of her early work a
character sticks out here and there, looking as though it
had been lifted whole from the actual world; for the young
satirist who has suffered a slight, whether at the hands of an
individual or of a class of people, is tempted to compensate
himself by putting a recognizable likeness of the offender
into his work, where—being imperfectly transmuted into
fit material for his art—it agrees very ill with its surround-
ings, and is usually to be known by something of acrimony
perceptible about it. Jane Austen (like Fanny Burney before
her) has some characters of this kind among her self-satisfied
young men, but, unlike Fanny Burney's, they are to be
found only in her early novels. John Thorpe, Tom Musgrave, Robert Ferrars are of this company—and I suspect
that Darcy narrowly escaped joining it: the Darcy of Meryton assembly is quite inconsistent with the Darcy who is
described and developed in the rest of the book. Charles
Musgrove would certainly have joined it if he had appeared
in an earlier novel, and have served as a mere outlet for
Jane's exasperation with what she called 'sporting Mania'.[1]

The novels, then, were to bring about a more and more
satisfying reconciliation between jarring impulses; but during
a silence, when nothing fictitious was being written, these
impulses would still be at war. Jane Austen, when she
returned to fiction, had to write herself into a good humour
again.

Accord within herself was made more difficult after her
father's death by circumstances: there was in these a
change and demand for adaptation; the change (in particular) from a family party to the household of a widow and
spinsters. Martha Lloyd, left alone when her mother died,
joined Mrs. Austen and her daughters in 1805, and these
four found themselves settled in a little world peopled by
ladies in like circumstances. Outside it they adventured
little, unless to keep in touch with acquaintances who had
befriended, or might befriend, their brothers. 'What a
different set are we now moving in!' Jane writes to Cassan-

[1] *Letters*, p. 344.

dra in 1805. 'But seven years I suppose are enough to change every pore of one's skin, & every feeling of one's mind.'[1] It is not only the present that is changed; the future, too, wears a new aspect. 'I was truly glad to see her comfortable in mind and spirits', she writes, later, of an elderly spinster friend; 'at her age, perhaps, one may be as friendless oneself, and in similar circumstances quite as captious.'[2] She was to accustom herself to these changes: 'It was the same room in which we danced 15 years ago!—I thought it all over—& in spite of the shame of being so much older, felt with thankfulness that I was quite as happy now as then.'[3] That, however, was written after she had left Bath; and she was very glad to go. It was a removal to be remembered thankfully afterwards: 'It will be two years tomorrow since we left Bath for Clifton, with what happy feelings of Escape!'[4] That had happened on 2 July 1806; and, after a few visits—culminating in one paid to Stoneleigh, the home in Warwickshire of the head of Mrs. Austen's family—the Austen ladies, rejoined by their friend Martha, settled, in March 1807, at Southampton, in the house which they were to share with the Frank Austens for the next three years. This was more like family life than the last part of their stay in Bath had been. Moreover, the James Austens, at Steventon, were now within easy reach. It was in these Southampton years that the young James Edward, her future biographer, came to know something of his aunt. In these years, too, the tie with Edward at Godmersham was strengthened, and, after a while, changed in character. In October of 1808 Edward's wife died, leaving him with eleven children, and Cassandra and Jane found themselves not only welcome, but necessary, to these nephews and nieces. And this need did not lessen as the elder children began to grow up; they must still be ready with sympathy in every emergency, from a proposal of marriage to the loss of a dormouse.[5] Here was a circumstance to strengthen Jane's confidence in life, to make of it something more than the mere instinctive

[1] Ibid., p. 148.   [2] Ibid., pp. 242, 243.
[3] Ibid., p. 236.   [4] Ibid., p. 208.
[5] Memoir, pp. 99, 100; Letters, p. 472.

acceptance that it had been when she was the age of her own Elizabeth Bennet; for her heart was so inclined that she might have said with Lady Sarah '. . . my affections follow the generations as they arise',[1] and it delighted her to see this new generation succeeding to all the pleasing cares of her own, and to some that she had missed.

With the beginning of this new phase of life, talk of books begins to come back into Jane Austen's letters. Now she is introducing a favourite of her own to Frank's wife,[2] and now slips back into her old vein of mocking commentary on the family readings: 'We are now in Margiana, and like it very well indeed. We are just going to set off for Northumberland to be shut up in Widdrington Tower, where there must be two or three sets of victims already immured under a very fine villain.'[3] In another letter: 'To set against your new Novel of which nobody ever heard before and perhaps never may again, We have got *Ida of Athens* by Miss Owenson; which must be very clever, because it was written as the Authoress says, in three months.'[4]

Perhaps this recovery of spirits has something to do with the stirrings of a new hope and interest in her own work which began to be evident about this time. On 5 April 1809 she wrote (under an assumed name) to Crosby,[5] reminding him of the sale of *Susan*, and insisting that 'an early publication was stipulated for at the time of sale'. Had the manuscript been lost?—and, if she provided him with another copy, would he go forward with the publication? If not, she would try her fortune elsewhere. Crosby replied[6] promptly that he was not in any way bound to publish the manuscript he had bought, and that he would take measures to prevent any one else from publishing it, but that she could have it back for the price he had paid. Now, some turns of expression in this correspondence are interesting; Jane Austen says:

'I . . . am willing to supply you with another copy [of the manuscript] if you are disposed to avail yourselves of it, & will engage for no

1 *Letters of Lady Sarah Lennox*, ii. 91.
2 *Letters*, p. 173.   3 Ibid., p. 248.
4 Ibid., p. 251.   5 Ibid., p. 263.
6 Ibid., p. 264.

farther delay when it comes into your hands. It will not be in my power from particular circumstances to command this copy before the Month of August, but then, if you accept my proposal, you may depend upon receiving it.'

Dr. Chapman explains that Jane would not be able to lay hand on her papers, the manuscript among them, while away from home. When she wrote, from Southampton, to Crosby she was on the point of setting out to visit Henry in London, and would not be settled again before the summer; for Mrs. Austen, her daughters, and Martha were to move to a new home in July. The copy, therefore, that is to be ready by August is presumably one exactly similar to Crosby's of which she has kept possession. This is significant: she was not to recover Crosby's copy for another seven years; but with this one in her hands she could set about revision whenever she should choose.—This change of home had been resolved on by October of the preceding year, when Jane was already writing of Edward's offer to their mother of a choice of houses, one on his Kentish, the other on his Hampshire estate; and of Chawton, in Hampshire, as the one preferred.[1] With the establishment of the little party at Chawton on 7 July 1809[2] a new phase of her life begins.

Chawton stands in pretty country, softer than Steventon: there are more beeches and all the timber is heavier. The new home appeared, from the village street, to be little more than a large, solid cottage—it had been occupied by Edward's bailiff; but on the garden side it showed itself, when Edward had taken some pains with it, as a very pleasant little house.[3] The garden[4] itself was big enough to occupy Mrs. Austen's energies, and the aspect of the other side was no drawback to her. The road through the village was a highway, and coaches passed on it, sometimes carrying young Austens to Winchester. Here it was easier than at Southampton to keep in touch with the rest of the family: Steventon was even nearer than before, and Edward might bring his family for a while to the big house, or lend it to one of his brothers. And it was here that most of the

---

[1] Ibid., number LIX.   [2] *Life*, p. 242.
[3] *Personal Aspects*, pp. 139-141 (quoting Caroline).
[4] *Homes and Friends*, pp. 175, 176 (quoting 'Family MSS.'—Anna's daughter).

younger generation came to know Jane. Some of their impressions of her have come down to us, and this is fortunate: for although we have a fair number of letters from Jane to Cassandra written in these years[1] they are all of the kind that Johnson liked—'Such tattle as filled your last sweet letter', he tells Mrs. Thrale, 'prevents one great inconvenience of absence, that of returning home a stranger and an enquirer'[2]—and this is a kind that is likely to be unmeaning to later readers in proportion as it was precious to the one for whom it was intended. Many of them, more-over, are evidently family news-sheets, meant to be read aloud. When Jane writes to Cassandra 'Your Letter gave pleasure to all of us, we had all the reading of it of course, I *three times*—as I undertook to the great releif of Lizzy, to read it to Sackree, & afterwards to Louisa'[3]—we can guess that her own letters to Cassandra at this time were often designed for such an audience and that this is why, of all her later letters, these carry the faintest personal im-press.[4] And if they fail to content us we must resort to her nephews and nieces, to the letters they got from their aunt, and kept, and their recollections of her.

It is worth while to distinguish a few among these younger Austens.[5] James's wilful, clever, pretty Anna, who from her childhood had known her aunts well,[6] was still at Steventon and, a little while after her marriage,[7] was to settle nearer still to Chawton. She embarked on a novel of her own, and Jane's criticism of it is like a private view of the workshop in which *her* novels were made. Among her aunt's heroines, Anna preferred Emma. Edward's Fanny, on the other hand, could not abide Emma—whom she may possibly have resembled a little, for her mother's death had forced her to take charge, when only fifteen, of her father's

---

[1] With Martha to share their attendance on Mrs. Austen, Jane and Cassandra would often be free to leave home.

[2] *Letters*, ed. G. B. Hill, ii. 19 (letter of 13 August 1777).

[3] *Letters*, p. 343. Sacree was nursemaid at Godmersham.

[4] See R. W. C., Introduction to *Letters*, XL.

[5] Edward's children, of course, became Knights when he took the name in 1812.

[6] She was unhappy and rebellious under her stepmother's rule.

[7] To Benjamin Lefroy; they were settled at Wyards, a farm-house near Alton, by September 1815.

household. This early responsibility and forced growth had contracted the difference in age between her and her aunts; they treated her rather as a younger sister than a niece. Already in 1808 Jane is writing to Cassandra:

'I am greatly pleased with your account of Fanny; I found her in the summer just what you describe, almost another Sister—& could not have supposed that a neice would ever have been so much to me. She is quite after one's own heart; give her my best Love, & tell her that I always think of her with pleasure.'[1]

And after Jane's death Cassandra liked to trace a resemblance to her in Fanny.[2] Edward's sons, the 'agreeable, idle Brothers' with whom Fanny was apt to compare her suitors, were favourites too—especially Edward and George, who had stayed with Jane for a few days after their mother's death but even they can hardly have been so familiarly known and loved, so thoroughly at home in the Chawton household, as James's son, James Edward,[3] who (Jane writes to his sister Caroline) 'makes himself as agreeable as ever, sitting in such a quiet comfortable way making his delightful little Sketches'.[4] Caroline herself was but little older than the disorderly company of young children of whom her aunt wrote to her that, though they 'are sometimes very noisy & not under such Order as they ought & easily might, I cannot help liking & even loving them, which I hope may not be wholly inexcusable in their & your affectionate Aunt . . .'.[5] She was just old enough to be flattered with bantering notes, and with a gay pretence of equality, 'for *we* do not grow older of course'.[6] She was only twelve when her aunt died; but her recollections, and possession of her mother's diaries, made her a valuable helper to the author of the *Memoir*.

These are the nephews and nieces who between them show us Jane Austen as she appeared to her family in the last eight years of her life; and if their impression is more favourable than a reader of her early letters would expect,

[1] *Letters*, pp. 216, 217.   [2] Ibid., p. 507.
[3] After succeeding to some property in the Leigh family he took the name of Austen-Leigh (1837).   [4] *Letters*, p. 471.
[5] Ibid., p. 473. These were Charles's children; Edward and Francis, also, still had young families.   [6] Ibid., p. 460.

that casts no slur on their testimony. Looking back, they remembered nothing but gentleness and good humour. 'In addressing a child she was perfect.'[1] She can never have been quarrelsome; she would dislike the intimacy of quarrels. And for children she had always transmuted her satiric gift into a faculty for entertaining: from the days when Anna lived at Steventon, onwards, she was gratefully remembered as an entertainer, whether she were inventing stories or 'giving a conversation as between myself and my two cousins, supposing we were all grown up, the day after a ball'.[2] And by the time that some of them, no longer children, were coming to know her as friend and equal she had found opportunity for making the critical apprehension that had once possessed her into a familiar spirit that would serve her; during those last eight years she was almost continuously engaged on her novels. Besides, she seems to have learnt how to use expression as a means of relief in her life as in her work. As to her way of talking about people, the author of the *Memoir* (who had heard her among her own generation) says that she never turned 'individuals into ridicule'. Her neighbours 'often served for her amusement; but it was her own nonsense that gave zest to the gossip'. (One remembers the inimitable burlesque-gossip in her letters: 'She told us a great deal about her friend Lady Cath. Brecknell, who is most happily married—& Mr. Brecknell is very religious, & has got black Whiskers.'[3])

'She was as far as possible from being censorious or satirical. She never abused them or *quizzed* them. ... The laugh which she occasionally raised was by imagining for her neighbours, as she was equally ready to imagine for her friends or herself, impossible contingencies, or by relating in prose or verse some trifling anecdote coloured to her own fancy, or in writing a fictitious history of what they were supposed to have said or done, which could deceive nobody.'[4]

This is significant; it makes intelligible the emphatic declaration of one of her nieces: 'I do not suppose she ever in her life said a sharp thing.'[5] For here, as in the novels, she is

---

[1] *Personal Aspects*, p. 114 (quoting Caroline).
[2] *Memoir*, pp. 90, 91; see also *Life*, p. 73.　　　　　　[3] *Letters*, p. 279.
[4] *Memoir*, pp. 92, 93. This seems to be founded on Caroline's account; which is quoted in *Personal Aspects*, p. 144.　　　　　　[5] *Life*, p. 240.

seen translating her critical impressions of individuals into
general terms, and so extracting the sting of exasperation.
The mood of these last eight years of her life was the mood
that Meredith attributes to the true comic artist: 'The
laughter of Comedy is impersonal and of unrivalled politeness.'[1]

Jane Austen probably found the way of life at Chawton
congenial; it was a country way, and she had always been
dissatisfied with life in a town, feeling that it had no natural
roots. (Anne Elliot, though she knew little of the sordid
aspects of it which oppressed poor Fanny Price, condemned
it for its want of 'duties and dignity', and its trivial human
contacts.[2]) She must very soon have been ready to dis-
count disappointments and begin work afresh, for in a little
while she was well on her way with it; but there is no means
of knowing exactly when she chose one from her three
manuscript novels and set about preparing it for the press.
We hear nothing of this until the fact is accomplished, and
the work accepted; for, unluckily, there are no letters surviving from the first year and three-quarters at Chawton. On
25 April 1811 Jane tells Cassandra that she is at work on
the proofs of *Sense and Sensibility*; and we are left to guess
what has brought her to this point, and why *this* should
be the manuscript chosen. Her reason for passing over
Northanger Abbey is easily guessed at; the right to publish
it would have cost her £10,[3] and Crosby's treatment of it
had not been encouraging: if he had thought its chances
poor in 1803, what would they be now that *Udolpho* was
eight years older? Besides, she may not yet have recovered
her pleasure in burlesque. It is harder to understand her
passing over *Pride and Prejudice*; but, in its first form, it had
met with a rebuff, and she was not in a confident mood:
she 'laid by a sum . . . to meet the expected loss'[4] on this her
new enterprise—which would, if it had proved unsuccess-
ful, probably have been her last. Compared with the other
novels, *Sense and Sensibility* has the air of a mere venture:
Cassandra knew of it, of course, when it was in the press,

[1] *An Essay on Comedy* (1897), p. 88.   [2] *Persuasion*, p. 138, ch. xv.
[3] The sum that Crosby had paid.   [4] *Life*, p. 255.

and very likely earlier, and both were concerned about its
success; but, for some while after publication, its authorship was kept a secret even from Anna.[1] It was never to
count for as much, to the author or her family, as the later
novels: she would—'if asked'—tell them what became of
Miss Steele,[2] but her own imagination did not linger in the
world of *Sense and Sensibility* as it was to do in that of *Pride
and Prejudice*.

Jane Austen must have set about the revision of *Pride and
Prejudice* out of sheer delight in the exercise of her own
rediscovered gift, for it was already far advanced before the
success of *Sense and Sensibility* could come to reassure her.[3]
There is another unlucky silence after June 1811, and when
the letters begin again in January 1813 *Pride and Prejudice* is
already on the point of publication.[4] Therefore we have no
direct evidence as to the degree of revision that it under-
went, beyond this reference in a letter of 29 January 1813:
'I have lop't and crop't so successfully . . . that I imagine
it must be rather shorter than S. & S. altogether';[5] but
of circumstantial evidence there is enough. It is so clearly
an advance upon *Sense and Sensibility* that it must, almost
certainly, be an advance upon its own first draft—which
had been written before *Sense and Sensibility* was cast in 'its
present form'. Moreover Dr. Chapman shows how particular examination confirms this general impression, his
principal argument being this: if *Pride and Prejudice* was
written, as certainly appears,[6] with an almanac of 1811 at
hand, 'we must infer', he says, 'that the book as we know it
was substantially rewritten in 1812; for it is certain that so
intricate a chronological scheme cannot have been patched
on to an existing work without extensive revision'.[7] One
more small argument suggests itself: on 29 January 1813

---

[1] *Life*, p. 241. In a letter of February 1813 J. A. tells Cassandra that Anna is to
be let into the secret (*Letters*, p. 303).

[2] *Memoir*, pp. 157, 158.

[3] *Life*, p. 243: 'by April 1811 *Sense and Sensibility* was in the printers' hands, and
Pride and Prejudice far advanced.'

[4] It was announced in that month—R. W. C., *Pride and Prejudice*, p. xi.

[5] *Letters*, p. 298. (It is not.) R. W. C. points out that it may have been either
First Impressions, or a later version, that was so abridged (*Pride and Prejudice*, p. xiii).

[6] R. W. C., Appendix to *Pride and Prejudice*, Chronology (developing a suggestion
of Sir F. MacKinnon's).   [7] *Pride and Prejudice*, p. xiii.

Jane tells Cassandra that the first copy of *Pride and Prejudice* has arrived: 'I have got my own darling child from London';[1] eleven days later she is writing to her: 'I am exceedingly pleased that you can say what you do, after having gone thro' the whole work.'[2] Cassandra, then, had not 'gone thro' the whole' of *Pride and Prejudice* before its publication; but Jane had teased her about her frequent re-readings of *First Impressions*.[3] This seems to imply a real difference between them.

It may have been about this time[4] that Jane Austen began, in her recovered confidence, to write more freely about her own work. The reticence that was a part of her would of course remain, but she was ready to speak of those artistic problems that would interest this or that one of her family, and of her own novels—at least so soon as they were in print.[5] (Her family might read, or hear, something of them while they were still in manuscript, but I doubt whether this signified an invitation to advise.) While Cassandra is reading the newly published *Pride and Prejudice*, Jane interposes with the mocking suggestion that it would have been improved by 'an essay on writing, a critique on Walter Scott, or the history of Buonaparté' worked into it.[6] And she enters gaily into the pretence that her imagined world, of Longbourn or Pemberley, is one with which they are all familiar. *Pride and Prejudice* lent itself admirably to this fiction; it had lived in its author's imagination for so long that she had developed a peculiar relation to its characters, and could say of her own Elizabeth Bennet 'I must confess that I think her as delightful a creature as ever appeared in print, and how I shall be able to tolerate those who do not

---

[1] *Letters*, p. 297.   [2] Ibid., pp. 302, 303.
[3] Ibid., p. 52.
[4] The gap in the letters leaves it uncertain.
[5] She could never, I am convinced, have asked her friends for contributions to a half-formed character, as Richardson did to Sir Charles Grandison. As to Cassandra —'with this dear sister—though, I believe, with no one else', her nephew says, 'Jane seems to have talked freely of any work that she might have in hand' (*Memoir*, 2nd edit., p. 364); but he bases this conjecture on Cassandra's knowledge of the plan of *The Watsons*—which Jane may have related to her only after the work had been laid aside.
[6] *Letters*, p. 300. For this fashion of introducing discursive stuff into novels, see Miss Tompkins's *Popular Novel in England, 1770–1800*, 1932, p. 18.

like *her* at least I do not know'.[1] And, in another letter:
'We have been both to the Exhibition & Sir J. Reynolds',—
and I am disappointed, for there was nothing like Mrs. D.[2]
at either. I can only imagine that Mr. D. prizes any Picture
of her too much to like it should be exposed to the public
eye.—I can imagine he w[d] have that sort of feeling—that
mixture of Love, Pride & Delicacy.'[3] This latter is a message
to Fanny Knight; for the younger generation entered into
the pretence with spirit, giving it fresh impetus. 'She would,
if asked, tell us many little particulars about the subsequent
career of some of her people.'[4] At Chawton Jane Austen's
work seems to recover that character of family entertainment to which it owes (I believe) several of its charms, and
one fault.

The conditions under which she worked, and the way
in which she adapted herself to them, may have strengthened
this characteristic. Her nephew remembered that most of
her writing 'must have been done in the general sitting-
room, subject to all kinds of casual interruptions'; that, not
wishing any one outside her own family to know what she
was doing, she wrote on small sheets of paper and put them
away when a creaking door warned her of one of these interruptions.[5] That was at Chawton, in comparative security;
even when paying a visit, however—and many were paid
within these years—she would contrive to go on with her
work. One of Edward's younger daughters, speaking of
her aunt's visits to Godmersham, recalled how she 'would
sit quietly working[6] beside the fire in the library, saying
nothing for a good while, and then would suddenly burst
out laughing, jump up and run across the room to a table
where pens and paper were lying, write something down,
and then come back to the fire and go on quietly working as
before'.[7] She must have developed to a remarkable degree
her faculty for living (when she chose) apart in her imagined
world—and, further, for keeping the regions of that world

---

[1] *Letters*, p. 297.   [2] Mrs. Darcy—Elizabeth.
[3] *Letters*, p. 312.   [4] *Memoir*, p. 157.
[5] Ibid., p. 102.   [6] This, of course, means sewing.
[7] Marianne Knight's reminiscence, given in talk to one of her cousins, and quoted
by C. Hill, *Homes and Friends*, p. 202.

distinct in her imagination. To be engaged at once on *Pride
and Prejudice* and *Mansfield Park*—and that while still correcting the proofs of *Sense and Sensibility*—and to preserve entire
the peculiar atmosphere of each—this is an achievement
which shows that she could project her imagination into
one or another of these fragile bubble worlds, and let it
dwell there.

Jane Austen's way of life at Chawton seems to have been
little disturbed, or animated, by contact with the human
world outside her own family: Mrs. Austen, now growing
old, gave up visiting; her daughters, who chose to consider
themselves middle-aged, may have lost the habit of adven-
turous social intercourse, and certainly could not afford to
go far in search of it. But when Jane visited her brothers—
particularly Edward and Henry—her range of acquaintance
extended itself. In London there would be intercourse with
Eliza's French friends, and visits to public places of entertainment, where 'my preference for Men & Women, always
inclines me to attend more to the company than the sight'.[1]
After Eliza's death in April 1813 Henry came to depend
more on his sisters, and their visits became more important,
Jane's giving her opportunity to see her work through the
press under his direction. On one score she objected to this
widening of her social world: all her work was published
anonymously, but Henry would not be persuaded to keep
her secret. '. . . In the warmth of his Brotherly vanity &
Love', she tells Francis, he has disclosed the authorship of
Pride and Prejudice. 'A Thing once set going in that way—
one knows how it spreads!—and he, dear Creature, has set
it going so much more than once. I know it is all done from
affection & partiality—but at the same time, let me here
again express to you & Mary my sense of the *superior* kindness which you have shewn on the occasion, in doing what
I wished.'[2] She was always shy with strangers[3]—'. . . though
I like Miss H. M. as much as one can at my time of Life

[1] *Letters*, p. 267.   [2] Ibid., p. 340.
[3] *Life*, p. 240, quoting one of the younger nieces. This is the most probable
explanation of the unpleasant account of J. A. in middle age which reached Miss
Mitford. *Life of Mary Russell Mitford Related in a Selection from her Letters to her
Friends*, ed. A. G. L'Estrange, i. 305.

after a day's acquaintance, it is uphill work to be talking to those whom one knows so little';[1] and if they wished to meet her on account of her authorship she was even less bold and sanguine than usual.[2] After all, the compensation for this effort was to be meagre; the tide of her fame flowed for so little a while that it only served to carry her as far as the Prince Regent's librarian.

This, however, is to look forward. *Mansfield Park*, 'begun about February 1811',[3] had been finished 'soon after June 1813'.[4] But it is not until March 1814 (when *Emma* is already on the stocks) that we hear of the manuscript of *Mansfield Park* being shown to Henry.[5] This is significant; in his *Biographical Notice* Henry implies that this was always his sister's way: after referring to the novels which had been 'the gradual performance of her previous life',[6] he explains that 'though in composition she was equally rapid and correct, yet an invincible distrust of her own judgement induced her to withhold her works from the public, till time and many perusals had satisfied her that the charm of recent composition was dissolved'.[7] And her treatment of the manuscript of *Persuasion*[8] shows that this continued to be her practice until the end. I suspect that the fortunes of the earlier novels had done much to form this habit; Jane Austen had found that she was able to return, cool and critical, to work that she had laid by, and to better it. In any case, it is clear that such a pause after the completion of any of the later novels signifies no dissatisfaction nor want of confidence. The mood in which *Mansfield Park* was begun may well have been diffident and anxious; it was thirteen years since she had last drafted a novel which was to reach completion, and though she had meanwhile found that she could recast old work successfully this was another kind of undertaking. But by the time that she reached the

[1] *Letters*, p. 419.
[2] Ibid., p. 311, and Henry's *Biographical Notice*, which, in the version of 1833 (p. ix), gives the story of the invitation to meet Mme de Staël refused.
[3] *Life*, p. 290, n. 2.   [4] Ibid., p. 290.
[5] *Letters*, p. 376; see R. W. C.'s note showing that this must be MS., not proofs.
[6] This seems to confirm my conjectures as to gradual revision.
[7] The version of 1818, prefixed to *Northanger Abbey* and *Persuasion*, ed. R. W. C.,
p. 4.   [8] See p. 38.

end she can hardly have needed the successful publication of *Sense and Sensibility* and *Pride and Prejudice* to reassure her. She must have known that *Mansfield Park* excelled *Pride and Prejudice* in its subtler conception of human relations— by as much *Pride and Prejudice* had excelled *Sense and Sensibility* in its more subtly planned construction.

Mansfield Park must have appeared soon after the announcement by the publisher (Egerton) in May.[1] Meanwhile, on the 21st of January,[2] *Emma* had been begun; either rising confidence or easier circumstances may have quickened its growth, for it was finished on the 29th of March 1815[3] (though it probably did not appear until early in 1816).[4] I suspect, moreover, that Henry was a little impatient of the maturing process. And so far as his sister's practice was the outcome of diffidence, he could urge against it her steadily growing success: *Mansfield Park* had been favourably received; *Emma* was noticed in the *Quarterly*.[5] There was a sting, for her, in some of its criticisms, but the review was, as a whole, complimentary, and it was a mark of attention; and, if she had known who was the writer, she could not but have been flattered, for it was Scott himself.[6] She had received besides another sort of notice: while *Emma* was yet in the press permission to dedicate 'any future work' to the Prince Regent was conveyed to her by his librarian, the Rev. J. S. Clarke.[7] It was accompanied and followed by compliments; Mr. Clarke's praise was unstinted—but it cannot have been altogether gratifying. At a time when her true province was discovering itself ever more clearly to her,[8] he suggested that she would be far better employed on one of several subjects proposed by himself—'. . . any historical romance, illustrative of the

---

[1] R. W. C., Introduction to *Mansfield Park*, p. xi.
[2] *Life*, p. 290.   [3] Ibid., p. 306.
[4] R. W. C., Introduction to *Emma*, p. xi.
[5] In the number for October 1815; which did not, however, appear until March 1816 (R. W. C., Introduction to *Emma*, p. xi).
[6] Lockhart says so, *Life of Scott*, v. 158, n. His statement was questioned, but has now been confirmed by Mr. C. B. Hogan: *Publications of the Modern Language Association of America*, xlv. 1264. It is such uncertainties as this that make us regret Jane's lost correspondence with Henry.   [7] *Letters*, p. 429.
[8] She was nevertheless diffident about this venture, fearing *Emma* would not please. *Letters*, pp. 443 and 449.

history of the august House of Coburg, would just now be very interesting'.[1]

James Stanier Clarke, however, though a dabbler in letters himself, was no very alarming critic. His proposals merely gave point to Jane Austen's delightfully satirical 'plan of a novel',[2] for she was recovering her delight in burlesque. She had been for some while interesting herself in the younger Austens' ventures in novel-writing;[3] and the sort of intimacy so developed may have led to the gay partnership in burlesque invention which Anna remembered:

> 'It was my amusement during part of a summer visit to the cottage to procure novels from the circulating library at Alton, and after running them over to narrate and turn into ridicule their stories to Aunt Jane, much to her amusement . . . We both enjoyed the fun, as did Aunt Cassandra in her quiet way though, as one piece of nonsense led to another, she would exclaim at our folly, and beg us not to make her laugh so much.'[4]

The outcome of one of these sessions was the mock-letter to Mrs. Hunter[5] which survives to illustrate their mood:

> '. . . Miss J. A.'s tears have flowed over each sweet sketch in such a way as would do Mrs Hs heart good to see, & if Mrs H. could understand all Miss Austen's interest in the subject she would certainly have the kindness to publish at least four volumes more about the Flint family. . . .'[6]

This recovered pleasure in burlesque may account for Jane Austen's renewed wish to get possession again of *Northanger Abbey*—and yet not be the sole reason. She had been reading Barrett's burlesque novel, *The Heroine*, in March of 1814; and her own enjoyment of it[7] must have shown her that the time for mocking false romance was not yet past. Henry bought back the copyright of *Northanger Abbey* for her,[8] and she was now free to prepare one of its manuscripts, if she chose, for publication. Clearly, she had

---

[1] *Letters*, p. 451.   [2] *Life*, pp. 337–340; and ed. R. W. C.
[3] At least from May or June 1814, when she acknowledges a part of Anna's manuscript novel (*Letters*, p. 387), onwards; Edward and Caroline also showed her their work.   [4] *Homes and Friends*, quoting 'Family MSS.', p. 195.
[5] A very obscure novelist.   [6] *Letters*, pp. 406, 407.
[7] Ibid., pp. 376, 377. The passage suggests a first reading; *The Heroine* had come out in 1813, and a second edition appeared in 1814.
[8] He is mentioned by name in the first edition of the *Memoir*, p. 171, and Brabourne, *Letters of Jane Austen*, i. 77.

this in mind in 1816,[1] for she wrote in that year the note which was to stand as 'Advertisement by the Authoress to Northanger Abbey' in the first printed version; she may even have given it yet another polishing[2]—her apology in the 'Advertisement' for 'those parts of the work which thirteen years have made comparatively obsolete' need refer to no more than time's action on what had been of topical interest when Crosby bought the manuscript; and 'we are not bound to believe', Dr. Chapman says, 'that nothing was altered after 1803'.[3] Therefore one should be cautious in drawing a line between the so-called earlier and later novels, and in asserting that 'Jane Austen could write at twenty as well, or better, or very nearly as well, as at forty':[4] we cannot be quite sure of knowing how she wrote at twenty.

She had a bigger undertaking on her hands at this time than any revision. *Persuasion* had been begun before she went to stay with Henry in London, in October 1815.[5] It was not to be written in such leisure or comfort as *Emma*. During much of October, November, and December Jane was nursing Henry through a severe illness. The spring brought another anxiety: Henry's business was failing, and in March of 1816 he was declared a bankrupt. By May, Jane's own health and spirits were beginning to decline— so her friends thought, on looking back.[6] But she went steadily on with *Persuasion*, and, on 18 July 1816, brought the story to a close.[7] The tenth chapter of the second volume,[8] however, did not satisfy her. She cancelled the greater part of it, and used the rest in a new draft, of two chapters, now the tenth and eleventh, the original eleventh chapter now standing twelfth (in the second volume).[9] The arrangement of her first draft now obliged her to make a fair copy of this last chapter.[10] Thus, she was in possession

---

[1] Though she seems to have hesitated later; see p. 38.
[2] R. W. C., Introduction to *Northanger Abbey*, pp. xii, xiii.
[3] Ibid., p. xiii.
[4] H. W. Garrod, 'Jane Austen: A Depreciation', *Transactions of the Royal Society of Literature*, 1928, p. 28.
[5] *Life*, p. 333.   [6] Ibid., p. 334.
[7] At the end of the first draft, she wrote 'Finis', and this date. See *Two Chapters of Persuasion*, ed. R. W. C., Introduction.
[8] i.e. the last chapter but one in the original draft.   [9] *Memoir*, pp. 166, 167.
[10] i.e. the original tenth and eleventh chapters. See R. W. C., Introduction to *Two*

of a rough copy of two chapters, and, very fortunately, this manuscript survives[1] to give us a little insight into her mode of revision. With that amendment, *Persuasion* achieved (so far as we know) its final form; but so long afterwards as 13 March 1817 she seems anxious that it should still rest in her possession, for she writes to Fanny: 'I have a something ready for Publication,[2] which may perhaps appear about a twelvemonth hence';[3] and, in a letter of ten days later, implies that she had been anxious to keep its existence a secret from Henry: 'Do not be surprised at finding Uncle Henry acquainted with my having another ready for publication. I could not say No when he asked me. . . .'[4] This may well signify no more than a mood of despondency and self-distrust; even *Northanger Abbey*, which had been prepared for publication the year before, was now dejectedly laid aside: 'Miss Catherine[5] is put upon the Shelve for the present,' Jane tells Fanny in the earlier of these two letters, 'and I do not know that she will ever come out.' She was by now very ill; it was only three days later that she relinquished her last work. On the other hand, these references to *Persuasion*[6] may witness only her resolve to follow her usual practice; she will keep the manuscript by her, not because she has seen faults in it—those she has discovered she has already remedied—but in order to find out what faults yet lurk there. The proposed period of probation, longer than *Emma*'s, may perhaps signify a distrust of Henry's affectionate impetuosity—or else a consciousness of the less favourable conditions in which *Persuasion* has been written.

The last work (which came to be known among her

Chapters of Persuasion. This introduction corrects, moreover, the *Memoir*'s account of the manuscript (of these two chapters) and gives its later history.

[1] It was left to Anna.

[2] That is, not a rough draft, such as the last work.

[3] *Letters*, p. 484. She asks Fanny to keep it secret—but that need imply no more than a natural distaste for gossip.   [4] Ibid., p. 487.

[5] 'Catherine' must have superseded 'Susan' as title. Was 'Northanger Abbey' Henry's choice? *Persuasion*, also, was left for him to publish; but *that* is a title of the kind that J. A. evidently liked—she had praised Anna's 'Enthusiasm' (*Letters*, p. 393).

[6] The identification of this unnamed novel with *Persuasion* is, of course, conjectural, but there is circumstantial evidence: it is described as 'about the length of Catherine' (*Letters*, p. 484), and 'the Heroine'—Jane tells Fanny—'. . . is almost too good for me' (ibid., p. 487). Besides, it cannot well be anything else.

family as *Sanditon*[1]) is a very surprising outcome of those last six months of her life (it had been begun on 27 January 1817[2]): it is a hilarious comedy of invalidism, and (what was even less to be expected) a bold venture in a new way of telling a story. While each of the earlier novels had been, in some respect, an advance beyond its predecessors, none of them would, if broken off short at the eleventh chapter, have left us in such uncertainty as to the way in which it was going to develop; and her other piece of unfinished work, *The Watsons*, seems, by comparison, almost to foreshadow its own fulfilment. At the end of the manuscript of *Sanditon* stands the date 'March 18'.[3] It was in that month, Caroline remembered, that she first realized how ill her aunt was.[4] In May Jane, with Cassandra, settled in lodgings at Winchester, where she might be attended by the best reputed surgeon of that neighbourhood, Charles Lyford—who from the first seems to have had little hope of what his attentions could do.[5] Jane was still writing gay, mocking letters, describing herself as 'a very genteel, portable sort of an Invalid',[6] and proposing, if Mr. Lyford should fail to cure her, to ask the Dean and Chapter for redress,[7] so late as the end of that month. The last letter of hers that survives has this characteristic passage: 'You will find Captain—a very respectable, well-meaning man, without much manner, his wife and sister all good humour and obligingness, and I hope (since the fashion allows it) with rather longer petticoats than last year.'[8] In June, James's wife, Mary, came to help Cassandra in nursing. On 18 July, Jane Austen died.

A few years later Scott wrote to Joanna Baillie:

'I am delighted with the prospect of seeing Miss Edgeworth and making her personal acquaintance. I expect her to be just what you describe a being totally void of affectation and who like one other lady

---

[1] *Life*, p. 381, n. 2.   [2] Ibid., p. 381.
[3] R. W. C., Introduction to *Sanditon*.
[4] *Memoir*, p. 171. At the end of that month Jane made her will. Mrs. Austen's brother, James Leigh Perrot, died on 28 March; his will was a disappointment to the Austens: they were to benefit by his bequests only after his wife's death; and, their present circumstances being narrow, especially since Henry's failure, this was a hardship. J. A. felt dejected and anxious.   [5] Ibid., p. 172.
[6] *Letters*, p. 494.   [7] Ibid., p. 496.
[8] Ibid., p. 498. Quoted in the postscript to Henry's *Biographical Notice* in 1817, but left out of the—otherwise enlarged—1833 version.

of my acquaintance carries her literary reputation as freely and easily as the milk-maid in my country does the *leglen* which she carries on her head and walks as gracefully with it as a Duchess. Some of the fair sex and of the foul sex too carry their renown London-fashion on a yoke and a pair of pitchers the consequence is that besides poking frightfully they are hitting every one on the shins with their two buckets. Now this is all nonsense too fantastic to be written to any body but a person of good sense. By the way did you know Miss Austen Authoress of some novels which have a great deal of nature in them—nature in ordinary and middle life to be sure but valuable from its strong resemblance and correct drawing. I wonder which way she carried her pail?'[1]

It is a pity that he had had no chance to learn, and leave recorded, the answer to this question. But a single encounter might have been worse than none. It would be necessary to know more of her than could be learnt in that way.

This was her life, and these, in brief, the circumstances to which she must learn to accommodate herself. Something more may be discovered by watching her mind as it responds to what she reads, and as it tries to formulate and solve the problems of her art. Beyond this, there is no profitable going. Of her response to more private promptings, to the religious doctrines which she accepted with mind as well as heart, she would hold that—for herself as for the rest of the laity—this was nothing of general concern. And there the matter may well rest.

[1] Scott, *Letters*, ed. H. J. C. Grierson, vii. 60.

CHAPTER II

READING AND RESPONSE

'THEY who do not read,' Johnson writes to Miss Thrale, 'can have nothing to think, and little to say.'[1] What did Jane Austen read, and what did it give her, to think and to say?

When *Emma* was in the press, James Stanier Clarke, who had concerned himself with its dedication to the Prince Regent, wrote to offer advice on Miss Austen's next book. The hero, he suggested, should be a clergyman, of such-and-such habits, such-and-such idiosyncrasies of manner, 'Fond of, & entirely engaged in Literature'.[2] Miss Austen replied politely that she was honoured by his proposal, but did not feel able to take advantage of it:

'Such a man's conversation must at times be on subjects of science and philosophy, of which I know nothing; or at least be occasionally abundant in quotations and allusions which a woman who, like me, knows only her own mother tongue, and has read little in that, would be totally without the power of giving. A classical education, or at any rate a very extensive acquaintance with English literature, ancient and modern, appears to me quite indispensable for the person who would do any justice to your clergyman; and I think I may boast myself to be, with all possible vanity, the most unlearned and uninformed female who ever dared to be an authoress.'[3]

The reader who, having both letters—the proposal and the reply—before him, can take the reply literally must closely resemble Mr. Clarke himself.

A just estimate of what her reading meant to Jane Austen is a necessity, for it underlies comprehension of what she intended that her writings should mean to their readers. To read was a matter of course and habit, no less for her than for other people of her condition; but the way in which her reading coloured her imagination, and consequently her writing, was peculiar to herself. Moreover, an allusive habit of expression also peculiar to her—an outcome, perhaps, of the conditions in which she wrote—allows us to

[1] *Queeney Letters*, ed. Lord Lansdowne, 1934, p. 22 (letter of 18 July 1780).
[2] *Letters*, p. 430; see also pp. 444, 445.   [3] Ibid., p. 443.

perceive something of the quality of this individual response to books, and its significance.

One might, perhaps, have expected to find the traces which Jane Austen's reading left on her writing most clearly apparent in her use of the *narrative material* which had served other novelists. But I do not believe that a search in this direction would be profitable—even if it could be conclusive—and for this reason: she had chosen to limit her scene, and with it her range of possible incident, to a particular social world. Others were attempting to present this scene—had been busy with the attempt ever since *Evelina*'s appearance. When many story-tellers occupy themselves with a social world which offers no great variety of likely action, their stories will probably resemble one another as to many of the major incidents, and if they draw on these limited resources like spendthrifts such resemblances will be inevitable—and therefore not significant. Now Fanny Burney and her successors were prodigals of this kind: in their plots were to be found almost all the likely happenings[1] of family life among the English gentry—besides some that are not at all likely. Therefore, to find an episode or turn of plot in one of Jane Austen's novels which resembles one in some earlier novel—even though that precursor should be one of her favourites, and prompting be as likely an explanation as coincidence—*this* tells us very little of what the work of that earlier novelist meant to Jane Austen; for, so long as she remained content to build her plots of these major incidents, she could not but build them of material that had been used already. Maria Edgeworth and Susan Ferrier evaded this compulsion when they adventured into other social worlds, hitherto unexplored; Jane Austen, remaining among her 'Country Families',[2] was to escape from it in another way.

Her real debts acknowledge themselves in her style, both in the narrow sense, her management of words, and in the wider, management of her narrative material; and it is in relation to these that I shall try to assess them.[3]

---

[1] All, that is, which would count as 'action' to the novelists and novel-readers of that day.   [2] *The Watsons*, p. 1; *Minor Works*, p. 314.   [3] See Part II.

For the purpose of this chapter, it is the quality of her response to what she read that matters; and I believe that an attempt to appreciate this quality should begin with a scrutiny of her allusions to books and writers. Some among the most significant of these may be called tacit allusions— they are not spoken aloud in her published work. Her acceptance of Johnson's practical wisdom, though it colours the view of life which her novels present, is acknowledged only in the exceptionally caressing tone of the references in her letters to 'my dear Dr. Johnson'.[1] Cowper, too, holds a place in her imagination which would hardly be appreciable if it were not for her letters; she consciously associates her impressions of the actual world with those other impressions, in that world of images *behind* the eyes, which his poetry has formed. She must have syringas for their garden in Southampton: 'I could not do without a Syringa, for the sake of Cowper's Line.'[2] I think that these two stand apart from the rest; there is little less intimacy in the allusions to Scott and Crabbe—nearly as much light pretence of personal acquaintanceship; but she does not refer herself to them, test her impressions and opinions against theirs, as she uses to do with Johnson and Cowper.

The allusions audible in her published work are of two kinds, one not far in tone from those I have noticed in the letters. This kind never takes the *form* of direct acknowledgement or compliment, and yet (unlike those other allusions which assume that form) it always carries an implicit tribute. It is most often an allusion to some idiosyncrasy of a writer familiar to her, and then the implied compliment— all the more pointed for its sheath of satire—consists in its being fully intelligible only to those readers who share her familiarity with his peculiar habits of thought and expression. It is as elliptical and indirect as talk among friends, where intuitive understanding of implications can be counted on. Some book, some passage, provokes a response in her, and she records that response for her own satisfaction— and, inseparable from hers, Cassandra's: whether it will be for many others' seldom concerns her much.

---

[1] *Letters*, p. 181.   [2] Ibid., p. 178.

Johnson himself provokes (I think) one such response, by his thirty-eighth number of *The Rambler*, in which he warns his readers of the dangers of superfluity in health as well as in riches. In the summer of 1816 Jane Austen, struggling with the langour of her last illness, in narrow circumstances which would probably contract if she lived to be old, might well smile at this marked idiosyncrasy in her 'favourite moral writer',[1] and quietly record her amusement in the work she had then in hand.

'Mrs. Smith's enjoyments', she explains gravely, 'were not spoiled by this improvement of income, with some improvement of health, and the acquisition of such friends to be often with, for her cheerfulness and mental alacrity did not fail her; and while these prime supplies of good remained, she might have bid defiance even to greater accessions of worldly prosperity. She might have been absolutely rich and perfectly healthy, and yet be happy.'[2]

There spoke, not her 'dear Dr. Johnson' of the letters to Mrs. Thrale, but the anxious censor of his generation's morals. And likewise Cowper—not the Cowper of *The Task*, but the less easy, less charming Cowper of the formal satires —wakens a mocking echo when he leaves the little world he understands to censure the great world that he knows only by report, and draw a severe comparison between 'Voltaire and the religious Cottager'.[3] Even so Goldsmith, when he left his proper work for compiling of histories, had received a pert little gesture of acknowledgement from the 'partial, prejudiced, and ignorant historian'[4] of 1791. She possessed and had read his *History of England*;[5] very probably it was the school-room history book at Steventon (and I should guess that it was its facetious and long-drawn-out accounts of executions that gave Catherine Morland her distaste for history). Thus, it is likely enough that it was one of the books which prompted *The History of England from the reign of Henry the 4th to the death of Charles the 1st*[6]—and one sly allusion turns likelihood into certainty.

---

[1] *Biographical Notice*, p. 7—Johnson 'in prose, and Cowper in verse'.
[2] *Persuasion*, p. 252, ch. xxiv.   [3] *Sanditon*, p. 17; *Minor Works*, p. 370.
[4] *Love and Freindship*, p. 81; *Minor Works*, p. 139.
[5] *Life*, p. 29. It was the four-volume *History* of 1771; see G. L. Keynes, *Bibliography*, 1929.
[6] Another of them may well have been that most ridiculous of historical romances, *The Recess*, by Sophia Lee (1785); it is the story of a secret marriage between Mary

Below the dedication stands this note: 'N.B. There will be very few Dates in this History'—and indeed there are none at all until the story of 'Anna Bullen' is reached, when the historian turns aside to observe: 'Tho' I do not profess giving many dates, yet as I think it proper to give some and shall of course make choice of those which it is most necessary for the Reader to know, I think it right to inform him that her letter to the King was dated on the 6th of May.'[1] Now, Goldsmith actually gives this 'necessary date' in the closing sentence of Anne Boleyn's plea—'From my doleful prison in the Tower, this sixth of May'[2]—what is more, it is the only date that he gives in the course of those eight reigns.

Gilpin, opinionated, enthusiastic, persuasive, was bound to make his appearance in this company of writers whom Jane Austen liked so well as to delight in their foibles: already, in her *History of England*, he receives an impudent little curtsey[3]—which favour he must share with those other picturesque figures, Robert Earl of Essex[4] and Emmeline's Delamere.[5] And his dogmatic appreciation of 'the picturesque' in landscape surely inspired Henry Tilney's 'lecture on the picturesque . . . in which his instructions were so clear that [Catherine] soon began to see beauty in every thing admired by him, and her attention was so earnest, that he became perfectly satisfied of her having a great deal of natural taste'.[6] She became, in fact, so apt a pupil as to be sure that, in his absence, 'she should not know what was picturesque when she saw it'.[7]

Indeed, there are implicit allusions of many kinds—lying as it were, at various depths—in Jane Austen's writings; Dr. Chapman has already made that evident. And if my

Queen of Scots and the Duke of Norfolk, and of the twin daughters born to them, and may account for the two pointed references to the Duke of Norfolk's support of Queen Mary's cause (*Love and Freindship*, pp. 89 and 92; *Minor Works*, pp. 143 and 145).

[1] *Love and Freindship*, p. 89; *Minor Works*, p. 143.

[2] ii. 384 (1771). Except in this passage, Goldsmith spells her name 'Anne Bullen' —here 'Boleyn', perhaps because it is so spelt in No. 397 of the *Spectator*, from which he may have lifted this letter bodily. [3] *Love and Freindship*, p. 90; *Minor Works*, p. 144.

[4] Who makes a flamboyantly picturesque appearance in *The Recess*.

[5] Charlotte Smith, *Emmeline, The Orphan of the Castle*, 1788.

[6] *Northanger Abbey*, p. 111, ch. xiv.

[7] Ibid., p. 177, ch. xxii.

conjectures as to an elusive reference here and there are to
be trusted, then it seems likely that there may be many more
still lying perdu—not noticeable, because they sprang from
an impulse of expression rather than of communication,
were nothing but the spontaneous record of her response—
whether assent or protest—to what she read. There is, for
example, a passage in *Sanditon* which sounds like an echo of
The Task—the discussion between Mr. and Mrs. Parker as
to the proper situation for a house. Cowper, in the first and
third books of *The Task*, had made very good fun of the
'improvers', who could not be satisfied with

> th'abode
> Of our forefathers, a grave whisker'd race,
> But tasteless. Springs a palace in its stead,
> But in a distant spot; where more expos'd
> It may enjoy th'advantage of the north,
> And agueish East, till time shall have transform'd
> Those naked acres to a shelt'ring grove.[1]

He played with this fancy:

> Our fathers knew the value of a screen
> From sultry suns, and in their shaded walks
> And long protracted bow'rs, enjoy'd at noon
> The gloom and coolness of declining day.
> We bear our shades about us; self depriv'd
> Of other screen, the thin umbrella spread,
> And range an Indian waste without a tree.[2]

I cannot but think that *The Task*, long familiar, was still fresh
in Jane Austen's mind when she made Mrs. Parker look
regretfully back to the sheltered, shady house they had left,
and Mr. Parker reassure her: 'My dear, we shall have shade
enough on the Hill & more than enough in the course of a
very few years;—The Growth of my Plantations is a general
astonishment. In the mean while we have the Canvas Awn-
ing, which gives us the most complete comfort within
doors—& you can get a Parasol at Whitby's for little
Mary . . .'[3]—until she meekly admits: 'I have not the smallest doubt of our being a great deal better off where we are
now.'[4]

---

[1] Bk. iii, ll. 767–773.   [2] Bk. i, ll. 255–261.
[3] *Sanditon*, p. 46; *Minor Works*, p. 381.   [4] Ibid., p. 47; *Minor Works*, p. 381.

Even among Jane Austen's explicit allusions many present themselves almost as unobtrusively as these. For example, they are not of necessity made in her own person. Books and writers may be mentioned because they are bound up in some way with the story: they play an important part in the intercourse between Edmund and Fanny,[1] between Anne and Captain Benwick;[2] and taste in literature serves as a letter of introduction to the pleasantly bookish family at Barton Cottage—Willoughby's welcome is certain once he has assured Marianne 'of his admiring Pope no more than is proper'.[3] Robert Martin's relation to Harriet and her fortunes is lightly foreshadowed when she describes him as having read *The Vicar of Wakefield* and being about to attempt *The Romance of the Forest* on her recommendation.[4]

Taste in reading does, in fact, serve to differentiate character (each one, from Henry Crawford to Miss Bates, having his own manner of misquoting) in the social world of Jane Austen's novels, a world which offers small scope for difference of opinion in any other matter of general concern.[5] Indeed, it pleases Jane Austen to be so consistent and exact in this matter that one can confidently deduce *her* likes and dislikes from the distribution of opinions among her characters. Ironically reserved as are most of the references to novelists in her published writings—it is her letters, rather than *Northanger Abbey*, that disclose her real liking for Maria Edgeworth—an unmistakable compliment is paid in them to two favourites, Richardson and Fanny Burney: the Thorpes cannot read them.[6] And, at the last, Scott is distinguished in the same manner—for who would not wish to be thought insipid by Sir Edward Denham? 'Tender, Elegant, Descriptive—but *Tame*'[7]—Sir Edward's unconscious tribute is paid, it is true, to Scott's poetry—but paid

[1] *Mansfield Park*, e.g. p. 156, ch. xvi.
[2] *Persuasion*, e.g. p. 100, ch. xi.
[3] *Sense and Sensibility*, p. 47, ch. x.   [4] *Emma*, p. 29, ch. iv.
[5] See R. W. C., *Emma*, Appendix (on Manners), p. 510, as to the etiquette which forbade women (in that age and that social world) to express any opinion on politics.
[6] It is true that Richardson's novels are admired by Sir Edward Denham, but only for those elements in them which J. A. considered perishable; much as (I think) she points her intention by making John Thorpe abuse the best part of *Camilla*.
[7] *Sanditon*, p. 91; *Minor Works*, p. 397. Although a rough draft, it may fairly be called work intended for publication.

at a time when Jane Austen has come to respect him as a novelist. Before the appearance of *Waverley* she had been disposed to rally him as the favourite of such romantic enthusiasts as Marianne Dashwood and Fanny Price. (And yet, even that raillery had not been quite *un*-complimentary: Fanny's expectation that Sotherton chapel will answer to Scott's description of Melrose[1] is the airiest and prettiest of follies. No raillery of precisely this kind is ever directed towards Byron.) To *Waverley* Jane Austen surrendered: 'Walter Scott has no business to write novels, especially good ones.— It is not fair.— He has Fame and Profit enough as a Poet, and should not be taking the bread out of other people's mouths.— I do not like him, & do not mean to like Waverley if I can help it—but fear I must.'[2]

To set against these allusive, indirect expressions of her taste, and those direct expressions of taste that is not hers, but her creatures', there seems to be only one passage that presents itself as an explicit statement of opinion in the author's own voice—the bold defence of novel-reading in *Northanger Abbey*.[3] And is that passage really so simple as it looks? It may, as C. L. Thomson suggested,[4] be a retort to the 'Advertisement' to *Belinda*[5]—in which case there is a double edge to its reproof of disingenuous young ladies who push a novel out of sight with the shame-faced admission that 'it is only . . . Belinda'. But, whether Miss Edgeworth had provoked it or no,[6] there is surely, in its extravagant claims for the novel—which has 'afforded more

---

[1] *Mansfield Park*, pp. 85, 86, ch. ix.   [2] *Letters*, p. 404.
[3] pp. 37, 38, ch. v.   [4] See p. 19.
[5] 'Every author has a right to give what appellation he may think proper to his works. The public have also a right to accept or refuse the classification that is presented.
    'The following work is offered to the public as a Moral Tale—the author not wishing to acknowledge a Novel. Were all novels like those of madame de Crousaz, Mrs. Inchbald, miss Burney, or Dr. Moore, she would adopt the name of novel with delight: But so much folly, errour, and vice are disseminated in books classed under this denomination, that it is hoped the wish to assume another title will be attributed to feelings that are laudable, and not fastidious' (1801).
[6] If she had, her 'Advertisement' may yet not have been the sole provocation; letter XLII in the seventh volume of *Sir Charles Grandison* relates a conversation between Mrs. Shirley and her grand-daughters, in which she tells them: 'The reading in fashion when I was young, was Romances. You, my children, have, in that respect, fallen into happier days. The present age is greatly obliged to the authors of the Spectators.'

extensive and unaffected pleasure' than any other sort of writing, and which is so boisterously preferred above the classics of the age—some suspicion of overstatement, pendant to the demure understatement in Catherine's eventual criticism of Mrs. Radcliffe. (Of Jane Austen's attitude towards Mrs. Radcliffe I have not thought it necessary to speak, unless incidentally, because it has already been closely scrutinized.[1])

It is clear, then, that allusions to books run like an undercurrent through Jane Austen's writing; her preoccupation with them is constant, but it is seldom, if ever, quite directly expressed. Now, this unforced habit of implicit allusion does not belong to the kind of reader who is unaware of the relation between his impressions of the actual world and impressions of that world of illusion which his reading has created in his imagination. And that is a relationship of which Jane Austen is acutely conscious. And we, having this consciousness disclosed to us by her allusive undertones, can find her apprehension of that relationship intelligibly expressed in the element of burlesque that is in almost all her work. There she formulates in her own way her criticism of what she has read. Her burlesque writing is like the visible part of an iceberg—the more formidable submerged part to which it bears witness being her deliberate attempt to avoid the faults she here satirizes. Therefore, in so far as these are technical faults, it will be well to study her burlesque pieces together with her technical achievement: to lay her early mockery of unsound artistic methods alongside her mature rejection of those methods,[2] her juvenilia beside her novels—even at the risk of seeming to treat too seriously those airy sports of wit. But in so far as her burlesque writing expresses criticism of the false vision of life that books seem to her to present, it is well to examine it in this chapter, for this criticism lies at the root of her intention as a novelist. To such an inquiry, one measure is necessary: burlesque speaks the language of its age, and therefore the temper of that age, and above all of its novel-

[1] Especially, of course, by Mr. Sadleir, in his Introduction to *Northanger Abbey* (Oxford, 1930).   [2] See Part II.

ists, novel-readers, and critics of the novel, demands, at
this point, a cursory examination. These people—most of
the writers unprofessional, or of small pretensions, most
of the readers casual and uncritical—belonged to the larger
community of literate but unliterary readers, which was
then awakening to a new consciousness of the part that
reading plays in the growth of the ordinary person's mental
constitution.

A symptom of this consciousness is the impulse (it is
deeper-rooted than a mere fashion) to introduce quotations
from familiar literature into all kinds of writing. Passages
from her favourite authors lie so thick among Mrs. Grant's
letters as to need the apology she offers for another of her
enthusiasms: 'Tombs . . . have a particular attraction for
me, I cannot get quietly past them.'[1] That is the trouble
with all of them—they cannot get quietly past a quotation
or allusion. While Scott (truly a man of letters, for all his
pretence of amateurishness) seems, when he quotes poetry,
to be merely slipping into his native language,[2] the lesser
novelists introduce quotations or set their puppets to talk
of books with a self-conscious air. 'To . . . [Morano] indeed',
says Mrs. Radcliffe, 'might have been applied that beautiful
exhortation of an English poet, had it then existed . . .'[3]
And even Miss Burney and Miss Edgeworth fall into this
uneasy style when they try to bring the imaginative posses-
sions of which they are conscious to the surface of their
writing.[4] Sharing as she did this consciousness, Jane Austen
yet perceived what was absurd in her contemporaries' expression of it. Mrs. Elton, displaying quotations, like framed
certificates of culture, in her talk;[5] Sir Edward Denham,
sprinkling his with fragments of half-remembered poetry
and half-understood criticism; Mr. Parker, backing his argument with an inappropriate line snatched ragged from its

---

[1] *Letters from the Mountains; being the real Correspondence of a Lady between the years
1773 and 1807* (1807). (J. A. knew them.)
[2] Witness the undercurrent of Shakespearian allusion and quotation in his
Journal.
[3] *Udolpho* (1794), ch. xvii.
[4] Surprisingly, this self-consciousness seems to persist and cramp even George
Eliot, for all the depth of her familiarity with the world of books.
[5] *Emma*, p. 282, ch. xxxiii; and p. 308, ch. xxxvi.

context;[1] these variously seem to show why their author rarely, if ever, expressed her share of that consciousness directly. It is no wonder that she retorted to James Stanier Clarke's proposal with the boast that she was 'the most unlearned and uninformed female who ever dared to be an authoress'.

The awakening of this widespread consciousness was accompanied by a sharpened anxiety as to the influence of the novel. The periodical essayists and reviewers to whom Jane Austen pretends to retort in *Northanger Abbey*[2] had writers of more authority to back them. Johnson had argued that novels, being more plausible than other kinds of fiction, invited the reader to identify himself with their personages, and that they were addressed to those least able to resist this insidious invitation:

'These Books are written chiefly to the Young, the Ignorant, and the Idle, to whom they serve as Lectures of Conduct, and Introductions into Life . . . when an Adventurer is levelled with the rest of the World, and acts in such Scenes of the Universal Drama, as may be the Lot of any other Man; young Spectators fix their Eyes upon him with closer Attention, and hope by observing his Behaviour and Success to regulate their own Practices, when they shall be engaged in the like Part. . . . If the Power of Example is so great, as to take Possession of the Memory by a kind of Violence, and produce Effects almost without the Intervention of the Will, Care ought to be taken, that . . . the best Examples only should be exhibited.'[3]

This argument still kept its force in Scott's day, and was developed by him in his review of *Emma*.

Cowper attacked the immoral persuasion of the popular novel, and the novelists

> Who kindling a combustion of desire,
> With some cold moral think to quench the fire.[4]

Crabbe returned to the attack again and again:[5] novels had meant too much to him in his starved youth; they must not be allowed to inflame and injure other minds.

---

[1] *Sanditon*, p. 17; *Minor Works*, p. 370.
[2] p. 37: 'Let us leave it to the Reviewers to abuse such effusions of fancy at their leisure, and over every new novel to talk in threadbare strains of the trash with which the press now groans.'
[3] *The Rambler*, number 4.
[4] *Progress of Error*, ll. 319, 320.
[5] *The Borough*, letters XII, XV, XX; see p. 58.

Indeed, he has all Mr. Woodhouse's kindly anxiety on others' behalf, and all his ignorance of robuster constitutions than his own—but it is their mental constitution that he is anxious to protect, and against Regina Maria Roche rather than wedding cake.

Thus, the novelists are frequently summoned to judgement by other writers,[1] only to be dismissed with a warning which they cannot but have found flattering: their influence is so strong that they must be careful as to its direction.

They *were* flattered. Bound as they were to consider their own work ephemeral,[2] they were willing to be persuaded that in its little day it could make some mark, if only an ugly one. At its best, this belief produces Maria Edgeworth's keen sense of responsibility—as moralist rather than as artist; more commonly, mere censoriousness: the novelists are very hard on one another. Susan Ferrier, so late as 1815, can call Mrs. Brunton's *Discipline* 'one of the very few novels I think fit for family use'.[3] Indeed, there is a stir of excited mutual curiosity among the members of this 'injured body'.[4] One recalls Miss Edgeworth's disconcerting first encounter with Mme de Genlis, who asked her visitor whether she knew the work of a fellow novelist—'and kissed my forehead twice because I had not read it'.[5] This is the excitement that accompanies a fancied sense of power. Whether that power was really so great; whether novels were read so immoderately by the young, and whether the young were so gullible—as the novelists supposed: these questions must stay open for the present. What we have to understand, now, is the part the novel played as a common ground of intercourse among readers of all sorts in

[1] e.g. Sir Thomas Bernard in *Spurinna or the Comforts of Old Age*. In the 1813 edition of this dialogue, novel-reading is not mentioned among the relaxations allowable in old age; in the 1816 edition it is suggested, challenged, and admitted 'speciali gratia'.

[2] Miss Tompkins, in the first chapter of *The Popular Novel in England, 1770–1800*, notices this current opinion, which the reviewers emphasized by their 'conviction that the novel was played out', that 'the works of Fielding and Richardson were . . . the culmination of a development' (p. 5).

[3] *Memoir and Correspondence of Susan Ferrier, 1782–1854*, ed. J. A. Doyle, 1898, p. 117.

[4] *Northanger Abbey*, p. 37.

[5] *Maria Edgeworth: Life and Letters*, ed. A. J. C. Hare, 1894, i. 131 (letter of 19 March 1803).

that age; it was ground on which men and women, the man
of letters and the common reader, could meet on comfortable terms. For there is one way in which the novel lends
itself to discussion among people who have not the necessary equipment for interchange of ideas on literary technique, or else (and this may be the greater handicap) are
unequally equipped. It is possible to treat the characters
as though they belonged to the actual world, and discuss
them, and their fortunes, as common acquaintances are
discussed in a circle of friends. I emphasize this hitherto
obvious possibility because it is now beginning to appear
outlandish and remote. It may be that to-day's novels offer
less opportunity for this treatment than those of the last
two centuries; it may be that we have lost the technique
proper to discussion of character, manners, style in conversation; it is certain that Jane Austen's contemporaries
possessed it and applied it to the creatures of fiction with
which they were familiar in a way that survives only among
the admirers of some one or another of a diminishing
company of novelists.

This kind of discussion had, of course, been current in
the novelists' own households almost from the beginning;
their friends' inquiries after their health and the fortunes of
their characters are made in the very same tone of voice;
Miss Mulso writes to Miss Highmore: 'You give me very
great pleasure in the account of your own happiness at
North End. I cannot envy my friends, but I wish to partake in their delights, which I always do when I hear of
them. I am very glad that poor Charlotte has extricated
herself from the confusion I left her in . . .'[1]—and so goes
on to discuss *Sir Charles Grandison*. But more significant is
the gradual dispersion of this sort of discussion. And even
the quantity and variety of the allusions to novels, in the
journals and letters of that age, tell us less than does their
tone. It is clear that they played an unobtrusively constant
part in the common intercourse of very various people.

Johnson sets the key, with his playful treatment of
Evelina. 'She no more minds me', he growls when Fanny

[1] *Richardson's Correspondence*, ed. A. L. Barbauld (1804), ii. 267.

Burney neglects him, 'than if I were a Brangton',[1] and his circle takes up the game, teasing Fanny by talking to her in Mme Duval's language, or the Branghtons', until her characters acquire a ghostly life of their own outside her books, and one of the children of her acquaintance comes to ask her gravely: 'Ma'am . . . will you . . . be so good as to tell me where Evelina is now?'[2] Scott's anecdote of a friend nicknamed after Mr. Bennet[3] is in the same vein; so is Maria Edgeworth's, of a party in Paris at which, when attempts to define an English dandy had failed, 'Madame d'Arblay's Meadows' was cited as an illustration.[4] These, it is true, may still be called novelists' circles; but look outside them, and still the tone of the allusions is the same— whether the grave Mrs. Carter unbends, in writing of the *Odyssey*, and calls Eumaeus 'Mr. Trulliber (I have forgot his Greek name)',[5] or likens her dear Miss Talbot to Richardson's Miss Howe[6]—or the still graver Mrs. Grant nicknames a disagreeable fellow traveller Smelfungus,[7] or calls moonlit nights 'Werter nights'.[8] Lady Louisa Stuart, looking back on her youth and the fashions that ruled then, can recall her first reading of *The Man of Feeling* and her 'secret dread [lest she] should not cry enough to gain the credit of proper sensibility'.[9]

And though we leave these literary people, and listen to women of fashion talking together, still the tone does not change—whether Lady Sarah Lennox compares a friend's situation with that of Joseph Andrews,[10] or Mrs. Lybbe Powys compares her own with that of Sir Charles Grandison,[11] or is reminded by two neighbours of Harriet Byron

---

[1] *Letters*, ed. G. Birkbeck Hill (1892), ii. 137. G. B. H. quotes in illustration from Fanny Burney's *Memoirs of Dr. Burney*; see also *The Queeney Letters*, ed. Lord Lansdowne, p. 22, for reported discussion of Captain Mirvan.

[2] *Diary and Letters of Mme d'Arblay*, ed. Austin Dobson (1904), i. 420.

[3] In his review of *Emma* for the *Quarterly*, p. 194.

[4] *Life and Letters*, ed. A. J. C. Hare, i. 298 (July 1820). See also her anecdote (op. cit. ii. 108) of the Highland guide who likened her sister to Sophia Western.

[5] *A Series of Letters between Mrs. Carter and Miss Talbot, 1741–70*, ed. M. Pennington (1809), i. 166.   [6] Ibid. i. 244.

[7] *Letters from the Mountains*, iii. 155.   [8] Ibid., ii. 143, 144.

[9] *Lady Louisa Stuart: Selections from her Manuscripts*, ed. J. A. Home (1899), p. 236.

[10] *Letters*, i. 182.

[11] *Passages from the Diaries of Mrs. Philip Lybbe Powys*, ed. J. Climenson (1899), p. 128.

and Lucy Selby.[1] Sensitiveness to a particular range of literary associations becomes common: Mrs. Lybbe Powys no more than Miss Edgeworth can see an old building without being reminded of Mrs. Radcliffe.

When allusions of this temper are to be found so dispersed, it seems possible to count not merely on a quick consciousness (in the mind of the common reader) of that province of the world of illusion which naturalistic fiction was then creating, but also on his capacity for responding to allusive comparisons between this world of illusion and the actual world. In such conditions burlesque can thrive; and this age produced its crop of burlesques of current fiction. There were, for example, Charlotte Lennox's *Female Quixote*, which, though it had been written in 1752 and aimed at the fading romances, was still read and enjoyed by Jane Austen; Maria Edgeworth's *Angelina*,[2] Sarah Green's *Romance Readers and Romance Writers*,[3] and Eaton Stannard Barrett's *The Heroine*,[4] all three falling between the date when *Northanger Abbey* was drafted and the date when it was published.

Thus, it is to an awareness of the world of illusion, rather than to an acquaintance with this or that novel, or school of novel-writing, that Jane Austen can, and does, appeal through the burlesque element in her work; and this is what makes that element imperishable—likely, at least, to last so long as the awareness itself survives. That may have lost, with its novelty, a little of its sharpness; but while there are common readers and imperfect novels it should not die.

Burlesque—by which I mean burlesque of fiction, since that is the limit of our present concern—must, at this point, be broadly defined, and its possible varieties discriminated. In such burlesque, mockery, critically directed, expresses itself by means of imitation. (The criticism may be trivially conceived—or else so seriously as to abash the mocking spirit; or the mockery owe little of its force to the imitation; but where any of the three is absent, the outcome is not burlesque.)

[1] Ibid., p. 134.   [2] 1801.
[3] 1810.   [4] 1813.

The most direct and obvious kind of burlesque consists in imitation to which exaggeration, displaced emphasis, or some other distortion has given a mocking turn—the object of its mimicry, therefore, being also the object of its mockery, which is not a necessary condition of all kinds of burlesque. It is best suited to criticism of technique—hence, it is the toy of scholars; and of patent improbability—and so, the sport of young wits. It is the staple of Jane Austen's juvenilia, but finds its way into her mature work only indirectly, in such passages as Henry Tilney's spirited skit on *Udolpho*. It threatens to cramp the creative artist, who, seeing the action develop in the theatre of his imagination, is impelled to cry out 'Ah, but that's not how it should be— look here . . .' and set over against his caricature of the world of illusion a faithful delineation of the actual world. This demands a kind of burlesque writing which shall have greater scope for subtlety; and two such kinds are remarkable especially for the use to which Jane Austen puts them.

In one, the contrast between false and true is reflected in the career of a character whose expectations, derived from fiction, are challenged and found false by experience. For all its subtle possibilities, this kind can become, in clumsy hands, as crude a type of burlesque as any. The burlesques which I have cited as representative of Jane Austen's age follow this pattern, and all (not excepting the two which she herself praised) are coarse-grained stuff. Arabella, the deluded heroine of Charlotte Lennox's *Female Quixote*, 'supposing Romances were real pictures of Life, from them . . . drew all her Notions and Expectations';[1] and a succession of ludicrous, painful, and dangerous misfortunes, followed by a very tedious and pedantic argument with a doctor of divinity, was needed to undeceive her. And though Charlotte Lennox knew the romances well enough to draw every one of Arabella's delusions from their conventions, these same 'notions and expectations' might, for all of point that remains to the mimicry, have arisen quite as satisfactorily from mere ignorance and giddiness, like those of Betsy Thoughtless;[2] so little of literary

---

[1] Ch. i.   [2] Mrs. Haywood's *History of Miss Betsy Thoughtless* (1751).

discernment has gone to the making of this and the following burlesque pieces. As for Maria Edgeworth's Angelina, she is brought by a surfeit of sentimental novels into a sordid and dangerous situation, and narrowly rescued from bailiffs and a drunken harridan—so narrowly that if we for a moment believed in her the story would come too near to tragedy; comedy it never approaches. Sarah Green's Margaret, having intoxicated herself with novel-reading until she is little better than an idiot, entertains disgusting conjectures as to the real people among whom she lives, and gets herself into squalid scrapes—it is a coarse piece of work. Barrett, though he is a smarter workman, treats his heroine no less brutally : like the rest, she can only be convinced of her folly by violent calamity and ponderous argument. These authors are impatient with the fools whom they have created and undertaken to reform, and there lies the danger of this pattern of burlesque; for the impatience of the writer is very apt to communicate itself to the reader. Peacock himself hardly escapes this impatience—until he reaches the serene mood of *Gryll Grange* and Miss Niphet, and is in no more hurry than a parent watching a child grow up.

In the other of these two burlesque patterns which have scope for subtlety, some fictitious situation or course of action is translated into terms of actual life—by which, of course, I intend, as always, a faithful representation of life as the writer sees it. Thus, suppose him to borrow a situation, he may offer to develop it; suppose a course of action, to tell what really happened. The first will very likely profess to be a sequel—such as Thackeray's *Rebecca and Rowena*;[1] the second, to be an exposure—such as *An Apology for the Life of Mrs. Shamela Andrews*. If a particular novel is aimed at, the chances are that it will be an ungracious piece of work, not subtle enough to be just; and yet, it has room for endless subtlety. It can oppose two worlds of illusion, as Thackeray opposes his own and Scott's; or it can suggest the contrast between illusion and actuality so allusively as to come very near to a kind of writing which, being independent

---

[1] It must, of course, be distinguished from the pretended sequel that is mere mimicry; that is, the first of the three kinds of burlesque which I have discriminated.

of mimicry, transcends burlesque altogether. And when it does, the critic is apt to complain fretfully that the author did not know his own mind. For in this kind of burlesque the creative artist finds his opportunity for setting his faithful representation of the actual world over against his caricature of the world of illusion; and, so occupied, he is apt to remember the world of illusion but fitfully, as Fielding does in *Joseph Andrews*. One circumstance, however, will keep him awake to it; he will not lightly let it escape his satiric attack if he comes to it with Crabbe's bitter belief in the power of a lie, and his determination to challenge it. Crabbe's tale of Ellen Orford, in *The Borough*,[1] makes a peculiarly interesting pendant to all other satire of fiction in that age. He complains in the prologue

> That Books, which promise much of Life to give,
> Should show so little how we truly live—

and goes on to mock the shams of current fiction, and above all the novelists' refusal to face the logical issue of the situations they have themselves devised. They lightly set their heroines in danger of seduction, but, with trivial inconsequence, arrange that they shall invariably

> Find some strange Succour, and come Virgins out.

Then he goes on to tell (with that angry thoroughness which has sometimes been mistaken for gusto) the pitiful tale of Ellen Orford. He sets her in each of the situations familiar to a heroine of fiction, and allows it to work itself out to its logical conclusion. The parallel is carefully drawn; Ellen experiences in its ugly reality every distress which, as an idle threat, had been used to tickle the fancy of contemporary novel-readers. And yet—so perishable is mimicry—this parallel seems to have escaped the notice even of M. Huchon, for, while he examines the prologue to Ellen Orford's story in relation to Crabbe's mockery of fiction,[2] he reserves the story itself for another part of his work, in which he offers it as an illustration of Crabbe's method in moral fable.[3]

---

[1] Letter xx.
[2] R. Huchon, *Un Poète Réaliste Anglais: George Crabbe*, 1906, pp. 332, 333.
[3] Ibid., p. 386.

To Jane Austen the intention of this letter[1] as a whole was probably clear, for she found this same fault in the popular novel, though she chose to attack it in another way. It is not idly that Scott, in contrasting the false conventions of the ordinary novel with the faithfulness of her representation, quotes from *Ellen Orford*.[2]

One further distinction may be made between these last two kinds of burlesque; in that kind which presents a character forced by life to abandon the illusions of fiction, it is necessary that this character, in suffering the birth-pangs of common sense and apprehension of reality, should co-operate with the author in pointing the contrast between false and true. But, in the other kind, when a situation is developed in deliberate opposition to the rules of fiction, it is not necessary that any of the characters involved should become aware of the contrast.

Now, veins of these two kinds of burlesque run through almost all of Jane Austen's mature work, and she grows steadily more skilful in her management of them—especially in making them an integral part of the narrative. It will be worth while to examine the development of this skill—first, with regard to the plans of the several novels, then as it shows itself in the crisis of each.

Northanger Abbey is a good point of departure, because of the boldness with which it flaunts its burlesque intention. The pattern of its burlesque element, however, is by no means simple. Though it is not subtly interwoven with the rest of the fabric, it is elaborately and ingeniously contrived.

It presents itself with a deceptive air of simplicity and broad, bold humour. The author herself seems to be explaining, in a clear, youthful, high-spirited voice, how her opening situation should develop according to the laws of the 'land of fiction'.[3] Since Catherine Morland is the heroine, it is her business to fit herself for this office, to emulate the

---

[1] She knew *The Borough*.   [2] In his review of *Emma*, p. 190.
[3] Scott's phrase, in his review of *Emma*, p. 190. The width of the satire in *Northanger Abbey*, its application to the novel of sentiment in Fanny Burney's tradition equally with the novel of romantic mystery in Mrs. Radcliffe's, has not been sufficiently recognized.

heroines of Mrs. Radcliffe, Mrs. Roche, and countless others
—to bring herself up after the pattern of Charlotte Smith's
Emmeline (for example),[1] who, besides forming correct
literary tastes in a ruined library, had 'of every useful and
ornamental feminine employment . . . long since made herself mistress without any instruction'.[2] But Catherine, alas,
'never could learn or understand any thing before she was
taught; and sometimes not even then, for she was often
inattentive, and occasionally stupid'.[3] And whereas Emmeline 'had learned to play on the harp, by being present when
Mrs. Ashwood received lessons on that instrument',[4] she, at
the height of her career as heroine, had advanced no farther
than to be able to 'listen to other people's performance
with very little fatigue'.[5] This was not all—'her greatest
deficiency was in the pencil';[6] here she fell miserably short
of Emmeline, who 'endeavoured to cultivate a genius for
drawing, which she inherited from her father'. It is true
that, 'for want of knowing a few general rules, what she
produced had more of elegance and neatness than correct-
ness and knowledge',[7] but when this small defect had been
remedied by a friend's communication of these few general
rules, she was able to execute a faultless portrait of her
Delamere (and leave it, wrapped in silver paper, on the
pianoforte, for him to discover there),[8] while poor Catherine,
her looking-glass image and opposite, 'had no notion of
drawing—not enough even to attempt a sketch of her
lover's profile, that she might be detected in the design'.[9]

It is to be hoped, however (the author suggests), that the
other characters will have a stricter notion of their responsibilities: Mrs. Morland will surely fill her daughter's mind
with 'cautions against the violence of such noblemen and

---

[1] *Emmeline, The Orphan of the Castle* (1788). I choose her as a good representative
of the type, and because, taking into account the fact that J. A. already knew the
book, I think it likely that she had this particular heroine present in her mind when
she wrote *Northanger Abbey*. But there is great similarity among the heroines of
that age.

[2] Vol. i, ch. vii.
[3] *Northanger Abbey*, p. 14, ch. i.
[4] Vol. i, ch. xiv.
[5] *Northanger Abbey*, p. 16, ch. i.
[6] Ibid.
[7] Vol. i, ch. vii.
[8] Vol. i, ch. xvi.
[9] *Northanger Abbey*, p. 16, ch. i.

baronets as delight in forcing young ladies away to some
remote farm-house'[1]—but she does not promise well. '. . .
Mrs. Morland knew so little of lords and baronets, that
she entertained no notion of their general mischievousness,
and was wholly unsuspicious of danger to her daughter
from their machinations.'[2] Indeed, being fully occupied in
rearing younger children, she had failed to put any ideas
into her daughter's head at all, and so fitted her admirably
for the part she was to play. Mrs. Allen may understand
better what is expected of her—but she proves so unhelpful
that it must be left to the reader 'to judge, in what manner
her actions will hereafter tend to promote the general distress of the work, and how she will, probably, contribute to
reduce poor Catherine to all the desperate wretchedness of
which a last volume is capable . . .'.[3] As for the hero, he
does not even know how to make a proper entrance:
Catherine

'had reached the age of seventeen, without having seen one amiable
youth who could call forth her sensibility; without having inspired one
real passion, and without having excited even any admiration but what
was very moderate and very transient. This was strange indeed! But
strange things may be generally accounted for if their cause be fairly
searched out. There was not one lord in the neighbourhood; no—not
even a baronet. There was not one family among their acquaintance
who had reared and supported a boy accidentally found at their door—
not one young man whose origin was unknown.'[4]

And so the best that Henry Tilney can do is to get himself
introduced to Catherine by the master of the ceremonies in
the Lower Rooms; and the small hope of mystery that this
leaves is dissipated by Mr. Allen's inconsiderate inquiries.

And now, by a delightful piece of ingenuity, the authoress
hands over to the newly arrived hero her own office of
interpreter: it is he, from now on, who will remind Catherine
of her duties as heroine, and point the difference between her
situation as it should develop under the laws of fiction, and

[1] *Northanger Abbey*, p. 18, ch. ii. J. A. may possibly have been thinking of Cowper's disapproval of heroines

Caught in a delicate soft silken net
By some lewd Earl, or rake-hell Baronet—
Progress of Error, ll. 313, 314.

[2] *Northanger Abbey*, p. 18.
[3] Ibid., pp. 19, 20, ch. ii.   [4] Ibid., p. 16, ch. i.

as it is actually developing. When the friendship between Catherine and Isabella breaks, he catechizes her:

' "You feel, I suppose, that, in losing Isabella, you lose half yourself: you feel a void in your heart which nothing else can occupy. Society is becoming irksome; and as for the amusements in which you were wont to share at Bath, the very idea of them without her is abhorrent. You would not, for instance, now go to a ball for the world. You feel that you have no longer any friend to whom you can speak with unreserve; on whose regard you can place dependence; or whose counsel, in any difficulty, you could rely on. You feel all this?"

' "No," said Catherine, after a few moments' reflection, "I do not— ought I?" '[1]

This is not all: it now begins to appear that Jane Austen has something in reserve—that she is going to use more than one of the possible burlesque patterns. (The pleasure of surprise is rare in burlesque.) Catherine, hitherto ignorant of the world of illusion, is instructed in its laws by Isabella, 'four years older than Miss Morland, and at least four years better informed',[2] and surrenders to its enchantment. It is characteristic of Jane Austen's delicate moderation that once this enchantment has mastered Catherine's imagination, Henry Tilney relinquishes for a while his office of interpreter; we do not need them both to point—he consciously, she with her author's help—the difference between Udolpho and Bath. Catherine now goes forward on her journey burdened with delusions which events must challenge. Daylight gives place to limelight—Beechen Cliff 'puts her in mind of the country that Emily and her father travelled through, in the "Mysteries of Udolpho".'[3] People begin to cast grotesque shadows: when General Tilney chooses another path than that which had been his wife's favourite, Catherine knows what to think about Mrs. Tilney.

'Of her unhappiness in marriage, she felt persuaded. The General certainly had been an unkind husband. He did not love her walk:— could he therefore have loved her? And besides, handsome as he was, there was a something in the turn of his features which spoke his not having behaved well to her.'[4]

---

[1] *Northanger Abbey*, p. 207, ch. xxv.
[2] Ibid., p. 33, ch. iv.
[3] Ibid., p. 106, ch. xiv.
[4] Ibid., p. 180, ch. xxii.

She does not stop here; before long she is dallying with

'the probability that Mrs. Tilney yet lived, shut up for causes unknown, and receiving from the pitiless hands of her husband a nightly supply of coarse food . . .[1] In support of the plausibility of this conjecture, it further occurred to her, that the forbidden gallery, in which lay the apartments of the unfortunate Mrs. Tilney, must be, as certainly as her memory could guide her, exactly over this suspected range of cells, and the stair-case by the side of those apartments of which she had caught a transient glimpse, communicating by some secret means with those cells, might well have favoured the barbarous proceedings of her husband. Down that stair-case she had perhaps been conveyed in a state of well-prepared insensibility!

'Catherine sometimes started at the boldness of her own surmises, and sometimes hoped or feared that she had gone too far; but they were supported by such appearances as made their dismissal impossible.'[2]

Indeed, they are as moderate as they are logical—judged by the canons of that world in which Madeline Clermont learns of her father's guilt by observing him look pointedly at a picture of Cain killing Abel.[3]

For all this, there is within Catherine herself an instinct, as of a wise child, that prevents her from abandoning her mind altogether to the world of illusion, and acquiring a taste for its poisonous magic fruit. Unlike Arabella, Cherubina, and the dreary company of heroines whom they ridicule, she is never deceived about those people in her little world who are true to themselves—she has a juster and more sensitive understanding of Eleanor Tilney than of Isabella Thorpe; nor is she deceived about herself: she never comes nearer to fancying herself a heroine than in the modest hope that 'since James's engagement had taught her what *could* be done'[4] Henry Tilney might in time return her affection. I believe Mr. Ralli to be at fault in finding Catherine and her folly incongruous: '. . . so delicate a mind' as hers, he says, 'requires less strong contrasts than the suggestions of Mrs. Radcliffe, the rough manners and want of sensitiveness of the Thorpes, and the rudeness of General Tilney . . .'.[5] This (if I have understood it) means that a more obtuse heroine would have served as well for the burlesque

[1] Ibid., pp. 187, 188, ch. xxiii.
[2] Ibid., p. 188, ch. xxiii.
[3] Regina Maria Roche, *Clermont* (1798), vol. iv, ch. i.
[4] *Northanger Abbey*, p. 138, ch. xvii.   [5] A. Ralli, *Critiques* (1927), p. 81.

element in *Northanger Abbey*. But it is essential to Jane Austen's purpose that Catherine's perceptions should be naturally just, merely clouded for a while by the perplexities of the passage from child to woman, so that she may take leave of her folly unregretfully:

'Charming as were all Mrs. Radcliffe's works, and charming even as were the works of all her imitators, it was not in them perhaps that human nature, at least in the midland counties of England, was to be looked for. Of the Alps and Pyrenees, with their pine forests and their vices, they might give a faithful delineation; and Italy, Switzerland, and the South of France, might be as fruitful in horrors as they were there represented. Catherine dared not doubt beyond her own country, and even of that, if hard pressed, would have yielded the northern and western extremities.'[1]

And so she enters the real world with a good heart—all the better because it is, appropriately, no doctor of divinity but Henry Tilney himself who leads her over the threshold.

Thus, the burlesque element in *Northanger Abbey* has a pretty intricacy and variety. Its strands are ingeniously interwoven with one another—but not so well woven into the rest of the fabric. There is weakness in the slight connexion between Catherine's fancied and her actual adventures at the climax of the story. The General's interference with her fortunes is neither a consequence of her foolish misconception of him (as it would be in any of the stock burlesques of the age), nor an amusing looking-glass version of it. And not all the light, gay references to her heroine-ship at the end[2] can draw these two together.

Now, the mockery of the world of illusion in *Sense and Sensibility* has not this pretty intricacy, and variety of pattern, but it is subtler, more allusive, and it is more closely inter-woven with the fabric of the story. For the misjudgement of people which causes Marianne so much suffering springs directly from her romantic vision of the world, as this from

---

[1] *Northanger Abbey*, p. 200, ch. xxv. I think that one of the threads of sympathy between J. A. and Scott shows itself in the similarity (both as to thought and expression) between this passage and a passage in Scott's life of Mrs. Radcliffe: '. . . she has uniformly selected the south of Europe for her place of action, whose passions, like the weeds of the climate, are supposed to attain portentous growth. . . .' *Miscellaneous Prose Works*, 1827, iii. 439. *Memoir of Mrs. Anne Radcliffe*, first published in *Lives of the Novelists*, 1820–4.

[2] e.g. p. 243, ch. xxx.

her reading. She has 'abandoned her mind to it' with the generous enthusiasm once admired and recommended. Cowper had spoken to William Unwin of 'the great complacency with which I read your narrative of Mrs. Unwin's smiles and tears; persons of much sensibility are always persons of taste; a taste for poetry depends indeed upon that very article more than upon any other'.[1] Marianne, who could hardly sit still through Edward's level reading of 'those beautiful lines which had frequently almost driven her wild', was a reader after Cowper's own heart. And she, 'who had the knack of finding her way in every house to the library, however it might be avoided by the family in general',[2] has built out of her favourite books an illusionary world which will not hold actual people. There is room in it for the simulacrum of Willoughby which her love has created; but there would be no room for Elinor, did not sisterly affection contrive to transform her. Such love as Elinor's for Edward has no place there; so long as it is prosperous, Marianne may hopefully call it 'blind partiality';[3] but Elinor's temperate expression of disappointment baffles her: 'When does she try to avoid society, or appear restless and dissatisfied in it?'[4] Jane Austen is at pains to bring Marianne's romantic notions into conflict not merely with Elinor's rules of good sense and expediency,[5] but also with Colonel Brandon's sobered sensibility, Edward's mildly humorous anti-romanticism and Margaret's simplicity. These qualities, though they are not essentially repugnant to her, have no place in her illusionary world; but the qualities that Willoughby allows her to see in him are proper to it. Having had the good fortune and tact to make an appropriate entrance,[6] he plays his part to admiration: his smart

---

[1] *Letters*, ed. Wright, i. 466 (letter of 18 March 1782). Surely it was such a conception of poetry as this that made Anne Elliot suppose it 'to be seldom safely enjoyed by those who enjoyed it completely' (*Persuasion*, pp. 100, 101, ch. xi).

[2] *Sense and Sensibility*, p. 304, ch. xlii.

[3] Ibid., p. 19, ch. i.   [4] Ibid., p. 39, ch. viii.

[5] It would be interesting to recover *Elinor and Marianne* and learn whether Elinor was from the beginning a 'sympathetic' character, or whether the young, lighthearted J. A. poked fun at her common sense, as she had at Charlotte Lutterell's in *Lesley Castle*.

[6] Deliciously set off by Margaret's reference to him 'with more elegance than precision' as 'Marianne's preserver' (*Sense and Sensibility*, p. 46, ch. x).

wit shows itself as ardent gaiety; he displays his taste and
sensibility to advantage.

'Marianne began now to perceive that the desperation which had
seized her at sixteen and a half, of ever seeing a man who could satisfy
her ideas of perfection, had been rash and unjustifiable. Willoughby
was all that her fancy had delineated in that unhappy hour and in every
brighter period, as capable of attaching her . . .'[1]

Against a native of her own world, a figment of her own
imagination, she has no defence. Thus the catastrophe
(though artificially and awkwardly precipitated) is the consequence of her surrender to illusion; and mockery of the
illusionary world is inextricably involved with the action.

Pride and Prejudice is not *bookish* in this sense. Books and
reading are indeed of some consequence in it: Mr. Bennet's
library, Mary's extracts, Elizabeth's rejection of books as a
subject of talk between herself and Darcy, and Miss Bingley's
choice of a book only because it was the second volume of
one Darcy was reading—all these in their variety make part
of the pattern of the comedy. But nobody strays from
Longbourn into the world of illusion.

Mansfield Park, though bookish enough, lies well outside
the province of burlesque, and so should seem irrelevant
here; but it is related to the burlesque-writer's art in one
respect, for it is an implied criticism, a reconsideration, as it
were, of a situation, a grouping of characters, which had
become familiar, almost commonplace, in the novel of
sentiment. Stevenson speaks of a 'temptation' which besets
the novelist to make his choice from among 'the old stock
incidents' of fiction '. . . as the mason chooses the acanthus
to adorn his capital, because they come naturally to the
accustomed hand'.[2] But such a stock incident may invite
the conscious artist to choose it, imagine it afresh, and
translate it—mockingly if he is intent on burlesque, gravely
if his intention is more critical and curious—into terms of
actual life. And so (I think) it was with this situation which,
by Jane Austen's day, had become an acanthus pattern in
sentimental fiction: Sir Charles Grandison, the first hero of

---

[1] *Sense and Sensibility*, p. 49, ch. x.
[2] *The Art of Writing : A Note on Realism* (1905), pp. 103, 104.

a novel who could well regard himself as both mentor and reward of the heroine, had set a fashion which was followed in *A Simple Story*,[1] in *Evelina* and *Camilla*, and several lesser novels. Jane Austen seems to accept this relationship between hero and heroine; but she develops it afresh, according to her own vision. In the first place, she devises it more naturally, making it spring from their situation in childhood. Such a device may have been suggested to her by the opening of *Camilla*; but, if it was, she has bettered the instruction, for the account of Fanny's childhood, while briefer than that of Camilla's (and therefore better proportioned to the rest of her story) is nevertheless more substantial, and leaves more firmly established in the reader's mind the impression of Fanny's childish dependence on Edmund and his protective tenderness for her. Further, this grateful devotion of Fanny's is the more natural in that it has not to satisfy every need of her being; for another kind of devotion, with more of romantic ardour in it, had long ago been given to William for his share. This grouping of the three is delicately suggested in the episode that opens Fanny's life at Mansfield Park, when Edmund (the only one of his family to discover their cousin's unhappiness) comforts her by encouraging her to talk about William and helping her to write to him. '. . . Edmund prepared her paper, and ruled her lines with all the good will that her brother could himself have felt, and probably with somewhat more exactness.'[2] And the impression of it is kept sharp by one of the author's rare (and therefore significant) generalizations: she dwells on the tenacity of the affection between brother and sister, the circumstances in which it may hold faster than that between husband and wife.[3] She gives, besides, to this relationship between hero and heroine a softness and warmth that it had wanted. There had been something repellent about the rectitude of those earlier heroes—Sir Charles, Lord Orville, Edgar Mandlebert; it had put them in too strong a position of

---

[1] Elizabeth Inchbald (1791): 'I am no longer engaged to Miss Milner' (Lord Elmwood tells his friend) 'than she shall deserve I should' (vol. ii, ch. vii).

[2] *Mansfield Park*, p. 16, ch. ii.

[3] Ibid., pp. 234, 235, ch. xxiv.

vantage for criticizing the heroine: faultless themselves, they could tell her whether it was the style of her letters, her dress, or her conduct at the opera house, that had cost her their regard. (Nothing could have prevented Edgar from declaring his love to Camilla 'but the unaccountable circumstance of her starting forth from a back seat at the play, where she had sat concealed, attended by the Major, and without any matron protectress'[1]—since he knows as much about the etiquette of being a heroine as though he had learnt it from experience.) It is therefore a relief to discover that Edmund (though a very Sir Charles Grandison to Fanny) is by no means faultless; that Fanny has the shrewder perception of what is consistent with the moral principles they share, and the greater steadiness in obeying their promptings.

Mansfield Park is not related to contemporary fiction at this point only. It reflects in its still waters some of the imaginary worlds which books create in the mind—the world of Scott's poetry which lends its brave colours to Fanny's vision of people and things; the shabby world of the comedy of intrigue which dupes Maria and Julia with its promise of pleasure in the make-believe flirtations of *Lovers' Vows*.[2] But these reflections are not used except as a means of opening the characters to us.

Emma, on the other hand, presents a deliberately contrived antithesis between the worlds of actuality and illusion which accords with Jane Austen's favourite pattern for burlesque, and yet—being of a subtler symmetry than *Northanger Abbey*, more complex than *Sense and Sensibility*—transcends our notion of burlesque-writing. Here it is no counterpart of Maria or Julia, no unsympathetic character, but the heroine herself who is deceived—more elaborately deceived than Marianne Dashwood, betrayed further into active folly than Catherine Morland—by the false notions current in the world of illusion. It is true that no reference is made to this world—because, I think, Jane Austen had no

[1] *Camilla* (1796), vol. ii, bk. iv, ch. ix.
[2] Jane Austen *may* have disapproved of amateur acting, as has been suggested (Reitzel, *Review of English Studies*, ix. 451); but all that *Mansfield Park* directly shows is her disapproval of make-believe that is *not* acting, like that of the Bertrams.

particular novel or comedy of intrigue in mind. But the
bookish origin of such follies does not need to be stated
explicitly. Such a young woman as Emma, so constituted
and so circumstanced, could have become acquainted with
illegitimacy as an interesting situation, infidelity as a comic
incident, only in her reading.[1]

Thus, Jane Austen has set herself a difficult task. Not
only has she made her heroine herself the dupe of the world
of fiction; she has allowed her to explore its ugliest region.
Here, surely, is a partial explanation of the diffidence that
her nephew remembered: although she was (he writes)
'very fond of Emma, . . . [she] did not reckon on her being
a general favourite; for, when commencing that work, she
said, "I am going to take a heroine whom no one but myself
will much like." '[2]

This was of consequence to her—as may be seen from
the pains she takes to make Emma's folly appear excusable
—the care with which the 'unconscious flattery' (as Mr.
Knightley calls it) not only of Harriet Smith but of all her
little family and social world is made to buzz in our ears as
it does in hers—the care with which the busy idleness of
that world is presented.[3] Contrariwise, the mysteries which
beset Arabella and Cherubina are all of their own making,
and usually spring from the perverse conviction that they
are themselves heroic figures—a disagreeable silliness of
which Emma has no more share than Catherine Morland,
for in Jane Austen's retort to sham romance it is the deception that is ugly, not the dupe.

And, in so far as she succeeds in this endeavour to make
us think not unfavourably of Emma, a characteristic which
distinguishes the point of view in her novels, not merely
from that in the popular novel of the day but also from that
in the satire it provoked, becomes clearly perceptible; for
here, in the last of them to be brought to its final state,[4] and

---

[1] Contrast her supposition—fanciful, as is everything that comes into her head,
but in no way coloured by the conventions of fiction—that the bad news that Mrs.
Weston has to break to her is news of 'half a dozen natural children . . . and poor
Frank cut off' (p. 393, ch. xlvi).

[2] *Memoir*, p. 157.   [3] See ch. iv.

[4] The state, that is, in which she was willing to see it published—a state *Persuasion*
does not seem to have reached.

therefore the most unambiguous expression of her mature
view of life, emerges her whole-hearted preference for the
actual world over that fictitious world with which she contrasts it. This is the preference which—allowing as it does
an altogether happy enlightment to the hood-winked characters—together with her care to make their follies excusable,
keeps their stories within comedy's true province. ('Comedy,'
Meredith says, 'justly treated, . . . throws no infamous
reflection upon life.'[1])

Now, if one should inquire why Jane Austen stands in
steady opposition to those burlesque-writers who, like herself, attacked the contemporary novel for giving a false view
of life, some things hitherto observed severally would show
themselves in intelligible relation to one another. First, a
reason becomes apparent for the ordinary burlesque-writer's
assumption that the deluded reader of shoddy fiction is
living in a fool's paradise: for such fiction, written without
artistic conscience (or even a moral purpose to steady it),
aims at presenting a vision of life, neither by obeying the
prevailing impulse in poetic fable and creating a new world,
nor by attempting to seize and keep that vision of the
familiar world which a sojourn in it has offered to the writer
—but by distorting this latter vision in a manner intended
to flatter the reader. For example, and this is an illustration
which might have been chosen by Charlotte Lennox or
Barrett, fiction written primarily for women will lean towards persuading them of their importance in the pattern
of human life by making courtship its pivotal business, and
surrounding it with the fictions of that kind of gallantry
which happens to be in fashion. (By writers of fiction,
Arabella 'was taught to believe that Love was the ruling
Principle of the World; that every other Passion was sub-
ordinate to this; and that it caused all the Happiness and
Miseries of Life'.[2]) So far the burlesque-writers' shrewd
glance has penetrated; but they do not see far enough into
this humbug. For, while they condemn the proffered flattery of the novelists as insincere,[3] they accept it at the novel-

---

[1] *An Essay on Comedy*, p. 33.   [2] *Female Quixote*, ch. i.
[3] Charlotte Lennox insists on woman's unimportance in man's life—unaware

ists' own valuation: perceiving (that is) that these writers
aim at presenting a rose-coloured view of life, they uncritically assume that the world they show is prettier than
actuality. Consequently, the discovery of the actual world
is, for their heroines, a dull, sad process of disenchantment,
hardly eased by the perfunctory reflection that reality may
have some pleasures of its own. Barrett's Cherubina, con-
stitutionally argumentative, sums up the case: 'Novels . . .
present us with incidents and characters which we can never
meet in the world; and act upon the mind like intoxicating
stimulants; first elevate, and at last enervate it.'[1] And in
this the burlesque-writers are (as I have shown) merely
reflecting current opinion—such as Sir Thomas Bernard
expresses when, in his revised edition of *Spurinna*,[2] he makes
one of his debaters challenge the novel in these terms: 'Is
not [its] tendency to enfeeble the mind, to give a false
estimate of life, and unfit us for the enjoyment of domestic
society—making every day that is not marked by some
striking and interesting occurrence, appear tame, heavy,
and insipid?'[3]—that is, to show the world in unnaturally
high relief, so that its real face must eventually appear
disagreeably flat to the disenchanted reader. This, indeed,
is the intention of the popular novel, but is it—as the
critics claim—its achievement? I will venture on this broad
generalization: that the vice of bad representational art (a
vice which, among the undiscriminating, has brought all
representational art into disrepute) is this intent to flatter;
and yet, while its censors cry out against its flattery, the
critical reader who penetrates farther will ask whether he is
indeed to consider himself flattered by such a representation
('Pray where, mamma, *are* the Emperor's new clothes?').
And so it should not be surprising to find Jane Austen, at
variance with other satirists of the world of illusion, main-
taining that to her the actual world appears the prettier and
pleasanter place. To Crabbe, however (as I have tried to
show), she does not stand opposed; since he, for his part, is

that the conventions she attacks suppose a relationship between men and women as
ungenial as that which she takes for reality.
[1] *The Heroine* (1813), vol. iii (letter XLVII).
[2] 1816; see p. 52, n. 1.   [3] pp. 125, 126.

bent on showing how ugly the actual world would look to
one who should find himself in the peculiar circumstances
postulated by the novelists. (That he probably thought them
less unlikely than she did is not to the purpose.) But it is
amusing to find Scott congratulating her on having presented a fictitious world which is not pretty enough to 'turn
the heads' of her youthful readers,[1] yet begging her to show
them a more romantically pretty picture of love—Scott,
who was to warn Margaret Laidlaw against romantic im-
prudence in love on the score that 'the world we actually
live in is not that of poetry and romance'.[2] What use had
Jane Austen for this double standard—she who preferred
the world's actual to its painted face? What cause had she
for even such light regret as Peacock's at the close of
Gryll Grange? 'It was the dissipation of a dream too much
above mortal frailty, too much above the contingencies of
chance and change, to be permanently realized.'[3]

It becomes worth while, now, to draw some comparison
between the catastrophes of the novels; for here Jane Austen
can be watched as she challenges the mastery of a false convention, subdues it, and makes it serve her purpose by standing as foil to the truth. Freedom from its tyranny does not
prompt her to part company with it altogether; it has
received life in her imagination, and this adventitious life
which the imagination of the creative artist lends to the
creature of a fellow artist's imagination is not lightly to be
extinguished, even though the creature itself be condemned
for a lying spirit: it persists—as Pamela's virtue did for
Fielding.

Such a comparison of the novels is made possible (if
Northanger Abbey is left out), and profitable, by the seeming
alikeness of their catastrophes. For Jane Austen accepts the
convention[4] of a climax to the action; that is, of tension
first increased, then snapped, by some act more violent

---

[1] *Quarterly*: review of *Emma*, p. 200: the young reader may come back to everyday life 'without any chance of having his head turned'.

[2] *Letters*, ed. Grierson, vii. 44 (letter to Margaret Laidlaw, about January 1822).

[3] *Gryll Grange* (1861), ch. xxxv.

[4] It may fairly be called a convention because of the matter-of-course acceptance
of it by English novelists of the eighteenth and nineteenth centuries. Sterne is the
sole exception—for even his imitators fail to follow him here.

than any that has preceded it. And the kinds of violent act that would lend themselves to the novelist's hand—and would appear likely in the life of an English country gentle-woman of that day—were, as I have suggested, very few. Unfortunately, Richardson had made it seem that, of those few, the violence of actual or attempted seduction might be the most apt and convenient for the novelist's purpose. The influence of this suggestion is seen in all of Jane Austen's novels—except *Northanger Abbey*, which shows rather impact than influence—but her response to it varies; and the variation reveals her development.

The catastrophes of *Sense and Sensibility* and *Pride and Prejudice* are particularly close to one another, and therefore show the direction in which she was moving. In *Sense and Sensibility* she accepts this convention almost uncritically—as though she were not yet conscious of her instinctive dis-satisfaction with it: Willoughby's habitual extravagance could well have kept him dependent on some relative who should forbid his marriage with Marianne; but the conven-tion demanded that he should lose her by a single violent act—and the moral pattern of the novel, that it should be as ugly an act as Jane Austen would consent to speak of—and so Colonel Brandon's Eliza is introduced into the story. Eliza is kept out of sight. This is well judged in a novel of comic intention; at the same time one may see in Jane Austen's very prudence an admission that she herself means to keep out of reach of Eliza. And her refusal to do anything more with Eliza's story than make use of it is apparent in her failure of power when Willoughby reappears after his part in it is known. His interview with Elinor is ineffectual, not because Jane Austen cannot contrive a crisis—it is not, for her, an exhilarating task, but she performs it well enough in the course of Marianne's illness; it is ineffectual because she has allowed the occasion of the interview to remain wholly unreal for her. This is betrayed by the very phrase she uses when Willoughby begins to show what he is—'deep in hardened villainy'[1]—which, as Jane would surely have told Anna had *she* used it, is 'such thorough novel

[1] *Sense and Sensibility*, p. 184, ch. xxix.

slang—and so old, that I dare say Adam met with it in the first novel he opened'.[1]

Comparison with the similar catastrophe of *Pride and Prejudice* throws this subject into relief. Clearly, there is a very great technical advance: Wickham's share in the story is much better contrived than Willoughby's; his character is opened to us gradually and deftly, in preparation for the part that he is to play,[2] and this part is evenly interwoven with the rest. Moreover, he does not break the comic mood of the whole, but, by the vanity of his petty intrigues and provincial gallantries, preserves it—until the crisis of the story is reached. And Lydia, who is to share this crisis with him, also belongs to the world of comedy—for just so long as he does. On the eve of it, she composes her nonsensical letter;[3] and, so soon as it is past, slips back with him into the comic world, to the accompaniment of appropriate comment from the rest of its natives. 'You ought certainly to forgive them as a christian,' is Mr. Collins's professional advice to Mr. Bennet, 'but never to admit them in your sight, or allow their names to be mentioned in your hearing.'[4] And Mary outdoes him: 'Unhappy as the event must be for Lydia, we may draw from it this useful lesson; that loss of virtue in a female is irretrievable—that one false step involves her in endless ruin—that her reputation is no less brittle than it is beautiful,—and that she cannot be too much guarded in her behaviour towards the undeserving of the other sex.'[5] The ironical undertones of Jane Austen's own voice in these comments are echoed clearly by the irony in her misappropriation of that passage from *The Vicar of Wakefield* in which Goldsmith makes Mrs. Primrose insist, with heartless sentimentality, upon Olivia's singing to him 'that little melancholy air your papa was so fond of'[6]—the song that describes too well her own forlorn condition. 'Goldsmith tells us', Jane Austen says (with a bluntness of

---

[1] *Letters*, p. 404. It is the rarity of this false touch in J. A.'s writing that makes it significant.

[2] The ignorance of Willoughby's character and intentions in which the reader is kept may be a surviving characteristic of *Elinor and Marianne*, for it is more in keeping with a novel-in-letters than with J. A.'s practice in direct narrative.

[3] *Pride and Prejudice*, pp. 291, 292, ch. xlviii.   [4] Ibid., p. 364, ch. lvii.

[5] Ibid., p. 289, ch. xlviii.   [6] Ch. xxiv.

manner to which she has not accustomed us) 'that when
lovely woman stoops to folly, she has nothing to do but to
die; and when she stoops to be disagreeable, it is equally to
be recommended as a clearer of ill-fame.'[1] For her, the
conventional reaction, whether of unthinking or of canting
folly, to such an act as the mutual seduction of Lydia and
Wickham, was essentially comic; but the act itself was not.[2]
And so, in obedience to an impulse which becomes more and
more clearly intelligible as we follow out this comparison
between the catastrophes in her novels, she closed her
imaginative consciousness against it. I believe that this
impulse had not always been so strong; that, when she wrote
First Impressions, she may have been willing to let her imagination realize Lydia's experience; and that, if she had been
encouraged *then* to go on writing, she might have embarked
on this imaginative voyage of discovery—with what success, it is impossible now to conjecture. But, by the time
she comes to write *Pride and Prejudice*, such an inclination,
if it has ever existed, is long dead; *now* such an act as Lydia's
cannot gain admission to her imaginative consciousness unless it presents itself as one of the incongruities over which
the comic spirit may hover, with 'unsolicitous observation';[3] and for this, it must have been differently conceived
from the beginning.

The way in which Jane Austen chooses to present the
catastrophe of *Mansfield Park* is significant: that Fanny
Price should close *her* imaginative consciousness against
Maria's experience—this was to be expected; that we should
see this episode only as Fanny sees it—this, though it is a
limitation not imposed by the mode of narration in *Mansfield
Park*, which allows us to see some things beyond the range
of Fanny's vision, is yet not inconsistent with it. But the
expression of Fanny's numb resistance to realization carries
overtones which only become clearly audible in that exceptional and therefore significant passage of direct speech:

[1] *Emma*, p. 387, ch. xlv.
[2] It could have been, in Restoration comedy; and Lydia sometimes seems like
Miss Hoyden strayed out of her proper world—until some word or phrase reminds
us that she illustrates Jane Austen's views on the bringing up of girls.
[3] Meredith, *Essay on Comedy*, p. 89.

'Let other pens dwell on guilt and misery. I quit such odious subjects as soon as I can, impatient to restore every body, not greatly in fault themselves, to tolerable comfort, and to have done with all the rest.'[1] There is certainly a more than customary coolness and aloofness in the tone of Jane Austen's voice when she sets about the business of 'restoring everybody . . . to tolerable comfort':

'I purposely abstain from dates on this occasion, that every one may be at liberty to fix their own, aware that the cure of unconquerable passions, and the transfer of unchanging attachments, must vary much as to time in different people.—I only intreat every body to believe that exactly at the time when it was quite natural that it should be so, and not a week earlier, Edmund did cease to care about Miss Crawford, and became as anxious to marry Fanny, as Fanny herself could desire.'[2]

Here in *Mansfield Park*, even more clearly than in *Pride and Prejudice*, the knot of the difficulty stands out: the violent act which precipitates the catastrophe (though carefully kept below the plane of tragedy) is not essentially comic; nor can it be made to appear so, without breach of the author's moral purpose.[3] Further, since she is now much older than the girl who devised the story of *First Impressions*, she cannot even slip back into the comic world with youthful inconsequence as soon as the catastrophe is past.

In *Emma* she contrives an opportune solution of the difficulty, without surrendering her position; for what *appears* to be the catastrophe is a mere figment of Emma's busy fancy, a happening in her own world of illusion: only there could Jane Fairfax engage in an intrigue with Mr. Dixon. And this mock catastrophe serves as foil to the real untying of the knot of misunderstandings, Emma's misinterpretation of the clues in Jane's mystery as foil to its real development, fancied misconduct as foil to actual indiscretion. The world of Emma's fancy fades in the clear, cool light of day.

This was, however, a device to be used but once. In *Persuasion*, new possibilities are seen opening out. The mockery of false taste is more subtly conceived, and finds

---

[1] *Mansfield Park*, p. 461, ch. xlviii. [2] Ibid., p. 470, ch. xlviii.
[3] To indict, not merely the fault, but also the fashion of education responsible for it. See R. W. Chapman, 'Jane Austen: a Reply to Mr. Garrod' (*Essays by Divers Hands*, R.S.L., 1931), p. 26.

its expression in a more intricate pattern of self-deceptions than Emma's. The key to this mockery is hidden in the episode on the Cobb, which, to the casual eye, looks so disconcertingly like a perfunctory bringing about of the conventional catastrophe—a clumsy contrivance to increase the tension to breaking-point. The young Musgroves, with Anne Elliot and their friends at Lyme Regis, walk out along the Cobb, and Louisa, exhilarated by the attentions of Captain Wentworth, begins to play childish pranks and insists that he shall 'jump' her from one ledge to the other; '. . . she was too precipitate by half a second, she fell on the pavement of the Lower Cobb, and was taken up lifeless!'[1] The rest believe her to be dead, and they react characteristically to this shock: Mary falls into hysterics, Henrietta faints; Anne and Captain Wentworth take command and arrange for Louisa to be carried indoors. And then, in the close of the episode, a familiar voice penetrates the babble of the poor Musgroves, a voice which no one who has heard it before can fail to recognize for Jane Austen's own: 'By this time the report of the accident had spread among the workmen and boatmen about the Cobb, and many were collected near them, to be useful if wanted, at any rate, to enjoy the sight of a dead young lady, nay, two dead young ladies, for it proved twice as fine as the first report.'[2] The mockery sheathed in that phrase—'nay, two dead young ladies'—pricks in an instant the bubble catastrophe; for its import is perfectly clear to any one who has observed Jane Austen's honourable dealings with her readers, her civil unwillingness to let them suffer (sympathetically) under a misapprehension. She will not allow them to misapprehend, here, the nature of the catastrophe: while it is not a mock climax to the action (like *Emma*'s), nor an anticlimax (like the farce of disinheritance in *Sense and Sensibility*), it is yet not quite what it seems to be. It is a climax to the earlier part of the action in that it brings to a head, and solves, a problem which that had set—the knot tied by Wentworth's fancied preference for Louisa, her fanciful

---

[1] *Persuasion*, p. 109, ch. xii.
[2] Ibid., p. 111, ch. xii.

infatuation with him. But the catastrophe which the spectators think they are witnessing is an illusion. Louisa is not
dead—nor even injured. True, she has fallen on her head;
but it had never been a very good one, and the blow seems
to have cleared it—for she acquires a taste for poetry and
learns to attach herself to a man who can return her affection. And yet Mr. Read offers this scene as an example of
Jane Austen's failure in serious emotional writing. Her
style, he complains, 'becomes almost ludicrous . . . under
the strain of dramatic action',[1] and he quotes a passage from
this episode, and goes on to pick from it phrases 'which are
not congruous with the tragedy of the situation'.[2] Moreover, he contrasts with its insignificance the urgency of the
scene in which Heathcliffe is found dead—a real with a
counterfeit catastrophe. His quotation, however, stops short
of the *two dead young ladies*, and so misses the key to the
ironical tone of the episode.

Here is not the irony of indifference—not that aloof tone
of voice which suggests the gradual withdrawal of the authoress from the darkening landscape of *Mansfield Park*. Jane
Austen can be careless in the contriving of violent action,
but I do not think it is carelessness that makes Louisa's
accident hardly plausible.[3] This irony is no mere symptom;
it is the very tongue in which *Persuasion* is written. Before
the episode, in the course of Anne's stay at Uppercross Cottage, a slender but tenacious thread of ironical suggestion
has begun to weave itself into the pattern of this novel: the
Musgroves of the 'Great House' are to visit the Musgroves
of the Cottage, and Louisa, with laborious, youthful tact,
explains that by bringing their harp she and Henrietta hope
to lighten the visit, and raise their mother's spirits: '. . . she
is thinking so much of poor Richard! And we agreed it
would be best to have the harp, for it seems to amuse her
more than the piano-forte.'[4] A chance allusion has recalled
'poor Richard' to her mind—'So we must all be as merry
as we can, that she may not be dwelling upon such gloomy

[1] Herbert Read, *English Prose Style* (1928), p. 119.
[2] Ibid., p. 120.
[3] For a suggestion as to the cause of this, see p. 129.
[4] *Persuasion*, p. 50, ch. vi.

things.'[1] Then follows directly a relentlessly matter-of-fact
explanation:

'The real circumstances of this pathetic piece of family history were,
that the Musgroves had had the ill fortune of a very troublesome, hope-
less son; and the good fortune to lose him before he reached his
twentieth year; that he had been sent to sea, because he was stupid
and unmanageable on shore; that he had been very little cared for at
any time by his family, though quite as much as he deserved; seldom
heard of, and scarcely at all regretted, when the intelligence of his
death abroad had worked its way to Uppercross, two years before'

—and that 'his sisters were now doing all they could for him,
by calling him "poor Richard"', while his mother, to whom
chance only has recalled him, has been 'thrown ... into greater
grief for him than she had known on first hearing of his
death'.[2] Mrs. Musgrove's creator, that is, has conceived of
her creature's retrospective grief as half fanciful, and means
to convey this conception of it to us: she shows what is
unreal in it, to us—allows perception of it to cool even
Anne's habitual warmth of sympathy—by the turn of Mrs.
Musgrove's lamentation. So long as grief lived, she would
surely be apt to forget the graceless boy in the child en-
dearingly dependent on her forbearance. Now she dallies
instead with the fiction of a brilliant future forestalled by
death, and, seeing the Navy personified in Wentworth,
laments to her ready sympathizer: 'Ah! Miss Anne, if it had
pleased Heaven to spare my poor son, I dare say he would
have been just such another by this time.'[3] And what is
'real and unabsurd' in her feelings—her author comments
uncompromisingly—rarely wins the sympathy which is its
right because it is awkwardly displayed: a comment which
would seem so little relevant as to be merely captious, if it
were not for the implied contrast which another character
in the book presents. There is to be something of ironic
reserve in the first mention of Captain Benwick: Wentworth's commendation of him 'had been followed by a little
history of his private life, which rendered him perfectly
interesting in the eyes of all the ladies. He had been engaged
to Captain Harville's sister, and was now mourning her

[1] Ibid.   [2] Ibid., pp. 50, 51, ch. vi.
[3] Ibid., p. 64, ch. viii.

loss.'[1] And his introduction to the Musgrove party confirms this impression: 'He had a pleasing face and a melancholy air, just as he ought to have, and drew back from
conversation.'[2] Anne's bent for sympathy impels her to
'begin an acquaintance with him', and they fall into talk
about books. When Jane Austen tells of taste in reading
we can be sure that she has something of character and
mood to disclose; we are to learn a little of Captain Benwick's character through his enjoyment of the lavish sadness
of Scott and Byron. (Had she conceived otherwise of his
sorrow, she might have allowed him to sympathize with
the disagreeable, the positively uncomfortable, melancholy
of Johnson and Cowper.) And a faint tone of ironical
detachment is perceptible when Anne tries to be of service
to him by discussing 'whether *Marmion* or *The Lady of the
Lake* were to be preferred, and how ranked the *Giaour* and
The Bride of Abydos; and moreover, how the *Giaour* was to
be pronounced', while he responds by repeating 'with . . .
tremulous feeling, the various lines which imaged a broken
heart . . .', and looking '. . . entirely as if he meant to be
understood'.[3] In fact, Captain Benwick, who can express
what is now only fanciful in his grief more gracefully than
poor Mrs. Musgrove could express what was still real in
hers, deceives not only himself but even those who should
know him best, the simple, feeling Harvilles. Anne alone
remains not wholly convinced;[4] the strong feelings which
she may not express make her sensitive to the force of feeling
in others; she penetrates to Captain Harville's undiminished
silent grief. If it were not for these two, and all that is implied in the talk between them, one might almost take *Persuasion* for a satire on the frailty of human sorrow and the
support it seeks from delusion; it is they who reveal it as a
delicate study in shades of distinction between the true and
the not quite true. And, as usual, Jane Austen associates
self-deception with wrong-headed reading. 'Yes, yes, if you
please, no reference to examples in books.'[5]

[1] *Persuasion*, p. 96, ch. xi.   [2] Ibid., p. 97, ch. xi.
[3] Ibid., p. 100, ch. xi.
[4] She remembers afterwards that she had not thought him inconsolable. (Ibid.,
p. 167, ch. xviii.)   [5] Ibid., p. 234, ch. xxiii.

What are we to make, however, of that crude farce—the mutual seduction of Mr. Elliot and Mrs. Clay—thrust into this delicate comedy? As an intrigue between rogues, diamond cut diamond, it has finer possibilities than it ever develops; so have the two characters themselves. Mrs. Clay begins admirably : her plausible, sly loquacity when she sets herself to win Sir Walter's favour surely promises well. Other men, she tells him, less fortunate than he as to rank and person, must expect to ' "lose the look of youth . . ." "Sailors do grow old betimes . . . Soldiers, in active service, are not at all better off: and even in the quieter professions, there is a toil and a labour of the mind, if not of the body, which seldom leaves a man's looks to the natural effect of time. The lawyer plods, quite care-worn; the physician is up at all hours, and travelling in all weather; and even the clergyman—" she stopt a moment to consider what might do for the clergyman'[1]—and there she is left, considering what may do for the clergyman, until that solemn, insinuating rogue, Mr. Elliot, is ready for her. What has become of the first comic inspiration? I think it is possible, with the catastrophes of the other novels in mind, to make a shrewd guess. The flaw lies here: these two could not receive full life unless they should be conceived of as comic in virtue of the part they had to play together.

In *Sanditon* this fault is done away. From the beginning, Charlotte Heywood sees Clara Brereton and Sir Edward Denham as people who may afford her the entertainment of a novel *come to life*. At first Clara seems the more promising—so charming were her person and address that 'Charlotte could see in her only the most perfect representation of whatever Heroine might be most beautiful & bewitching, in all the numerous vol:[s] they had left behind them on Mrs. Whitby's shelves'.[2] Besides, her situation promises appropriate fortune: 'She seemed placed with [Lady Denham] on purpose to be ill-used.'[3] But Charlotte has to shift the centre of her expectations, for 'while she pleased herself the first 5 minutes with fancying the Persecutions which *ough*[t] to be the Lot of the interesting Clara,

---

[1] *Persuasion*, p. 20, ch. iii.   [2] *Sanditon*, p. 75; *Minor Works*, p. 391.
[3] Ibid., p. 76; *Minor Works*, p. 391.

especially in the form of the most barbarous conduct on
Lady Denham's side, she found no reluctance to admit from
subsequent observation, that they appeared to be on very
comfortable Terms'.[1] That Sir Edward Denham, a fellow
novel-reader, has seen like possibilities in Clara's situation
does not at first occur to her, because it takes her a little
while to see through his plausibility to his absurdity : '... She
c^d not but think him a Man of Feeling—till he began to
stagger her by the number of his Quotations, & the bewilder-
ment of some of his sentences.'[2] (To Charlotte, as to her
author, idiosyncrasy in syntax is often an indication of
idiosyncrasy in character.) His talk of novels opens his
character still further :

'The Novels which I approve are such as display Human Nature with
Grandeur—such as shew her in the Sublimities of intense Feeling—
such as exhibit the progress of strong Passion from the first Germ of
incipient Susceptibility to the utmost Energies of Reason half-
dethroned,—where we see the strong spark of Woman's Captivations
elicit such Fire in the Soul of Man as leads him—(though at the risk of
some Aberration from the strict line of Primitive Obligations)—to
hazard all, dare all, atcheive all, to obtain her.'[3]

The author interprets this jargon (but, in the final draft, he
would surely have been made to explain himself) :

'His fancy had been early caught by all the impassioned, & most
exceptionable parts of Richardson's [novels]; & such Authors as have
since appeared to tread in Richardson's steps, so far as Man's determined pursuit of Woman in defiance of every opposition of feeling &
convenience is concerned, had since occupied the greater part of his
literary hours, & formed his Character.'[4]

And so he reveals himself, supremely comic in virtue of the
part which he is to play in unconscious burlesque of the
conventional catastrophe of the sentimental novel :

'. . . it was Clara whom he meant to seduce.—Her seduction was quite
determined on. Her Situation in every way called for it.'[5] . . . 'He knew
his Business.—Already had he had many Musings on the Subject. If he
were constrained so to act, he must naturally wish to strike out something new, to exceed those who had gone before him—and he felt a
strong curiosity to ascertain whether the Neighbourhood of Tombuc-
too might not afford some solitary House adapted for Clara's reception;
—but the Expence alas! of Measures in that masterly style was ill-

[1] *Sanditon*, p. 76; *Minor Works*, p. 392.   [2] Ibid., p. 89; *Minor Works*, p. 396.
[3] Ibid., pp. 106,107; *Minor Works*, p.403.   [4] Ibid., pp. 108,109; *Minor Works*, p. 404.
[5] Ibid., p. 111; *Minor Works*, p. 405.

suited to his Purse, & Prudence obliged him to prefer the quietest sort of ruin & disgrace for the object of his Affections, to the more re-nowned.'[1]

And so that false convention crumbles at last to dust, and is blown away by laughter.

In this rough draft, it is the laughter of farce rather than of comedy; in the final version, with Clara's story developed, it might have been less hilarious. But since we shall never see this version, we must go back, for Jane Austen's most delicate discrimination against insidious self-deception, to the finished (if not finally revised) *Persuasion*. In its network of imaginings, from Louisa's idlest fancies to Anne's autumn melancholy (tempered as this is with amused recollection of 'the farmer, counteracting the sweets of poetical despon-dence, and meaning to have spring again'[2]), lies her vision of reality and of the unrealities that humankind prefers. It is a vision so constantly held and consistently presented that, if she had been born a man then, or a woman in this more indulgent age, it might almost have been called Thought, and have lent its name to this chapter.

[1] Ibid., p. 112; *Minor Works*, pp. 405, 406.   [2] *Persuasion*, p. 85, ch. x.

PART II
JANE AUSTEN'S ART

VOLTAIRE (TO MADAME DU TOUR). *Oh! que voulez-vous donc?*
MADAME DU TOUR. *De la simple nature,*
  Un ridicule fin, des portraits délicats,
  De la noblesse sans enflure;
  Point de moralités; une morale pure
  Qui naisse du sujet, et ne se montre pas.
  Je veux qu'on soit plaisant sans vouloir faire rire;
  Qu'on ait un style aisé, gai, vif et gracieux;
  Je veux enfin que vous sachiez écrire
  Comme on parle en ces lieux.

Prologue to L'*Échange*

CHAPTER III
STYLE

I HAVE suggested that something may be learnt by watching Jane Austen as she finds her way towards realization and solution of the problems of her art; and it may be well to begin with the smallest and most definite of these problems, those connected with her 'manner of writing with regard to language'—we shall not at first need a definition of wider implications than this of Johnson's, with its illustration from Swift: 'Proper words in proper places make the true definition of a *stile*.'

Jane Austen expresses her realization of these problems explicitly in her letters to Anna, critical comments on the instalments of Anna's own novel; in the rest of her letters, seldom otherwise than implicitly, but clearly enough for any one who is familiar with these letters as a whole. Her preferences and opinions as to 'proper words in proper places' are implicit in all her literary satire: in her burlesque of bad style in *Volume the First* and *Love and Freindship*; in the vein of burlesque that is traceable in her letters to Cassandra; and in the idiosyncrasies of speech—and still more of letter-writing—of her disagreeable people. Direct satire of current abuses she leaves to her clever young men: 'Don't palm all your abuses of language upon me', Mr. Palmer says to his silly wife when she professes to be quoting him;[1] and when Henry Tilney has pounced on Catherine's misuse of *amazing* and *nice* Elinor warns her: 'Miss Morland, he is treating you exactly as he does his sister. He is for ever finding fault with me, for some incorrectness of language, and now he is taking the same liberty with you. The word "nicest", as you used it, did not suit him; and you had better change it as soon as you can, or we shall be overpowered with Johnson and Blair all the rest of the way'[2]—from which I infer that his author, like his sister, thought him 'more nice than wise'. Some others of her opinions can be inferred from

---

[1] *Sense and Sensibility*, p. 113, ch. xx.
[2] *Northanger Abbey*, pp. 107, 108, ch. xiv.

those small but invaluable pieces of evidence, the fragments
of her manuscripts that survive. *The Watsons* and *Sanditon*
are rough drafts, showing erasures and corrections. There
is a significant alteration here and there in *Volume the First*;
and *Love and Freindship* may have as much to tell us if the
manuscript becomes accessible. There is also the manuscript
of the first draft for the end of *Persuasion*, doubly interesting
in that it shows her corrections and offers itself besides for
comparison with the final version. To study it is—almost—
to watch Jane Austen at work, to see her arranging a sentence this way and that, and discovering her own preference.
Among the manuscripts, *Lady Susan* alone is a discreet, un-
revealing, fair copy.

But, it may fairly be said, 'among these pieces of evidence,
all that can be called direct and explicit are collected from
mere fragments of writing'. Nevertheless, regarded together
they show a particular characteristic—one that is to be
expected of the least fragments of Jane Austen's work—
a radical consistency. So, though the corrections in any one
of the manuscripts may show her struggling with an incidental difficulty—as those of *The Watsons* seem to me to
do—the preferences which a study of all the manuscripts
reveals answer, with a delightful precision, the preferences
expressed in the letters to Anna; while the dislikes which
emerge from such a comparison tally with her choice of
faults to ridicule in the burlesque writings. A few instances
will serve for the time being. It is evident, for example, that
she disliked unnecessary elaboration of sentence-structure.
At first (I think) this dislike took the form of an uncritical
suspicion of formality, and she found antithesis in itself
slightly absurd; there is some pert mimicry of it in *Volume
the First*[1]—but it is worth noticing that one passage of this
sort has been erased, as though she had lost patience with
it on re-reading. She was discovering that only certain kinds
of elaboration are disagreeable to the ear—those that go
against the grain of the language. The sentence that makes
a double bend where it had better have run straight is of

---

[1] In *A Fragment* (p. 132; *Minor Works*, p. 71) and *The Generous Curate* (p. 135; *Minor Works*, p. 73). There is a slight suggestion of Johnsonian mannerism in these.

this kind. 'A lovely young Woman lying apparently in great pain beneath a Citron tree', she writes in *Jack and Alice*, 'was an object too interesting not to attract their notice.'[1] And her *hollow* people have a taste for double negatives; indeed, General Tilney is hardly to be followed round their turns. 'No endeavours shall be wanting on our side', he tells Catherine, 'to make Northanger Abbey not wholly disagreeable.'[2] And Mr. Collins practises the same refinement: 'I cannot be otherwise than concerned', he writes to Mr. Bennet, 'at being the means of injuring your amiable daughters.'[3] As her touch grows surer and lighter she allows her tiresome talkers to embark on sentences that are too elaborate for their powers, and *stick*—as Mr. Elton and Mrs. Clay do in their complimentary speeches. Rhetorical questions are another favourite trick of General Tilney's; he never reckons on the interruption of an answer. There is a similar consistency in the little corrections that Jane Austen makes in her own work, and those she proposes to Anna. 'Your descriptions are often more minute than will be liked', she writes. 'You give too many particulars of right hand & left.'[4] Revising a passage of her own, in *The Watsons*, she had pruned her account of the Edwards' house of its minute particulars.[5] Moreover, in work which we know only in its finished state, she is noticeably sparing in her use of this sort of detail. She refers, for example, to William Price's distress at the neglect of 'some slight, but essential alteration of his uniform waistcoat, which he had been promised to have done for him' upon his promotion.[6] I surmise that she had a particular alteration in mind; but, as Dr. Chapman says, she 'knows all the details, and gives us very few of them'.[7]

These suggestions to Anna (and those to James Edward also) raise a problem of their own, which it is convenient to consider here. What are we to understand by the varieties of opening—'I think', 'we think', 'your aunt C. and I both

[1] *Volume the First*, pp. 34, 35; *Minor Works*, p. 20.
[2] *Northanger Abbey*, pp. 139, 140, ch. xvii.   [3] *Pride and Prejudice*, p. 63, ch. xiii.
[4] *Letters*, p. 401.   [5] p. 19; see note to l. 20.
[6] *Mansfield Park*, p. 381, ch. xxxviii.
[7] 'Jane Austen's Methods', *Times Literary Supplement*, 9 February 1922.

think', 'one guesses', and so on? It is safe, I am sure, to rule out the possibility that 'we think' ever means a family verdict; Mrs. Austen's perturbation at a breach of etiquette is mentioned in a tone of gentle raillery, and, for the rest, we have clearly only Jane and Cassandra to reckon with. I believe that, except in the single passage which explicitly dissociates them,[1] they may be counted as one; and even in that passage the suggested contrast between Cassandra's severity and Jane's leniency is at least half playful, corresponding with the pretended anticipation of censorship in an earlier letter to Cassandra herself: 'We walked to Weston one evening last week, and liked it very much. Liked *what* very much? Weston? No, *walking* to Weston. I have not expressed myself properly, but I hope you will understand me.'[2] Therefore it seems to me that, with this outstanding exception, these critical letters to Anna and James Edward express Jane Austen's own views with only so much reservation as comes of her anxiety not to daunt them.

The characteristics of Jane Austen's style are consistent one with another and with the opinions she expresses. But consistency need not hinder growth. It must be the brilliance of her early style that has blinded critics to her gradual and steady development. In one of the earliest among her surviving letters, earlier than any surviving draft of her novels, this sentence catches the eye: ' 'Tis really very kind of my Aunt to ask us to Bath again; a kindness that deserves a better return than to profit by it.'[3] Could there be a more neatly cut comment on an invitation from a rich relation who, by all accounts, did her duty by her nieces without any appearance of enjoyment? One can feel no surprise, after this, at the frosty sparkle of *Lady Susan*, nor at the edge which exact phrasing gives to the satire in *Sense and Sensibility*. One can only wonder whether a young lady who is able to write like this in her first published work will ever learn to write still better. And, indeed, to the casual reader it may sometimes seem that she will not always write so well as she does in the novels drafted before the close of

---

[1] *Letters*, pp. 395, 396.   [2] Ibid., p. 68.   [3] Ibid., p. 26.

her youth; that never again will she be so brilliantly idiosyn-
cratic, so unmistakably herself, as in *Pride and Prejudice*; that
she might almost say, as Dryden is made to say in *The Hind
and the Panther Transvers'd*, '. . . I fill the first part with
Flowers, Figures, fine Language, and all that; and then
I'gad sink by degrees, till at last I write but little better than
other People.' Nevertheless, Mr. Garrod's declaration that
'Jane Austen could write at twenty as well, or better, or
very nearly as well, as at forty', not only overlooks (as I have
said) our uncertainty as to what she really did write at
twenty, but misses essential qualities in her later style.

For the manner of her later novels those early sports of
wit, the juvenilia, were not very apt training, and her earliest
published writing bears signs of apprenticeship. She had to
gain—and *Sense and Sensibility* and *Pride and Prejudice* show
that she did not come by it all at once—command of a
variety of tones: the tone of voice, for example, proper to
different kinds of narrative; not merely for occasional passages
of emotional urgency but also for the sustained course of
grave, circumstantial relation of events. I suspect that a
sense of this need may be lightly expressed in her own pretended threat to Cassandra, that she will intersperse the 'playfulness and epigrammatism of the general style' of *Pride and
Prejudice* with something that will form a contrast to it.[1] The
satiric point of this passage is turned, of course, against
those authors from whom she is to learn this contrasted
style, but the phrase 'playfulness and epigrammatism' exactly
hits off the narrative manner of *Pride and Prejudice*, its charm
and its limitations. For a retrospect of Mr. Bennet's married
life it is admirable: 'To his wife he was very little otherwise
indebted, than as her ignorance and folly had contributed
to his amusement. This is not the sort of happiness which
a man would in general wish to owe to his wife; but where
other powers of entertainment are wanting, the true philo-
sopher will derive benefit from such as are given.'[2] But for
the prospect of Lydia's married life it is not so good: '. . .
how little of permanent happiness could belong to a couple
who were only brought together because their passions were

---

[1] Ibid., pp. 299, 300.   [2] *Pride and Prejudice*, p. 236, ch. xlii.

stronger than their virtue, she could easily conjecture.'[1] The antithesis jingles.

In dialogue also she has much to learn, in spite of the precocious quickness of ear that had early caught more than one tone in the talk of fools—the tone of sheer farce in the quarrel between Lady Williams and Alice Johnson,[2] the solemn nonsense which accompanies the entrance of the hero into *Love and Freindship*; in spite, too, of the witty invention that already delights us in the dialogue of *Sense and Sensibility*, and burns still more brightly in that of *Pride and Prejudice*. She has to discover the tones that express diverse moods, the undertones, for example, of anxiety and sense of loss, and—harder still, I suspect—of unreserved happiness. In *Pride and Prejudice* she seems sometimes to distrust her own ear for these tones; she allows the spirit of comedy to govern her characters' language as long as it may, and then takes the words from their mouths. 'My dearest sister,' Jane begs, when Elizabeth confesses her engagement, 'now be *be* serious . . . Will you tell me how long you have loved him?'

' "It has been coming on so gradually that I hardly know when it began. But I believe I must date it from my first seeing his beautiful grounds at Pemberley."

'Another intreaty that she would be serious, however, produced the desired effect; and she soon satisfied Jane by her solemn assurances of attachment.'[3]

Even less sure, I think, did she feel of her resources when talk was wanted for plain, sensible people. She was to congratulate Anna—more than once, and with unusual emphasis—on her success in serious dialogue, especially among such characters. 'I . . . am more particularly struck with your *serious* conversations', she writes,[4] and admits regretfully : 'I wish you could make Mrs. F. talk more, but she must be difficult to manage & make entertaining, because there is so much good common sence & propriety about her that nothing can be very *broad*.'[5] From the manner of their introduction I should guess that the Gardiners were to have

[1] *Pride and Prejudice*, p. 312, ch. l.   [2] *Jack and Alice* (*Volume the First*).
[3] *Pride and Prejudice*, p. 373, ch. lix.
[4] *Letters*, pp. 420, 421.   [5] Ibid., p. 402.

been all common sense and propriety, like Mrs. F., but when they appear their talk has a dry sparkle that would hardly discredit Mr. Bennet's side of the family. Not before *Emma* does Jane Austen achieve such dialogue as that between Mrs. Weston and Mr. Knightley, which accomplishes what it has to do with only the gentlest twinkle of humour on her side and no more than habitual irony on his. And when those two sensible women, Lady Russell and Mrs. Croft, talk together, she falls back on *oblique oration*.

Her later command of variety of tone in narrative and dialogue is well illustrated within small compass by the two scenes at the White Hart, in the rewritten part of *Persuasion*. There is the straightforward relation, so plain that it draws no undue attention to itself; level, too, as it must be for the contrast with the sequel, but never spiritless; there, also, the several tones of the talkers, from Charles's broad good humour to Mrs. Croft's cool sense, and from Mrs. Musgrove's easy absurdity to the highly charged mood of Anne and Captain Harville.

What have been the character and direction of Jane Austen's development in that short course from *Sense and Sensibility* to *Persuasion*? For the present it will be enough to suggest that her consciousness has grown more subtle, her apprehension of her subject more complex; she has learnt to say what she has to say through her books, above all through the medium of her characters' consciousness; and (this is our immediate concern) she has formed a style fit for her purpose.

This development of style may be seen in its plainest aspect by finding out how it is that she can tell her story— how she makes exactly intelligible to us the symmetrically posed, precisely interrelated happenings that she chooses for narrative pattern—through the talk of her characters, even the most unpromising of them. A character of marked idiosyncrasies of speech, for example, does not seem well fitted to convey to the reader information of any complexity: one would not, at first sight, choose Miss Bates as the likeliest person to make clear to us so prettily complicated a comedy of errors as *Emma*. Yet this is her office. 'What is

before me, I see', she says,[1] and she not only sees but conveys to us the exact circumstances at more than one turn
of her niece's fortunes. Who would suppose that Miss
Bates would be able to convey anything exactly? But, taking
her time about it, she does—and that without using any
mode of expression inconsistent with her usual habits of
speech. Fanny Burney, faced with a like problem in *Camilla*,
sacrifices consistency, and allows the muddle-headed Sir
Hugh Tyrold to be more or less articulate as the plot
requires; and it is not unusual to see a novelist slipping
furtively round this obstacle with the words 'He related
what had occurred'—and then giving his own account of
the affair. But it is a consequence of Jane Austen's method
that the obstacle itself should be much less formidable to her
than it appears: look closely at the idiosyncrasies in speech
of her characters, and they will show themselves to be
modelled, as it were, in very low relief. This is how it comes
about that Miss Bates's speech, while achieving an impression of inextricable confusion, is yet capable of making us
understand the finest intricacies of the plot; that it forms
a limpid element, in which its subject—her mother's spec-
tacles, or the Perrys' carriage, or even the order of events
at a crisis[2]—is clearly apparent. This *limpid confusion* is the
result of all its characteristics. First, she never misuses
words (unless when she is recognizably quoting Mrs. Elton);
then, not one of her sentences can fairly be called confused;
their structure and movement are as neat and brisk as her
person. In fact, the impression of confusion is given by
two habits which are so contrived as to counterbalance one
another: in the first place, she seldom completes a sentence,
though she usually carries it far enough to show how it
should have been completed (a familiar English idiom):
'. . . poor dear Jane could not bear to see anybody—anybody at all—Mrs. Elton, indeed, could not be denied—and
Mrs. Cole had made such a point—and Mrs. Perry had said
so much—but, except them, Jane would really see nobody.'[3]
In the second place, each sentence flies off at a tangent from

[1] *Emma*, p. 176, ch. xxi.   [2] See pp. 176–178.
[3] *Emma*, p. 390, ch. xlv.

the last, but so characteristic are the trains of thought that, when need is, every sentence elucidates its curtailed predecessor—as a very small quotation will illustrate: ' ... upon my word, Miss Woodhouse, you do look—how do you like Jane's hair?'[1] *This* use of fragmentary speech exacts more skill than does any other to which Jane Austen had turned it. She had employed it to suggest strong feeling, embarrassment—forces tugging against the impulse for expression—in Colonel Brandon's and Willoughby's accounts of themselves to Elinor, and was to use it for the same purpose in her first draft of Captain Wentworth's proposal of marriage. In such cases, its use is to alter the speaker's voice from its habitual tone—which in Willoughby's it had failed to do because we had not been allowed to hear enough of his ordinary voice. But for Miss Bates it *is* the habitual tone, and indicates not disorganization of the ordinary course of thought and feeling but that course itself. To represent a peculiar mode of progress requires greater delicacy of intimation than to represent arrest or disturbance of progress. And this delicacy of intimation is one consequence of that unemphatic treatment of idiosyncrasy which I have called low relief.

This same shallow modelling is discernible in all Jane Austen's dialogue. She tends to suggest social variants in speech by syntax and phrasing rather than by vocabulary, as appears when the elder, and less genteel, Miss Steele is compared with Fanny Burney's Branghtons; this is what Nancy makes of Edward's conversation with her sister, when she tries to report it to Elinor: ' ... it all came out ... how he had been so worried by what passed, that as soon as he had went away from his mother's house, he had got upon his horse, and rid into the country some where or other; and how he had staid about at an inn all Thursday and Friday, on purpose to get the better of it.' And 'Edward have got some business at Oxford, he says; so he must go there for a time; and after *that*, as soon as he can light upon a Bishop, he will be ordained. I wonder what curacy he will get!'[2] This, though it is broad enough to embarrass

---

[1] Ibid., p. 323, ch. xxxviii.   [2] *Sense and Sensibility*, pp. 273 and 275, ch. xxxviii.

her sister—who can manage the phrases of common talk pretty well, and is not likely to give herself away except in her letters—yet does not so differ in vocabulary from the speech of the Dashwoods as does that of the Branghtons from Evelina's. And it is syntax and phrasing likewise that differentiate the speech of the Thorpes from that of the Tilneys. Yet, in this shallow modelling, there is such exact keeping of scale that the distinctions remain clearly apparent: no sentence of Elizabeth Watson's could be transferred to her sister Emma, however their opinions may agree, because of their different upbringing; nor could a Steele vulgarism be mistaken for that of a Thorpe. Jane Austen never repeats herself. Each social shelf in her little world has its own slang—Isabella Thorpe's, Tom Bertram's, Mary Crawford's; and so have the professions, when they appear—Mr. Shepherd's language has a recognizable flavour, though (to the relief, surely, of a generation that was becoming well acquainted with the lawyer of fiction) very sparingly used.

How did Jane Austen come by this mastery of dialogue? She must have had, to begin with, a fine and true ear. 'She is one of the greatest,' Dr. Chapman says, 'because one of the most accurate, writers of dialogue of her own or any age.'[1] And even Mr. Garrod, in his *Depreciation*, calls her writing 'truthful and apt'.[2] Evidently she was an alert observer of mannerism in speech—at first, I suspect, because it irritated her; there is a note of exasperation in her treatment of Margaret Watson.[3] Later she learned how to draw its sting. Mannerism, especially when it takes the form of recurrent word or phrase, is by no means easy to represent; there is but a hair's breadth between the point at which the reader delightedly recognizes it as a revealing habit of speech, and the point at which its iteration begins to weary him. But even as Mr. Elton's 'Exactly so' is ready

[1] *Miss Austen's English (Sense and Sensibility)*, p. 389.
[2] H. W. Garrod, 'Jane Austen: A Depreciation' (R.S.L.), p. 30.
[3] '. . . her manner was all affection & her voice all gentleness; continual smiles & a very slow articulation being her constant resource when determined on pleasing. —She was now so "delighted to see dear, dear Emma" that she could hardly speak a word in a minute' (*The Watsons*, p. 87).

to catch the attention as an expression of his unfeeling complaisance, and before it can threaten tediousness, Emma transfixes it by her mimicry beyond the need of repetition: ' "This man is almost too gallant to be in love," thought Emma. "I should say so, but that I suppose there may be a hundred different ways of being in love. He is an excellent young man, and will suit Harriet exactly; it will be an 'Exactly so,' as he says himself . . ." '[1] Again, just as Miss Bates's idiom is beginning to tease the ear, Emma relieves pent feelings by her outrageous parody: she supposes Miss Bates to be thanking Mr. Knightley ' "for his great kindness in marrying Jane . . .—'So very kind and obliging!—But he always had been such a very kind neighbour!' And then fly off, through half a sentence, to her mother's old petticoat. 'Not that it was such a very old petticoat either—for still it would last a great while—and, indeed, she must thankfully say that their petticoats were all very strong.' "[2]

Where this tact is wanting, a quick and retentive ear can be tiresome; where artistic sensibility and conscience are wanting, it can even be a serious disadvantage, for it will hardly allow its possessor to realize the need for transmuting stuff of memory into stuff of art. Even an intuitive faculty for selection will not be enough for this purpose—as Fanny Burney demonstrates, in her double part of novelist and memoirist. She selects shrewdly and remembers faithfully—contemporary memoirs, tallying with hers, show how faithfully—the idiosyncrasies of speech which seem to her characteristic; and, having a keen eye for the surface of character, she uses them with capital effect in her journal and letters. But when she turns novelist this very facility, both in retaining and selecting, may become a snare. It is all very well in *Evelina*, a supposed series of journal-letters, where Madame Duval's 'Ma foi' and Captain Mirvan's 'Holloa, my lads' will pass for the mannerisms noticed by a diarist with a gift of mimicry and a disposition to malice. But for the direct narrative of *Cecilia*, *Camilla*, and *The Wanderer* it is not so fit. Horace Walpole, when he com-

[1] *Emma*, p. 49, ch. vi. [2] Ibid., p. 225, ch. xxvi.

plains of *Camilla*'s inferiority to *Evelina*, attacks its dialogue:
'The great fault is that the authoress is so afraid of not
making all her *dramatis personae* set in character, that she
never lets them say a syllable but what is to mark their
character, which is very unnatural . . .'[1] But it is the abandon-
ment of journal-letter form, the assumed responsibilities
of direct narration, that have discovered this weakness to
him. 'There is little in her works', Hazlitt says, 'of passion
or character, or even manners, in the most extended sense
of the word, as implying the sum-total of our habits and
pursuits; her *forte* is in describing the absurdities and affec-
tations of external behaviour, or the *manners of people in
company*.'[2] For the instinctive selective faculty of the mimic,
bent on seizing the recognizable turn of expression, waits
for the prevailing mood (which is by no means the same
thing as the manners that indicate 'the sum-total of our
habits and pursuits')—for Lady Louisa Larpent at her most
languid, Mr. Lovel at his most foppish, Miss Larolles at her
most hoydenish; and so the fine point of interaction between character and circumstance is likely to be missed.
And the symptom by which this may usually be recognized
is the failure of the characters to surprise us; nothing they
say can give us that tingling shock of the unexpected which
will create the illusion of the living voice.

    This surprise must be delicately contrived, however, if it
is not to blur the impression they have made on our imagination. And here again Jane Austen's use of 'low relief'
proves its worth. For such relief can be momentarily
heightened: a character may of a sudden—not casually, but
under pressure of some sense of urgency—speak with
deeper idiosyncrasy than usual. Such a pressure disturbs
the habitual unaffected formality of Mr. Woodhouse's speech
when 'according to his custom on such occasions' he is
'making the circle of his guests, and paying his particular
compliments to the ladies', last among them Jane Fairfax.
For even as he generalizes, and allegorizes, and addresses

---

[1] *Letters*, ed. Toynbee (1903–25), xii. 339. (Letter of 1 October 1782.)
[2] *Works*, ed. P. P. Howe (1930–4), vol. xvi (contributions to the *Edinburgh
Review*), *Standard Novels and Romances*, p. 21.

her in the third person—momentarily, under the immediate pressure of his kindly solicitude, his voice alters in tone: 'I am very sorry to hear, Miss Fairfax, of your being out this morning in the rain. Young ladies should take care of themselves.—Young ladies are delicate plants. They should take care of their health and their complexion. My dear, did you change your stockings?'[1]

By what method did Jane Austen achieve this discreet use of idiosyncrasy in speech? The corrections in her rough drafts seem to have something to tell. Both in *The Watsons* and in *Sanditon* she can be seen sketching out first what her characters have to communicate, and then marking, by gradual little touches, the manner of communication—as though a draftsman should first set a human figure in a certain attitude, and occupying a certain position in his composition, and then develop it into a particular figure, with proper characteristics of person and dress. In the opening of *The Watsons*, Emma and Elizabeth are introduced to us as they are driving together, 'in the old chair', 'to the town of D. in Surrey'; and the task of explaining the family's character and situation is given to Elizabeth, with the least possible help from the author's own voice. Now, looking into the corrections, one perceives that, while in the first draft Elizabeth simply tells what has to be told, this plain account is afterwards so modified by a number of minute touches—above all, by the substitution of little vulgarisms and colloquialisms for unaffected formal speech—as to indicate also the peculiar tone of the speaker. A reference to Tom Musgrave's habit of 'philandering' becomes: '. . . he is always behaving in a particular way to one or another.'[2] Penelope's making 'no secret of wishing to marry' becomes: 'There is nothing she w^d not do to get married—she would as good as tell you so herself.'[3] And there is a steady and consistent substitution of short, plain words for longer synonyms throughout Elizabeth's speech. In *The Watsons*, it is true, Jane Austen seems to be struggling with a peculiar oppression, a stiffness and heaviness that

---

[1] *Emma*, p. 294, ch. xxxiv.
[2] *The Watsons*, p. 4; see Dr. Chapman's note.   [3] Ibid., p. 6.

threaten her style, and so the corrections show a general trend towards shorter, more colloquial words, in narrative as well as dialogue. But this does not hold good for *Sanditon*, nor does it sufficiently account for the systematic deepening, in the corrections of both manuscripts, of the idiosyncrasies in the speech of almost every character. Tom Musgrave's gallantry is a little broadened as he smirks at Emma in the assurance that he is making himself particularly agreeable: he has not, he easily admits, troubled to visit her family before her arrival: 'But I am afraid I have been a very sad neighbour of late. I hear dreadful complaints of my negligence wherever I go, & I confess it is a shameful length of time since I was at Stanton.—But I shall *now* endeavour to make myself amends for the past.'[1] And a sharper edge is given to Mrs. Watson's malice, a more sickly flavour to Margaret's affectation, through such small changes. By the same means, of course, Jane Austen accentuates the amiable characteristics of her pleasant people: in recasting the end of *Persuasion* she uses some passages from the original draft, merely rewriting them; if one such passage—Wentworth's confession to Anne—is read in the two versions,[2] it will be found that, by little corrections in the first, and little alterations when she comes to make the second, she has heightened the vehemence and candour with which he blames himself for his pride and obstinacy. The corrections in the manuscript of *Sanditon* show this same gradual differentiation in the speech of the several characters: Mr. Parker's idiom, his habit of thinking *in phrases*, becomes more marked; the relation of her past history by Lady Denham to Charlotte acquires her peculiar intonation through vulgarisms in syntax: 'We lived perfectly happily together' becomes 'Nobody could live happier together than us';[3] and a little button of absurdity is fastened on top of Sir Edward's pretentious vocabulary by the substitution of 'anti-puerile' for 'sagacious' in his description of the ideal novel-reader—that is, of himself.[4]

[1] *The Watsons*, pp. 51, 52: 'I confess' and 'I shall *now* endeavour' are inserted in revision.
[2] *Two Chapters of Persuasion*, pp. 20, 21 (for corrections, see notes); *Persuasion*, pp. 242, 243, ch. xxiii.   [3] *Sanditon*, p. 97.   [4] Ibid., p. 108.

'I hate re-writing,' Scott said, 'as much as Falstaff did paying back.'[1] I should not be surprised to learn that Jane Austen positively enjoyed it.

This style, with its quick and light response to idiosyncrasy, allows Jane Austen's characters to be, so far as we are concerned, *communicative*—and that in a natural and probable manner. Their faculty of observation varies, of course; nicety of perception belongs only to her favourites; but they can all tell us something about one another. 'I do not think Mr. Knightley would be much disturbed by Miss Bates', Mrs. Weston says. 'Little things do not irritate him. She might talk on; and if he wanted to say any thing himself, he would only talk louder, and drown her voice.'[2] Yet these communications never appear to come from the author's own fund of knowledge, because they so faithfully observe the idiom of the character through whom they reach us, whether in the form of dialogue, letter, or reflection. Few novelists can be more scrupulous than Jane Austen as to the phrasing of the thoughts of their characters. Mr. Bennet, believing that his brother-in-law had borne the cost of Lydia's marriage, wished that he had made provision for his daughters: 'Had he done his duty in that respect, Lydia need not have been indebted to her uncle, for whatever of honour or credit could now be purchased for her. The satisfaction of prevailing on one of the most worthless young men in Great Britain to be her husband, might then have rested in its proper place.'[3] His letters are equally characteristic, and, like all the letters in Jane Austen's novels, nicely differentiated from the speech of the writer. The men's letters always show a very little increase of formality, which sharpens the point of Mr. Bennet's wit, lends weight to Darcy's assertions, and elaborates Frank Churchill's compliments; the women seldom attempt this formality, unless, like Lucy Steele, they are straining after gentility; nevertheless, a passage from one of their letters could rarely be mistaken for a passage of dialogue, since these letters catch and hold a mood as speech can rarely do—

[1] *Chronicles of the Canongate*, ch. v. [2] *Emma*, pp. 225, 226, ch. xxvi.
[3] *Pride and Prejudice*, p. 308, ch. l.

Lydia's exhilaration in eloping, Jane's distress and confusion in telling Elizabeth of the elopement. It may be
worth noticing here that Jane Austen had no very useful
model for her fictitious letters. The novel-in-letters, being
obliged to relieve the density of narrative by dialogue,
formed a convention which only this need could justify:
the convention of long conversations reported word for
word. The letters of stage-comedy were not subject to this
convention, but they must be concise and crucial. Neither
offered a precedent for the lifelikeness of Mary Musgrove's
letter, with its translation of others' talk into her own
idiom, and its news in the postscript.

The virtue of this style which Jane Austen has made to
be the means of communication of her characters lies in its
equitable settlement of conflicting claims; not only does it
allow her people to be constant without becoming static,
but it gives them a language in which they may speak to us
as they would while telling us what she means that they
should. Moreover it achieves harmony with her narrative
manner. Mr. Morgan speaks of the tyranny of convention
over 'the means employed to pass from dialogue to narrative and back again' in the early novel, the jarring sensation
of a transition, consciousness that 'the narrative planes were
being shifted'; and he holds that 'this passing from plane to
plane is one of the everlasting difficulties of a novelist'.[1] Jane
Austen's narrative style seems to me to show (especially in
the later novels) a curiously chameleon-like faculty; it varies
in colour as the habits of expression of the several characters
impress themselves on the relation of the episodes in which
they are involved, and on the description of their situations. The very arrival of the Bertrams' party in the midst
of the solemn grandeur of Sotherton seems to weigh it
down:

'Mr. Rushworth was at the door to receive his fair lady, and the whole
party were welcomed by him with due attention. In the drawing-room
they were met with equal cordiality by the mother, and Miss Bertram
had all the distinction with each that she could wish. After the business
of arriving was over, it was first necessary to eat, and the doors were

---

[1] *Epitaph on George Moore* (1935), pp. 47, 48.

thrown open to admit them through one or two intermediate rooms into the appointed dining-parlour, where a collation was prepared with abundance and elegance.'[1]

As they make their progress through the house, with its 'solid mahogany, rich damask, marble, gilding and carving', this abundance and elegance seem to lie like an increasing load upon the imagination, until, half stupefied with the air of Sotherton, we reach the appropriate anti-climax of Mrs. Rushworth's 'relation': 'This chapel was fitted up as you see it, in James the Second's time. Before that period, as I understand, the pews were only wainscot; and there is some reason to think that the linings and cushions of the pulpit and family-seat were only purple cloth; but this is not quite certain.'[2]

This aptitude that I have likened to a chameleon's is, however, no more than a symptom of the pliability of Jane Austen's narrative style; and that pliability is due to the essential simplicity of its staple. Here she was fortunate and judicious; she inherited a good tradition, and she was content with it. As for prose, her brother tells us that 'Her reading was very extensive in history and belles lettres; and her memory extremely tenacious'; that she was acquainted with 'the best essays and novels in the English language'; and among the graver writings he singles out Johnson's.[3] She was brought up, in fact, on the standard authors of her own and the preceding age, and their habits of thought and expression might become hers, if she were so disposed.

She did not look to the novelists for direction as to style; and this was well, for the great novels of the mid-eighteenth century had too strong individuality, and their successor, the novel of sentiment, did not know its own business. It wanted, not merely a grand style for its more ambitious passages, but also an unaffected, level style for plain relation of fact and circumstance. This is Fanny Burney's notion of a matter-of-fact introductory statement:

'In the bosom of her respectable family resided Camilla. Nature, with a bounty the most profuse, had been lavish to her of attractions; Fortune, with a moderation yet kinder, had placed her between luxury and

---

[1] *Mansfield Park*, p. 84, ch. ix.   [2] Ibid., p. 86, ch. ix.
[3] *Biographical Notice*, 1817, p. 7.

indigence. Her abode was the parsonage-house of Etherington. . . .
The living, though not considerable, enabled its incumbent to attain
every rational object of his modest and circumscribed wishes; to bestow
upon a deserving wife whatever her own forbearance declined not; and
to educate a lovely race of one son and three daughters, with that liberal
propriety, which unites improvement for the future with present
enjoyment.'[1]

Fanny Burney takes pains to be ridiculous. Her followers
are often merely slovenly. Jane Austen neither strains after
grandiloquence[2] nor slips into slovenliness. She practises
but one grammatical irregularity which is uncomfortable
to the ear now—what may be called the dislocated clause.[3]
Of this I have found instances in the prose of every one
of those writers who seem likely to have influenced her—
as a slip; it is occasional, and usually to be found in casual
writing—in Goldsmith's task-work, in Gibbon's letters.
Jane Austen, however, uses it as freely as though she had
never heard it condemned; and Beckford parodies it savagely
as an habitual fault of style in women's novels.[4] Was it a
licence which had been tacitly permitted to them? Did
James and Henry Austen regard it as a fault which they
would not have allowed to stand had they noticed it in
their own writings, but which might be passed over in
their sister's with the apology that Fielding had offered for
faults of style in *David Simple*?—'. . . some small Errors,
which Want of Habit in Writing chiefly occasioned, and
which no Man of Learning would think worth his Censure
in a Romance; nor any gentleman, in the writings of a young
Woman'.[5] At all events, it may fairly be said that Jane
Austen's sentences are rarely if ever ambiguous; a pronoun
may sometimes go astray, but the drift of the paragraph
always makes the writer's intention clear. Beckford's general
satire of the novelists' style does not in fact apply to her.

---

[1] *Camilla*, ch. i.
[2] Her rare inversions sound to me Johnsonian; that is, an unconscious reflection
of her reading.
[3] e.g. Lady Catherine, speaking of her daughter and Darcy, says: 'While in their
cradles, we planned the union' (*Pride and Prejudice*, p. 355, ch. lvi).
[4] *Modern Novel Writing* (under the pseudonym of Lady Harriet Marlow), 1796.
[5] Sarah Fielding, *David Simple*, 1744 (2nd edit.)—with a preface by Henry
Fielding, in which he mentions his correction of these errors. (They are seldom worse
than colloquialisms or awkwardnesses.)

To the essayists and historians, on the other hand (to adopt Henry Austen's division), his sister seems to have apprenticed herself, even in childhood. Already in *Love and Freindship* echoes of Goldsmith's voice are heard—echoes, at least, of some of those tones of his voice that belong to his task-work for booksellers. This summary account of Edward IV—'His best qualities were courage and beauty; his bad, a combination of all the vices'[1]—might equally well come from his *History of England* or from the pert little burlesque version of it in *Love and Freindship*, in which I seem to hear a tinkling echo of this very phrase: 'This Monarch [Edward IV] was famous only for his Beauty and his Courage, of which the Picture we have here given of him,[2] and his undaunted Behaviour in marrying one Woman while he was engaged to another, are sufficient proofs.'[3]

This tone of sly simplicity is not, however, audible to me in Jane Austen's later writing. The simplicity of her novels, with that other quality, slyness or shrewdness, which gives this simplicity its value, seems to belong to another tradition and, even so, to belong with a difference. The essayists of the eighteenth century had been kindly masters to the young Jane Austen; the turn of wit, the phrasing, of their lighter moods had come easily to her—and this may perhaps account for that precocious assurance in style which has half hidden her later development. Even in her childish burlesque pieces every sentence is almost as deliberately and neatly turned (on its small scale) as are those of her masters. From the lightest piece of nonsense—'Our neighbourhood was small, for it consisted only of your Mother'[4] —to the sharpest prick of satire—'I expect nothing more in my wife than my wife will find in me—Perfection'[5]—each stands firmly, its weight exactly poised. Here already is the sharp definition of *Lady Susan*, and here the promise which *Pride and Prejudice* was to fulfil. 'Next to being married,' Mr. Bennet says to Elizabeth, when he hears of Jane's

---

[1] Goldsmith, *History of England* (1771), ii. 250.
[2] i.e. one of Cassandra's medallions, made, perhaps, in playful imitation of those in the 1771 *History*.
[3] *Love and Freindship*, p. 86; *Minor Works*, pp. 140, 141.
[4] Ibid., p. 7; *Minor Works*, p. 78. [5] *Volume the First*, p. 46; *Minor Works*, p. 26.

cross fortunes, 'a girl likes to be crossed in love a little now and then. It is something to think of, and gives her a sort of distinction among her companions. When is your turn to come? You will hardly bear to be long outdone by Jane. Now is your time. Here are officers enough at Meryton to disappoint all the young ladies in the country. Let Wickham be *your* man. He is a pleasant fellow, and would jilt you creditably.'

'Thank you, Sir, but a less agreeable man would satisfy me. We must not all expect Jane's good fortune.'[1] This, like many other passages in Jane Austen's novels, tingles with a rhythm which stage comedy[2] could never quite forget, though it might sound but faintly for a generation at a time—rhythm which is justified (as prose rhythm needs to be) by excitement. Instant perception of the absurd charges word and phrase with all the forces which in ordinary talk are dissipated, giving an impression of speed and simplicity not alien from the temper of verse. Such an impression must be elusive; no reader can vouch for more than his own experience. To me this rhythm seems audible in every one of Jane Austen's novels—even where I should least expect it, where no pulse of bodily well-being keeps time with it, in *Sanditon*. For it is appropriated by no one kind of comic dialogue. It tingles in the wit of Mr. Bennet —'Wickham's a fool, if he takes her with a farthing less than ten thousand pounds. I should be sorry to think so ill of him, in the very beginning of our relationship.'[3] It is perceptible in the shrewd or droll saying that may be occasionally allowed to 'plain matter-of-fact people, who seldom aim at wit of any kind'—'And very nice young ladies they both are; I hardly know one from the other.'[4] And yet it is not out of place in the merely absurd talk of fools. '*We*', Mr. Parker assures his wife, when she envies their more sheltered neighbours, 'have all the Grandeur of the Storm, with less real danger, because the Wind meeting with nothing to oppose or confine it around our House, simply

---

[1] *Pride and Prejudice*, pp. 137, 138, ch. xxiv.
[2] J. A. was probably an habitual reader of plays.
[3] *Pride and Prejudice*, p. 304, ch. xlix.   [4] *Persuasion*, p. 92, ch. x.

rages & passes on.'[1] For it is their creator's delight in
absurdity that vibrates in their talk. But if Jane Austen
learnt from the dramatists the turn of phrase proper to
comedy she learnt also, in writing *Pride and Prejudice*, how
to differentiate her dialogue from that sort she would
associate with the stage; how to make it more reflective on
the one hand, more inconsequent on the other, according
to the bent of the speaker. And what she learnt from the
essayists she likewise transmuted to her own use; that,
indeed, is the way in which they were good masters, and
she an apt pupil—they taught her to make something of her
own. Lady Middleton and Mrs. Dashwood 'sympathised
with each other in an insipid propriety of demeanour, and
a general want of understanding'.[2] That might come from
one of the early periodical essays. It has the formality, the
preponderance of general and abstract terms, which seems to
have repelled Mrs. Meynell[3]—but which we are less likely
to take amiss. To us Jane Austen appears like one who
inherits a prosperous and well-ordered estate—the heritage
of a prose style in which neither generalization nor abstrac-
tion need signify vagueness, because there was close enough
agreement as to the scope and significance of such terms.[4]
Character and motive, for example, might be presented in
them—a practice best illustrated, and very likely familiar to
Jane Austen herself, in the *Lives of the Poets*. 'His mind was
not very comprehensive, nor his curiosity active; he had no
value for those parts of knowledge which he had not himself cultivated.'[5] This, surely, and countless passages like
it, represent the school in which she trained herself. Lady
Russell forms and expresses her judgement on Mr. Elliot in
these terms: 'Every thing united in him; good understanding, correct opinions, knowledge of the world, and a warm
heart . . . He was steady, observant, moderate, candid'; he
possessed 'sensibility', and 'a value for all the felicities of

[1] *Sanditon*, p. 48; *Minor Works*, p. 381.
[2] *Sense and Sensibility*, p. 229, ch. xxxiv.
[3] Alice Meynell, 'The Classic Novelist' in *The Second Person Singular* (1921).
[4] It is, I believe, want of realization of this element in Jane Austen's style that
has made critics such as Mr. Forster find a reflection of her point of view in the
thoughts of all her heroines; see *Abinger Harvest* (1936), p. 149.
[5] *Life of Shenstone*.

domestic life'[1]—and so on. Here, of course, the ear catches
an inflexion of irony in the use of such exact and emphatic
terms for a misapprehension; but that implies no dissatisfaction with the terms themselves. They are used to express
the opinions on their fellow characters of all the *reflective*
heroines (Catherine being a child, and Emma, as she calls
herself, an 'imaginist'): for Elizabeth Bennet's criticism of
her father's 'ill-judged . . . direction of talents . . . which
rightly used, might at least have preserved the respectability of his daughters, even if incapable of enlarging the
mind of his wife';[2] for the shrewd observations of Elinor
Dashwood and Charlotte Heywood; even for Anne Elliot's
gentler judgements. But, more and more freely, they are
combined with other kinds of expression in that interplay of formal and colloquial, abstract and concrete, general
and particular, to whose interaction are due the firmness and
suppleness of the style in which the great prose writers of
the eighteenth century could address the Common Reader.
Fanny Price, eager to find in her own shortcomings the
reason for her mother's early neglect of her, supposed
that 'she had probably alienated Love by the helplessness
and fretfulness of a fearful temper, or been unreasonable
in wanting a larger share than any one among so many
could deserve'.[3] Sometimes there is a humorous purpose
in the juxtaposition: 'They had a very fine day for Box
Hill; and all the other outward circumstances of arrangement, accommodation, and punctuality, were in favour of
a pleasant party. . . . Nothing was wanting but to be happy
when they got there.'[4] Sometimes it marks the centre of a
comic episode—as in Sir Thomas's attempt to give 'Mr.
Rushworth's opinion in better words than he could find
himself'—and his author's comment: 'Mr. Rushworth hardly
knew what to do with so much meaning.'[5] That commonplace turn of expression—the neutral verb mobilized by the
preposition—goes with the grain of the language, would
not be out of place in dialogue, yet is wholly in keeping

[1] *Persuasion*, pp. 146, 147, ch. xvi.
[2] *Pride and Prejudice*, p. 237, ch. xlii.
[3] *Mansfield Park*, p. 371, ch. xxxvii.
[4] *Emma*, p. 367, ch. xliii.   [5] *Mansfield Park*, p. 186, ch. xix.

with the narrative passage to which it belongs. Scott, the only one of Jane Austen's contemporaries who has a lively appreciation of the prose tradition they inherited, is at a drawback here: the language of his narrative passages must always remain distinct from the dialogue of his Scots-speaking characters, and from the Ossianic drone by which he distinguishes his Gaelic speakers.

If Jane Austen trained herself in Johnson's school, that was not, I think, the limit of her debt to him; something more personal remains—some tones of his voice seem to be echoed in her style. An echo is too elusive to be certainly identified; but conjecture may be worth offering. I think I see in her familiarity with, and love of, his work the explana-tion of her aptitude for coining pregnant abstractions—such phrases as Miss Bates's *desultory good-will*, of which the sounds pursued her visitors as they mounted her stairs;[1] Mrs. Elton's *apparatus of happiness*, her large bonnet and basket;[2] and Sir Walter's advance towards his grand cousins 'with all the eagerness compatible with anxious elegance';[3] these, surely, may be called Johnsonian phrases and may fairly remind us of such passages in *The Rambler* as the description of the leisurely travellers who 'missed . . . the Pleasure of alarming Villages with the Tumult of our Passage, and of disguising our Insignificancy by the Dignity of Hurry'.[4] From Johnson she may have learnt also a liking for antithetic phrasing, coming to perceive his antitheses closing on his subject as large hands may close on a creature which must be held before it can be set free; coming to distinguish this formality as one congenial to English idiom. Anne Elliot, advising Captain Benwick, 'ventured to hope that he did not always read only poetry; and to say, that she thought it was the misfortune of poetry, to be seldom safely enjoyed by those who enjoyed it completely; and that the strong feelings which alone could estimate it truly, were the very feelings which ought to taste it but sparingly'.[5] I will suggest another small accomplishment which Jane

---

[1] *Emma*, p. 239, ch. xxvii. I think this is not a very common idiom in women's writings, though Mrs. Thrale learnt it from the same master.
[2] Ibid., p. 358, ch. xlii.   [3] *Persuasion*, p. 184, ch. xx.
[4] *The Rambler*, number 142.   [5] *Persuasion*, pp. 100, 101, ch. xi.

Austen may possibly owe to 'her dear Dr. Johnson': while
he has been criticized for making all the fictitious correspondents in his periodical essays address him in his own
stately language, his lively mimicry of idiom in *oblique oration*
has passed unnoticed. Thus Anthea, who thought nothing
so elegant as a display of timidity, 'saw some Sheep, and
heard the Weather clink his Bell, which she was certain was
not hung upon him for nothing, and therefore no Assurances nor Intreaties should prevail upon her to go a Step
farther; she was sorry to disappoint the Company, but her
Life was dearer to her than Ceremony'.[1] Now Jane Austen
has an aptitude, not very common among the earlier novelists, for these satirically reported conversations: Mrs. Elton
on strawberries, and Lady Bertram on the ball, are probably
the best-remembered; but these merely confirm impressions
already made; her slighter essays in this kind are quite as
shrewd, and, within small compass, create the impression
in our minds of the talk of some minor character who would
otherwise be silent—of Mrs. Philips with her promise of
'a little bit of hot supper',[2] or Mr. Shepherd, with his account
of his chosen tenant—'quite the gentleman'.[3]

Among these elusive echoes of the tones of voice of her
favourites I seem to detect one that may be worth a moment's
notice. The train of possibilities begins with Richardson's
realization that a parenthetical phrase, most often built
upon a present participle, if introduced abruptly into the
midst of a speech—that is, not qualifying the introductory
'he said' or its equivalent, but indicating change of tone
or gesture as a stage-direction might do—gives the air of
eyewitness to any one who reports the speech; and since,
in his novels, the narrator is always, for the moment,
autobiographer, that reporter is always supposed to be an
eyewitness, and therefore needs this illusion. (Thus, conversations reported by Miss Harriet Byron are not seldom interrupted by the parenthesis 'Snatching my hand'.)
Fanny Burney appears to perceive this advantage and follow
Richardson, so long as she also lets one of the characters tell

[1] *The Rambler*, number 34.
[2] *Pride and Prejudice*, p. 74, ch. xv.   [3] *Persuasion*, p. 22, ch. iii.

the story—that is, in Evelina's letters. (Need it be said that here, too, 'Snatching my hand' is a not infrequent parenthesis?) But it seems to be Boswell who, in his own double character of author and eyewitness reporting an affair, introduces this device into direct narration, in his *Tour to the Hebrides* and, still oftener, in his *Life of Johnson*. Thus, in Johnson's speeches occur such parenthetical phrases as: '(looking to his Lordship with an arch smile)'. Whether or no Jane Austen's ear really caught from one of these three among her favourite authors the impression of immediacy which this device is able to lend to dialogue, her frequent and apt use of it is worth remarking. Nancy Steele's tale of her sister is brought within earshot by such parentheses as '(Laughing affectedly)' and '(giggling as she spoke)',[1] and poor Miss Bates's of her niece by '(twinkling away a tear or two)';[2] while we seem indeed to see Captain Harville's attention divided between Anne and Captain Wentworth: 'There is no hurry on my side', he tells Wentworth. '"I am only ready whenever you are.—I am in very good anchorage here," (smiling at Anne) "well supplied, and want for nothing.—No hurry for a signal at all.—Well, Miss Elliot," (lowering his voice) "as I was saying, we shall never agree I suppose upon this point."'[3]

Evidence as to Jane Austen's *dislikes* in word or phrase is less elusive, for it consists not only in her avoidance of such habits of expression but also in her ridicule of them in her burlesque writings, and in her warnings to Anna against them. Any close observer of her ways must have noticed that she is, so to speak, *shy* of figurative language, using it as little as possible, and least of all in her gravest passages. I do not think it extravagant to find some suggestion of the amusement and discomfort which idle use of figurative expressions caused her in this small quip to Cassandra: 'He ... poor man! is so totally deaf that they say he could not hear a cannon, were it fired close to him; having no cannon at hand to make the experiment, I took it for granted, and talked to him a little with my fingers. . . .'[4] For this use of

---

[1] *Sense and Sensibility*, pp. 274, 275, ch. xxxviii.   [2] *Emma*, p. 378, ch. xliv.
[3] *Persuasion*, p. 234, ch. xxiii.   [4] *Letters*, p. 242.

stale, unmeaning figures of speech is a common mark of
insincerity in her disagreeable people—in Mrs. Elton, with
her borrowed plume of poetic image, her chatter of 'Hymen's
saffron robe';[1] in General Tilney, whose imagery belongs to
the conventions of a heartless gallantry: "'I have many
pamphlets to finish," said he to Catherine, "before I can
close my eyes; and perhaps may be poring over the affairs
of the nation for hours after you are asleep. Can either of
us be more meetly employed? *My* eyes will be blinding for
the good of others; and *yours* preparing by rest for future
mischief"'[2]—a manner of speech that almost seems to excuse
Catherine's suspicions; above all, in Mrs. Norris: 'Is not
she a sister's child?' she asks, rhetorically, of Fanny Price;
'and could I bear to see her want, while I had a bit of bread
to give her?'[3] And one sees a grotesque vision of those
two—the child and the woman—confronting one another
across the shining expanse of the parsonage dining-table,
with a 'bit of bread' between them. But Mrs. Norris did
not see that vision; she saw nothing—metaphor was to her
a screen for the meaninglessness of her generous words.

I suspect that it was Jane Austen's practice of denying
herself the aid of figurative language which, as much as any
other of her habits of expression, repelled Charlotte Brontë,
and has alienated other readers, conscious of a dissatisfaction
with her style that they have not cared to analyse. What
prompted her to such a denial? Did she distrust all figurative language because she was sharply aware of the aptitude
of the most languid figurative expressions for persisting
as a mere habit of speech, after they have lost even the
feeble life they had for the imagination?—a not unreasonable distrust, so large is the element of figurative idiom in
our tongue. And was she further aware that, since such
language commonly carries in the first using some emotional
suggestion, it cannot *fossilize* without turning into a lie?
Even if this should seem a rashly conjectural explanation of
her apparent distrust of all figures of speech, her evident
dislike of all that are *ready made*, it is certainly worth while

---

[1] *Emma*, p. 308, ch. xxxvi.
[2] *Northanger Abbey*, p. 187, ch. xxiii.   [3] *Mansfield Park*, p. 7, ch. i.

to notice her quick ear for all those ready-made phrases, whether figurative or no, which creep so insidiously into our habitual speech. She had always held aloof from slang:[1] 'Miss Fletcher and I were very thick', she writes to Cassandra in Steventon days, 'but I am the thinnest of the two.'[2] She makes fossil phrases the staple of Lady Bertram's accustomed style of letter-writing—'a very creditable, commonplace, amplifying style':[3] 'We shall greatly miss Edmund in our small circle', she writes to Fanny when he has gone to fetch his sick brother; 'but I trust and hope he will find the poor invalid in a less alarming state than might be apprehended...'[4]—a style that breaks up and dissolves under the influence of real feeling: 'He is just come, my dear Fanny, and is taken up stairs; and I am so shocked to see him, that I do not know what to do.'[5] They are a mark also of the talk of Mr. Parker—who was not 'a man of strong understanding':[6] 'Here were we, pent down in this little contracted Nook, without Air or View, only one mile and 3 q^{rs} from the noblest expanse of Ocean between the South foreland & the Land's end, & without the smallest advantage from it. You will not think I have made a bad exchange, when we reach Trafalgar House—which by the bye, I almost wish I had not named Trafalgar—for Waterloo is more the thing now.'[7] And she is at pains to emphasize this habit: 'The Growth of my Plantations is a general astonishment'[8]—*that* was substituted in revision for 'My Plantations astonish everybody by their Growth'.

What it is that disgusts in Mrs. Elton's speech is not so obvious. It is not merely the idle figurative expressions— the recluse torn reluctant from her instrument and crayons, and the rest, though they are many; nor the slang, with its uneasy pretensions, nor the wilful use of concrete and particular expressions where there is no occasion for them: 'A most pitiful business!—Selina would stare when she

---

[1] It is Mary Crawford's slang that persuades me she was never meant to be very agreeable.
[2] *Letters*, p. 14.
[3] *Mansfield Park*, p. 425, ch. xliv.
[4] Ibid., p. 426, ch. xliv.
[5] Ibid., p. 427, ch. xliv.
[6] *Sanditon*, p. 23; *Minor Works*, p. 372.
[7] Ibid., p. 44; *Minor Works*, p. 380.
[8] Ibid., p. 46; *Minor Works*, p. 381.

heard of it.'[1] It is rather a general and insidious misuse of
language in the interests of an ugly smartness, which produces much the same sort of unpleasant sensation as seeing
a tool misused.

Jane Austen's sharpest critical satire is aimed, however,
at the contemporary novelists' peculiar phraseology—commonly a rank weed in the aftermath of a great age of fiction.
Miss Clavering, who was to have collaborated with her
friend Miss Ferrier, noticed it. 'I don't like those high life
conversations', she says shrewdly; 'they are a sort of thing
by consent handed down from generation to generation in
novels, but have little or no groundwork in truth . . . [they]
could at best amuse by putting one in mind of other novels
not by recalling to anybody what they ever saw or heard in
real life. . . .' And she is pretty severe on her friend's more
ambitious writing in this kind, 'which is the style of conversation of duchesses only in novels'.[2] A conversational
style handed down from one generation of novelists to
another—that is a pitfall, as Jane Austen gently reminds
Anna: 'I do not like a Lover's speaking in the 3[d] person;—
it is too much like the formal part of Lord Orville, & I think
is not natural.'[3] She had made fun of fossilized phraseology
in her earliest pieces, sometimes tilting a fragment of it
gently to let the light fall on it: 'his Mother had been many
years no more'.[4] Even more unobtrusively it makes its way
into her early novels: 'the lenient hand of time did much
for [Catherine] by insensible gradations in the course of
another day.'[5] Beckford had parodied these stock phrases;
but his hand had been heavy: '. . . the finer feelings of the
celestial Arabella suffered a new and more terrible shock,
which the lenient hand of time could alone hope to mollify.
The original breaking of his collar bone, by the fall from
his famous hunter, which had once so cruelly alarmed the
ladies in the park, was no longer an object of material

[1] *Emma*, p. 484, ch. lv. I think that Jane Austen positively disliked this idiosyncrasy—of which she gives variants to Sir Edward Denham and John Thorpe.
[2] *Memoir and Correspondence of Susan Ferrier*, ed. J. A. Doyle, pp. 114–118 (letter
of 10 May 1813).
[3] *Letters*, pp. 387, 388. Charlotte Brontë slipped back into this awkward practice.
[4] *Love and Freindship*, p. 10; *Minor Works*, p. 80.
[5] *Northanger Abbey*, p. 201, ch. xxv.

magnitude, but . . . the innumerable difficulties he might labour under, was indeed a stroke which required the utmost fortitude, and every religious consideration to combat and sustain.'[1] Where he makes nonsense, Jane Austen with a lighter touch makes something that is *almost sense*. She sees where exaggeration is not needed, where demure imitation will serve. She allows Henry Tilney to hit off the style of Mrs. Radcliffe's descriptive passages in his mock forecast of Catherine's arrival at the Abbey,[2] and of the novel of sentiment in his pretended investigation of Catherine's feelings upon the arrival of Isabella's letter.[3] She never lost her taste for mimicry, but her later novels gave her less scope for it. Her consciousness of this particular pitfall is most forcibly expressed in her watchful avoidance of it, most pointedly in that stricture on Anna's novel in which she comes nearest to severity: 'Devereux Forester's being ruined by his Vanity is extremely good; but I wish you would not let him plunge into a "vortex of Dissipation". I do not object to the Thing, but I cannot bear the expression;—it is such thorough novel slang—and so old, that I dare say Adam met with it in the first novel he opened.'[4]

Behind this explicit expression of aversion we can perceive her steady rejection of 'novel slang', and behind this consistent practice her sensitiveness to the entity of the word. Her corrections show her mind moving among words, arranging and rearranging them, until she gets them phrased to her liking; and so every one of them remains exquisitely whole, like a falling drop of water, and no two or three are allowed to run together and settle into stagnant pools.

Delicate precision, resulting from control of the tools chosen—one could almost be content to claim no more than this for Jane Austen's style, surmising that she would hardly claim as much. She might have been willing to accept Richardson's compliment to Lady Bradshaigh: 'The pen is almost as pretty an implement in a woman's fingers as a needle.'[5] She would probably have been puzzled by John

---

[1] *Modern Novel Writing*, ch. i.
[2] *Northanger Abbey*, ch. xx.
[3] Ibid., p. 207, ch. xxv.   [4] *Letters*, p. 404.
[5] *Correspondence*, ed. Barbauld (1804), vi. 120 (no date).

Bailey's tribute: 'She wrote . . . well, because she could write well and liked it, and all the better because she did not know how well she wrote.'[1] For I think that she would have been satisfied to transfer to her style her playful boast of her own manual dexterity: 'An artist cannot do anything slovenly.'[2]

[1] *Introductions to Jane Austen*, 1931, p. 25.
[2] *Letters*, p. 30.

CHAPTER IV

NARRATIVE ART

I. THE NARRATOR AND HIS MATERIAL

(i) *Substance*

IN that burlesque play *The Rovers* (in the *Anti-Jacobin*), there is a stage-direction:

'Companies of Austrian and Prussian Grenadiers march across the stage confusedly, as if returning from the Seven Years' War.'[1]

It has been a surprise to more than one generation of Jane Austen's readers that her naval officers do not march across her stage confusedly, as though returning from the Napoleonic wars. Instead, they enter very composedly, as though returned from walking up partridges in the stubble.

There is certainly some significance, alike in the constancy with which readers and critics have thought they could perceive the absence of something essential from the composition of her novels—assumed, too, that it must likewise have been absent from her own composition—and in the constantly changing conception of that essential thing. Her contemporaries had not asked for any reference to those 'moving accidents by flood and field' which, to the generations that directly followed, seemed to have been the subjects most worth writing about in that age; neither do we. They were more apt to remark a want of ideal heightening, moral and emotional—'that elevation of virtue, something beyond nature,' Lady Romilly calls it in a letter to Maria Edgeworth, 'that gives the greatest charm to a novel'.[2] Lady Shelley, in taking Scott to task for his failure to give his heroes and heroines 'a higher tone of feeling' than accords with common experience, complains that 'the same objection may be made to all Jane Austen's novels. . . . Surely works of imagination should raise us above our

---

[1] Act II, scene ii.
[2] *Romilly-Edgeworth Letters, 1813–1818*, ed. S. H. Romilly, 1936, p. 92 (letter of November 1814, referring to *Mansfield Park*).

every-day feelings, and excite in us those *élans passagères* of
virtue and sensibility which are exquisite and ennobling. . . .'[1]
And Scott himself, though he makes fun of this very
heightening in the novel of sentiment—whose characters,
he says, were habitually 'presented . . . in the most sentimental mood, and with minds purified by a sensibility which
often verged on extravagance'—pleads nevertheless for its
preservation wherever love and courtship are the novelist's
theme.[2]

All such charges could, of course, be answered. To
Scott's complaint of want of sensibility in Jane Austen's
novels her own complaint of his review of them would be
sufficient reply: it overlooks *Mansfield Park*. It is more to
the purpose that, in reading the novel that particularly provokes his censure, he has failed in attention and missed the
distinction between Charlotte Lucas's cynicism and Elizabeth Bennet's ironical affectation of it with regard to marriage.
Another novelist's criticism, graver because more heart-felt
and more deeply consistent with the critic's own practice—
Charlotte Brontë's—can be met by explanation. For it was
in very unfavourable circumstances that she first encountered
Jane Austen's work. George Henry Lewes had insisted that
she should read *Pride and Prejudice*, and profit by its example;
and coming to it under this compulsion she found it, and
thought she found Jane Austen, commonplace and sophisticated, with no more than a knack of shrewd observation to
her credit, and said so;[3] whereupon Lewes hastened to confirm the harm he had done by a defensive apology: an
admission that Jane Austen had neither poetry nor sentiment
in her composition, a claim that she was nevertheless 'one
of the greatest artists . . . that ever lived';[4] thus exasperating
his correspondent by the implication that these two qualities,
which she valued in a novelist above all others, were of no
consequence. It is not therefore a surprise to find that two
years later Charlotte Brontë has advanced no farther in

[1] *The Diary of Frances Lady Shelley*, ed. R. Edgecumbe, 1912–13, ii. 64 (letter of
16 August 1819).
[2] Review of *Emma* in the *Quarterly*, p. 191.
[3] Clement Shorter, *The Brontës: Life and Letters*, 1908, i. 386, 387 (letter of 12
January 1848).   [4] See Charlotte Brontë's answer: op. cit. i. 388.

making Jane Austen's acquaintance; but it is disappointing
to observe her directing her next attempt towards *Emma*[1] —
with just such an outcome as might have been predicted:
she is confirmed in her dislike of the author, and provoked
to analyse the work that stirs her antipathy:

'She does her business of delineating the surface of the lives of genteel
English people curiously well. There is a Chinese fidelity, a miniature
delicacy in the painting. She ruffles her reader by nothing vehement,
disturbs him by nothing profound. The passions are perfectly unknown
to her . . . Even to the feelings she vouchsafes no more than an occasional graceful but distant recognition . . . Her business is not half so
much with the human heart as with the human eyes, mouth, hands, and
feet. What sees keenly, speaks aptly, moves flexibly, it suits her to
study; but what throbs fast and full, though hidden, what the blood
rushes through, what is the unseen seat of life and the sentient target
of death—this Miss Austen ignores.'[2]

And back she comes to the still rankling exhortation of
Lewes; for it had reached a keenly sensitive spot: whereas
Scott had asked for a certain heightening proper to fiction,
she demanded heightening throughout as true to life.

Now this of course can be answered, not by such a defence
as Lewes's, but by such a witty dismissal of attackers and
defenders together as Katherine Mansfield's:

'Can we picture Jane Austen caring—except in a delightfully wicked
way— . . . that people said she was no lady, was not fond of children,
hated animals, did not care a pin for the poor, could not have written
about foreign parts if she had tried, had no idea how a fox was killed
. . . —was, in short, cold, coarse, practically illiterate and without
morality? Mightn't her reply have been, "Ah, but what about my
novels?" '[3]

But a profound and more reasoned discontent has been
growing articulate with the passage of time: a distrust of
the range and depth of Jane Austen's imagination, an appre-

---

[1] In a letter of 2 February 1850 to W. S. Williams (op. cit. ii. 111) she asks for a
copy of any of Jane Austen's novels, except *Pride and Prejudice*, which she has read,
and mentions Miss Martineau's preference for *Persuasion*. If Williams had sent her
Persuasion, would she have found something in it that *Emma* could not give her?
[2] Op. cit. ii. 127, 128 (letter of 12 April 1850 to W. S. Williams).
Mr. Read, quoting this passage without its context, finds it 'unanswerable'. (So
would Sir Edward Denham.) 'The justice of that analysis', he says, 'remains, to
confront the present sophisticated rage for Jane Austen' (H. Read, *Collected Essays in
Literary Criticism*, 1938, p. 296).
[3] *Novels and Novelists*, ed. J. M. Murry (1930) (reprinted from the *Athenaeum*).

hension lest her vision may be limited in such a way as to be
falsified. Lord David Cecil has not let this pass unchallenged.

'For aesthetic reasons she limits herself', he says, '. . . to the mood of
comedy and the world of the small gentry in England. But comedy can
deal . . . with themes as important and significant as those of tragedy:
while the life of an English squire's wife is as serious as the life of any
one else: it can no more avoid the central problems that face mankind
during its sojourn on this planet. The visible structure of Jane
Austen's stories may be flimsy enough; but their foundations drive
deep down into the basic principles of human conduct. On her bit of
ivory she has engraved a criticism of life as serious and as considered
as Hardy's.'[1]

And he proceeds to sum up this 'criticism of life':

'In none of her books is it stated more fully than in *Sense and Sensibility*
. . . Jane Austen lived at a period of intellectual revolution. The standards of reason and common sense which had guided the larger part of
educated opinion during the eighteenth century were being over-
thrown; and a new race of thinkers was rising who referred all their
opinions to the guidance of the instinctive movements of the heart. . . .'

Sense and Sensibility is 'an attack on the fundamentals of the
Romantic position'. It is a protest against the high value
that the romanticists set on 'passion and sensibility and a
heart responsive to the beauties of nature', especially as
'guides to conduct'. It is an assertion that 'Emotion un-
controlled by reason leads you into ludicrous mistakes,
involves you in trouble that brings misery both to yourself
and any one you have to do with; and, in the end, it does
not last'.[2]

This suggestion, however, is thrown out at the end of a
short essay, where there is no room to develop it; and as it
stands it does not seem truly to represent the case. I do not
believe the vital issue between Elinor and Marianne—nor
between the wise and foolish virgins in any other of Jane
Austen's novels—to be the issue between head and heart,
old-fashioned rationalist and new-fashioned romanticist. I
have tried to show it rather as (in part) an expression of her
constant tranquil preference for a true over a false vision
of life, particularly with regard to ideas of happiness. And
I do not think that we can now get any farther without

[1] Introduction to *Sense and Sensibility*, Oxford, 1931, p. xiii.
[2] Op. cit., pp. xiii, xiv.

looking into those 'aesthetic reasons', and some impulses besides, on account of which she limited her range to the world of comedy and of the English country gentry—and accepted also some other limitations.

Jane Austen expressed her sense of the novelist's need to *select* emphatically, and more than once. Of the most explicit of these expressions one is heard in the letters to Anna containing advice on her novel. Anna is urged to stay within the social world that is familiar to her: '. . . You had better not leave England. Let the Portmans go to Ireland, but as you know nothing of the Manners there, you had better not go with them. You will be in danger of giving false representations. Stick to Bath & the Foresters. There you will be quite at home.'[1] This is no more than one would expect of a delineator of manners who drew from Charlotte Brontë scrupulous praise of her 'Chinese fidelity'. But a later passage is more illuminating: 'You are now collecting your People delightfully, getting them exactly into such a spot as is the delight of my life;—3 or 4 Families in a Country Village is the very thing to work on.'[2]

Another explicit expression of this conviction and preference is heard in the correspondence with J. S. Clarke (the Prince Regent's librarian), which composes, together with the *Plan of a Novel* which it helped to provoke, so delightful a little comedy that it should be regarded as a whole—even though it must raise some problems besides this of choice of subject. It opens demurely with Jane Austen's letter consulting Mr. Clarke as to the etiquette of dedicating *Emma* to the Prince Regent.[3] This brings in return praise of her talent, with voluble suggestions as to how she may best employ it; he begs her to 'delineate in some future Work the Habits of Life and Character and enthusiasm of a Clergyman', whose disposition and manners he sketches, complaining (not very reasonably) that neither Goldsmith nor La Fontaine has 'delineated an English Clergyman, at least of the present day—Fond of, & entirely engaged in Literature—no man's Enemy but his own'.[4] Much of Miss Austen's

[1] *Letters*, p. 395.   [2] Ibid., p. 401.
[3] Ibid., p. 429.   [4] Ibid., p. 430.

reply to this invitation, denying that she has the equipment for representing a character of such intellectual range, I have already quoted.[1] And it answers just as one would expect to her preference for family life in a country village as a subject. But her objection to Mr. Clarke's proposal is two-fold; the mood of such a project would be alien to her: 'The comic part of the character I might be equal to, but not the good, the enthusiastic, the literary.'[2] Did she, when she blandly reckoned herself equal to 'the comic part of the character', realize that Mr. Clarke had been offering himself as her model? If not, she may have been enlightened by his following entreaty:

'Do let us have an English Clergyman after *your* fancy—much novelty may be introduced—shew dear Madam what good would be done if Tythes were taken away entirely, and describe him burying his own mother—as I did—because the High Priest of the Parish in which she died—did not pay her remains the respect he ought to do. I have never recovered the Shock. Carry your Clergyman to Sea as the friend of some distinguished Naval Character about a Court ...'

—naval chaplaincy and court appointment being alike part of Mr. Clarke's own experience—'you can then bring fore-ward like Le Sage many interesting scenes of Character & Interest'.[3] All of which proposal, of course, finds its way into the hilarious *Plan of a Novel, according to hints from various quarters*—with a marginal acknowledgement of its source. No answer to this letter survives; and when he writes again it is to propose that 'any historical romance, illustrative of the history of the august House of Cobourg, would just now be very interesting'.[4] And that word *romance* stirs up his correspondent to define what she believes to be her proper province:

'I am fully sensible that an historical romance, founded on the House of Saxe Cobourg, might be much more to the purpose of profit or popularity than such pictures of domestic life in country villages as I deal in. But I could no more write a romance than an epic poem. I could not sit seriously down to write a serious romance under any other motive than to save my life; and if it were indispensable for me to keep it up and never relax into laughing at myself or other people, I am sure I should be hung before I had finished the first chapter. No, I must

[1] p. 41.
[2] *Letters*, p. 443.
[3] Ibid., pp. 444, 445.
[4] Ibid., p. 451.

keep to my own style and go on in my own way; and though I may never succeed again in that, I am convinced that I should totally fail in any other.'[1]

There her adviser seems to have relinquished his attempt; and the last echo of the argument is heard in the *Plan of a Novel*, of which the heroine is to be a 'faultless character . . . with much tenderness & sentiment, & not the least Wit', and her father a clergyman, 'the most excellent Man that can be imagined . . . without the smallest drawback or peculiarity . . .'—unless, of course, one could count as a drawback his habit of conversing with his daughter 'in long speeches, elegant Language—& a tone of high serious sentiment'—and his propensity for autobiography.[2]

In effect, then, Jane Austen's resolve to 'go on in her own way' means deliberate choice both of subject and of mood—deliberate and whole-hearted: she will take as subject for her art a certain region in the social world because it is (as subject) 'the delight of her life'—not, as her critics have loosely inferred, the safest thing for her to write about.

Her practice bears out this claim, refutes this inference; for not only does she confine herself, as she recommends Anna to do, to that small part of the human world which the circumstances of her life have brought under her observation;[3] but within it she marks out for her province a yet smaller region; and when the bounds of her experience widen there is no directly corresponding expansion of this province. Life in Bath and Southampton, the company of Frank and Charles at Chawton, opened windows into a region of their lives, the world of naval society on shore, and in *Mansfield Park* she glances through these windows— brings William Price to Mansfield, lets him talk of his profession (as Colonel Brandon could not have done), and even carries Fanny into the midst of such talk at Portsmouth: it ripples round her, laps against her incomprehension: '. . . You lost a fine sight by not being here in the morning to see the Thrush go out of harbour. . . . If ever there was a perfect beauty afloat, she is one; and there she lays at Spithead,

---

[1] Ibid., pp. 452, 453.   [2] *Plan of a Novel*, p. 9; *Minor Works*, p. 428.
[3] Not so small as was once thought; Dr. Chapman has made that evident.

and anybody in England would take her for an eight-and-twenty.'[1]   There is a stir of expectancy in the air, as Mr. Price and his author watch the *Thrush* out to sea; and then it subsides, and *she* turns to Highbury and a narrower prospect than that of any of the earlier novels. And though her visits to Henry and Eliza in London brought her acquainted with *émigré* society—and Fanny Burney was then writing, in her dedication of *The Wanderer*, that it was quite impossible 'to delineate . . . any picture of actual human life without reference to the French Revolution'—Jane Austen turned back, in *Persuasion*, to the country villages and Bath society of her earlier experience; while *Sanditon*, in so far as it drew on memory and observation, cast back to the sea-side places that she visited while her father was still alive.

Moreover, corresponding with her choice of a subject of small extent, we can perceive her contentment with a narrow range of narrative patterns. She is quite incurious about the form of the novel: that is, she tries on (as though they had been dresses) the two shapes that are in current use—the novel-in-letters, and the story directly and methodically related by an impersonal narrator—and then, having ascertained which is the better fit, adopts it and makes no further experiment. Within this framework, too, she feels little need for variety; much as a painter may choose a fresh subject but repeat a composition that contents him, she repeats a device, one that had long lost its freshness on the stage, for bringing about her climax: a proposal of marriage precipitated by a misunderstanding as to an engagement. (But, characteristically, she never allows the misunderstanding to arise from coquetry, not even in its contemporary disguise of excessive sensibility; her contentment with the device may be uncritical, her mode of using it is not.) In *Sense and Sensibility* the supposition of Edward's marriage does not so much precipitate as set off his proposal to Elinor; but in *Emma* the fullest, most elaborate use is made of such a misunderstanding. It is the misconstruction which Mr. Knightley puts on Emma's admission as to her ignorance of Frank Churchill's intentions that forces him to express

[1] *Mansfield Park*, p. 380, ch. xxxviii.

his feelings for her; while it is her supposition of his attachment to Harriet, and her determination to act on it, that
brings him to propose marriage to her.[1]

And then, in her next novel, Jane Austen repeats this very
pattern: in the climax of *Persuasion* (as it was first drafted)
Captain Wentworth is compelled to speak to Anne of the
engagement that Bath rumour has fabricated between her
and Mr. Elliot; and her manner of denying this rumour
encourages him to tell her of the change in his own feelings
towards her. This part of the story was, of course, rewritten,
and this episode altered—but not, I am persuaded, because
Jane Austen was uneasy in repeating a pattern.

She was impelled (I think) to make the alteration by two
distinct kinds of incentive, personal and artistic; and to
understand the strongest of these personal impulses is to
learn something of the habit of mind that gave them birth.
Perhaps this understanding may be reached by means of a
comparison with one of Scott's moods. When Scott drew
back from the end of *Marmion*, protesting

> I do not rhyme to that dull elf,
> Who cannot image to himself . . .
> Nor sing I to that simple maid
> To whom it must in terms be said . . .[2]

that the love of Wilton and Clare prospered at last, he was
only expressing, lightly and not very gracefully, his habitual
and deliberate preference for leaving his avowed lovers alone
in one another's company. And when Jane Austen lightly
misquotes and misapplies these jingling lines[3] she is echoing,
whether chance or intuition prompts her, the expression of
a mood with which she is wholly in sympathy. The assurance
in the close of *Mansfield Park*, that 'exactly at the time when
it was quite natural that it should be so, and not a week
earlier, Edmund did cease to care about Miss Crawford, and
became as anxious to marry Fanny, as Fanny herself could
desire',[4] might almost be a reminiscence of her original
response to this passage. Until she wrote that first draft
of *Persuasion* she had never[5] written what could be called a

---

[1] Ch. xlix.
[2] *Marmion*, 1808, canto vi, stanza xxxix.
[3] *Letters*, p. 298.
[4] *Mansfield Park*, p. 470, ch. xlviii.
[5] So far as her surviving work shows.

scene between lovers. There had been scenes of courtship—but only where there could be no mutual acknowledgement of love: Mr. Collins may make his proposal of marriage to Elizabeth in our hearing, and no lovers' rights of privacy will be invaded; Darcy, too, may pay his addresses to her—so long as they awake no response. But when at last the response comes, when there is a spark and conflagration—then the lovers walk away into a friendly cloud. The dialogue gives place to direct narration and reported talk—we hear only the story-teller's voice—until those most private moments are past; and when the lovers become audible again they are still walking, and give the impression that if we were to press upon them they might draw away once more out of ear-shot. In *Emma*, indeed, Jane Austen implies as much: the opportunity of mutual understanding comes within reach, and Emma catches at it. 'What did she say?—Just what she ought, of course. A lady always does.'[1] And away they walk into their private cloud, leaving us, mere eaves-droppers, behind them.

And yet, in the first draft of *Persuasion*, Jane Austen sets her lovers face to face before us—keeps them there, too, still seated (surely it is not idle to remember that all the others were on their feet, and walking?). It is well done, and yet it is, somehow, uncomfortable. But, when this part of the story is rewritten, Wentworth's account of the change in his feelings—which cannot be given summarily in the author's own voice—is cast into the form of a letter; and, the extrication thus accomplished, he and Anne are free, upon the instant of mutual recognition, to walk away and leave us behind them.

With this reticence which was instinctive in Jane Austen must be ranked other motives for limiting her province, which may be called personal in that they were the outcome of her circumstances and of her habitual reaction to them. It is easy to forget, now, what sort of trial the novelists of that day had to face: how unhesitatingly the reviewers, especially if their subject were a woman, would take it for granted that she had nothing to draw on but the stuff of experience, and

[1] *Emma*, p. 431, ch. xlix.

how little they would allow for such process of transmutation of that stuff as might baffle identification. Whately, in his review of *Northanger Abbey* and *Persuasion* for the *Quarterly*, drew this inference from the account of Fanny's attachment to Edmund:

'The silence in which this passion is cherished—the slender hopes and enjoyments by which it is fed—the restlessness and jealousy with which it fills a mind naturally active, contented and unsuspicious—the manner in which it tinges every event and every reflection, are painted with a vividness and a detail of which we can scarcely conceive any one but a female, and we should almost add, a female writing from recollection, capable.'[1]

If this is the manner of approach of a responsible and courteous critic, what is to be expected from the apprentice or hack reviewer? Surely a lady of no more than usual reticence will take into account this likelihood of unlicensed interpretation? Miss Edgeworth (in a very interesting letter on the shortcomings of 'facsimile copying') recorded her own strict custom of altering any character of which the first idea had been 'taken from life from some ORIGINAL . . . from propriety, to avoid individual resemblance', as well as for artistic reasons.[2] Miss Edgeworth, it is true, published her stories under her own name; but anonymity was not impenetrable; and it was most likely to break within that circle of personal acquaintance who, with the reviewer's example before them, and knowledge of circumstance that he lacked, would indeed be formidable. Fanny Burney ('a sad prude', her sisters called her) wondered how Mrs. Thrale would regard her once she learnt of her authorship:

'. . . Won't she think it strange, where I can have kept such company, to describe such a family as the Branghtons, Mr. Brown, and some others? Indeed, (thank Heaven!), I don't myself recollect ever passing half an hour at a time with any one person *quite* so bad; so that, I am afraid she will conclude I must have an innate vulgarity of ideas, to assist me with such coarse colouring for the objects of my imagination.'[3]

[1] January 1821, pp. 366, 367.
[2] *Life and Letters*, ed. A. J. C. Hare, ii. 251 (letter of 6 September 1834).
[3] *Diary and Letters of Madame d'Arblay*, ed. Austin Dobson, 1904, i. 9 (letter of 25 July 1778). Her fears were not quite idle; Mary Russell Mitford writes: 'I have . . . been reading "The Wanderer." The first observation which strikes every one on the perusal of this disappointing work is, what bad company Madame

Such an interpretation is most to be feared if the novelist has indeed used stuff of personal experience—or even figments that resemble it: if Jane Austen had introduced a French *émigré* into any of her stories, those acquaintance to whom her authorship was known would have glanced at once towards Eliza Austen's friends. It is clear from the 'Opinions' which Jane Austen recorded that such readers did sometimes amuse themselves with the game of conjectural identification—a fact which shows her anxious care for her anonymity to have been no morbid excess of sensitiveness, but mere social common sense. All these considerations support Sir Frank MacKinnon's finding: ' Jane Austen, I feel sure, never copied a character from a known person; I am sure that she never delineated a known place under a fictitious name'[1]—that, in fact, thorough in this as in all else she undertook, she left no traces that could give her acquaintance fair cause[2] to suspect a likeness, and be made uncomfortable.

Moreover, it may be worth noticing at least one situation very apt for her purpose of which nevertheless she made no use—and which in fact occurred within her family. What a young woman needs, if she is to become a heroine of fiction, is a little neglect and ill usage; and who so fit to neglect and ill use her as the stepmother of fiction? But some such part James's second wife seems to have played to poor Anna; and if that unhappy relationship ever casts its shadow on any of Jane Austen's novels it is discreetly transformed by the contrivance of transplanting Fanny Price into her cousins' home, and bringing her within reach of her Aunt Norris.

So much is legitimate inference; at the risk of seeming frivolous I will offer one conjecture that goes farther: I should guess that Louisa Musgrove was originally meant to suffer injury in some sort of carriage accident—perhaps to be spilt from a gig, as Mrs. Croft so often was, but with

d'Arblay must have kept since she wrote "Camilla!" Where could she find such gentlemen and ladies as she has chosen to represent?' (op. cit. i. 291).

[1] F. D. MacKinnon, *The Murder in the Temple and other Holiday Tasks*, 1935, pp. 86, 87.

[2] I doubt whether Miss Mitford's informant was scrupulous as to this point.

more serious consequences; that Jane Austen had this purpose still in mind when she made Louisa exclaim to Captain Wentworth: 'If I loved a man . . . I would be always with him, nothing should ever separate us, and I would rather be overturned by him, than driven safely by anybody else.'[1] The mood of that exclamation, and of his delighted response, comes back into Anne's memory at the catastrophe. But I think that, before reaching that episode, Jane Austen was turned from her purpose by remembrance of two such accidents,[2] which had caused the death of her friend Mrs. Lefroy and her cousin Jane Williams, and contrived instead that fall from the Cobb which wears, to me, the air of an improvisation. This, however, is mere surmise.

When Jane Austen has chosen a region within that little world of the English gentry as most fit for her purpose, she has yet accomplished the lesser part of what is implied in the phrase 'going on in her own way'. Her choice of the mood of comedy is a less simple affair. What does she do with the world she knows in order to make of it a fit substance to compose the world of comedy? On what principle does she select, by what process does she transmute, the stuff for this purpose?

Before looking into this problem it may be worth while to notice the ironical tone of her references to anything with which she does not mean to be concerned. Henry Tilney, having completed his 'lecture on the picturesque', 'suffered the subject to decline, and by an easy transition from a piece of rocky fragment and the withered oak which he had placed near its summit, to oaks in general, to forests, the inclosure of them, waste lands, crown lands and government, he shortly found himself arrived at politics; and from politics, it was an easy step to silence.'[3]—And that, she seems to say, is just so much of *that* subject as shall lie within my province; for the right of selection is mine.

Selection means, of course, exclusion; and her most

---

[1] *Persuasion*, p. 85, ch. x.
[2] That in *Sanditon* is, from the start, obviously trifling.
[3] *Northanger Abbey*, p. 111, ch. xiv.

evident exclusion is that of death. Out of her stories death takes no one whom we know: the elder Mr. Dashwood is gone before he can become any more than a name to us; Mrs. Churchill remains a name, threatening but impalpable; and Fanny Harville has been dead some months when we first hear of her. What is more, death's action, in the earlier novels, affects vitally no one whom we have come to know. Report of it casts no such strange shadows as fall across the end of *Love's Labour's Lost*. We first meet the Dashwoods when Henry Dashwood's death is already a fact in their lives; Mrs. Churchill's death touches merely the fortunes of that one of her family with whom we are acquainted. In *Persuasion*, indeed, death has left a mark; but its scar on Captain Harville's heart is but indicated in ironical contrast with his friend's cherished melancholy.

Moreover, in these stories no Goddess Fortune has unchallenged power; there is neither simple nor ironical imagining of 'destinee, that may nat been eschewed'. Even coincidence—so accommodating a device as sorely to tempt a narrator of commonplace events—is used sparingly; seldom unless for the purpose of bringing two people to such a place, at such a time, for the sake of their encounter; and always discreetly. It is usually to be found at the beginning, where it properly makes part of the inevitable initial agreement between story-teller and reader. Thus, Wickham's militia regiment is stationed at Longbourn when Darcy visits a friend in that neighbourhood; Frank Churchill meets at a sea-side place a lady who turns out to be the niece of his father's neighbour. As to Mrs. Smith's previous association with Mr. Elliot, however, I am not sure that her author saw it as sheer coincidence. I should surmise that she rather took it for a probable occurrence in fashionable society, the country lady assuming that there, where some are more intimate than they should be, all must be acquainted.

Money, that villainous agent in so many of Crabbe's tales, has here no such prestige. Already in Steventon days the young Jane Austen had begun to mock the conventional use of this motive in fiction, writing to Cassandra: 'The partnership between Jeffereys, Toomer, and Legge is dissolved; the two latter are melted away into nothing, and it is to be hoped that Jeffereys will soon break, for the sake of a few heroines whose money he may have.'[1] And wherever in her novels it appears portentously we may be sure of an anti-climax. In the opening of *Sense and Sensibility* it threatens to govern the action; Crabbe himself makes no nicer calculation as to income than occupies those first chapters. But John Dashwood's denial of dowries to his half-sisters proves of little consequence to any of them: to Marianne's fortunes it matters less than Willoughby's previous misconduct, while for Elinor the God Mammon plays the part of the clown whose tricks never come off; his activity culminates in the farce of disinheritance, executed in Jane Austen's most sparkling early manner. To Mrs. Ferrers her money seems to mean limitless power over her sons' lives—but it is a bubble power, pricked in the ironic summary of her achievements:

'Her family had of late been exceedingly fluctuating. For many years of her life she had had two sons; but the crime and annihilation of Edward a few weeks ago, had robbed her of one; the similar annihilation of Robert had left her for a fortnight without any; and now, by the resuscitation of Edward, she had one again.

'In spite of his being allowed once more to live, however, he did not feel the continuance of his existence secure, till he had revealed his present engagement; for the publication of that circumstance, he feared, might give a sudden turn to his constitution, and carry him off as rapidly as before.'[2]

It is the youngest of the sisters who has set the key for all mention of money in this story:

'"I wish," said Margaret, striking out a novel thought, "that somebody would give us all a large fortune apiece!"'[3]

Mammon is no more reverently treated in *Northanger Abbey*; the rhythm of hilarious laughter beats in the account of John Thorpe's manipulation of the Morland fortunes for the sake of his own consequence:

'By merely adding twice as much [as he wished them to possess] for the grandeur of the moment, by doubling what he chose to think the

[1] *Letters*, p. 53.
[2] *Sense and Sensibility*, p. 373, ch. l.
[3] Ibid., p. 92, ch. xvii.

amount of Mr. Morland's preferment, trebling his private fortune, bestowing a rich aunt, and sinking half the children, he was able to represent the whole family to the General in a most respectable light.'[1]

As to the entail in *Pride and Prejudice*, it threatens to be the bugbear of Longbourn—only to dwindle into insignificance in Mrs. Bennet's confused imaginings.

There is but one of Jane Austen's stories in which a turn of worldly fortune seems as though it may really prove crucial—*The Watsons*; and that she abandoned incomplete. In each of the rest she has set her people in such a situation that, whatever appearances may suggest, they will never be at Mammon's mercy.

We are to notice also the absence of another tall shade— collective humanity, whether in its more obviously terrifying form, the mob, or menacing as organized society. (It was well that she avoided even indirect representation of public disturbance, which gives abnormal importance to humanity in gross.)

The sole agents, indeed, in the action of her novels are individual human beings. And the comedy is the outcome of their making fools of themselves and of one another. This, after all, is no upstart idea of comedy. 'He is a person indeed of great acquir'd Follies', Dorimant says contentedly, almost lovingly, of Sir Fopling Flutter; and Medley answers: 'He is like so many others, beholding to his Education for making him so eminent a Coxcomb; many a Fool- had been lost to the World, had their indulgent Parents wisely bestow'd neither Learning nor good breeding on 'em.'[2] It pleases Jane Austen, however, to follow this rule more steadily and more strictly than the Restoration dramatists themselves had done—or, indeed, than it is necessary for comedy to do. For comedy is able to represent infirmities which are in themselves by no means ridiculous but of which the comic representation may provoke laughter. Jane Austen's people do not suffer these infirmities.

On her men and women no incalculable force is exerted. They do not feel the impact of ideas. It is true that she offers,

[1] *Northanger Abbey*, p. 245, ch. xxx.
[2] Etherege, *The Man of Mode, or, Sir Fopling Flutter*, Act i, scene i.

lightly but not idly, a reason for this which has nothing to do with artistic principle—her want of a classical education; true, besides, that her characters belong to a class in which ideas do not sensibly vibrate—in which (not for the ladies alone) 'from politics it is an easy step to silence'. Nevertheless, there is a noticeable artistic consistency between the free play of her individual men and women on one another and the absence of such currents of thought as play on George Eliot's men and women.

Further, Jane Austen's characters have not to react to strange and moving impressions, the impact of the unfamiliar. Charlotte Brontë asked for herself that peculiar stimulus: of the remote and alien—even if no better represented than by Rochester's foreign mistresses; of that part of the natural world that does not own man's sovereignty; of intercourse with those who 'can call spirits from the vasty deep'. She demanded of life that it should, by such shocks, liberate the sullen inmate who inhabits the imagination of most of us, but will not speak to, nor at the will of, the householder; will not answer any summons but from without. Jane Austen summoned no such agency. Whether her house of imagination harboured no such inmate—that is another question altogether.

These seem to me the most important ways in which Jane Austen chooses to fashion and control, by the limitations she imposes on her subject, both its shape and its substance. I will not linger over those that are less significant, because the subject has been canvassed very often already.[1] And now the question arises—do these limitations falsify her vision? In the literal sense, of course, they cannot. Not even the simplest reader, that is, could take such a world as she presents for a complete image of the actual world. And to quarrel with her for choosing to impose any limits surely implies an incapacity to apprehend life except in the mirror of fiction, and an immoderate appetite for vicarious experience. This is a folly which her

---

[1] For example, her refusal to represent, unless by hearsay, an occasion upon which no woman is present. It is left to Mr. Knightley to tell us of Mr. Elton's 'general way of talking in unreserved moments, when there are only men present' (*Emma*, p. 66, ch. viii).

deceptive naturalism of presentation can merely excuse. But the real issue remains : does what she leaves out distort by its absence the impression made by what she puts in ?

This question, delicately examined by Mrs. Woolf, would seem to need no further scrutiny. Analysing the scene of the ball, in *The Watsons*, she says :

'We have been made to see that if Emma acted so in the ball-room, how considerate, how tender, inspired by what sincerity of feeling she would have shown herself in those graver crises of life which, as we watch her, come inevitably before our eyes. Jane Austen is thus a mistress of much deeper emotion than appears upon the surface. She stimulates us to supply what is not there. What she offers is, apparently, a trifle, yet is composed of something that expands in the reader's mind and endows with the most enduring form of life scenes which are outwardly trivial. Always the stress is laid upon character. How, we are made to wonder, will Emma behave when Lord Osborne and Tom Musgrave make their call at five minutes before three, just as Mary is bringing in the tray and the knife-case? It is an extremely awkward situation. The young men are accustomed to much greater refinement. Emma may prove herself ill-bred, vulgar, a nonentity. The turns and twists of the dialogue keep us on the tenterhooks of suspense. Our attention is half upon the present moment, half upon the future. And when, in the end, Emma behaves in such a way as to vindicate our highest hopes of her, we are moved as if we had been made witnesses of a matter of the highest importance. Here, indeed, in this unfinished and in the main inferior story, are all the elements of Jane Austen's greatness. It has the permanent quality of literature. Think away the surface animation, the likeness to life, and there remains, to provide a deeper pleasure, an exquisite discrimination of human values. Dismiss this too from the mind and one can dwell with extreme satisfaction upon the more abstract art which, in the ball-room scene, so varies the emotions and proportions the parts that it is possible to enjoy it, as one enjoys poetry, for itself, and not as a link which carries the story this way and that.'[1]
... 'In her masterpieces, the same gift is brought to perfection.' [She examines an episode in *Mansfield Park*.] 'Here is nothing out of the way; it is midday in Northamptonshire; a dull young man is talking to rather a weakly young woman on the stairs as they go up to dress for dinner, with housemaids passing. But, from triviality, from commonplace, their words become suddenly full of meaning, and the moment for both one of the most memorable in their lives. It fills itself; it shines; it glows; it hangs before us, deep, trembling, serene for a second; next, the housemaid passes, and this drop, in which all the happiness of life has collected, gently subsides again to become part of the ebb and flow of ordinary existence.'[2]

[1] *The Common Reader* (1925): 'Jane Austen', pp. 174, 175.   [2] Op. cit., p. 178.

This would seem enough; and yet, excused by the fact that it is merely a passage in a too brief essay, I should like to press the inquiry a little further. 'She stimulates us to supply what is not there.' Yes; and she does this partially, perhaps principally, by holding with steady consistency to a clear and precise scale of moral values. 'We have been made to see . . .' that, as such a scale regulates Emma Watson's least action, so it would regulate her conduct 'in those graver crises of life which, as we watch her, come inevitably before our eyes'. Yes—but is this (with its implication of the mode of allegory) a full explanation of Jane Austen's method and achievement? Mrs. Woolf's further delicate probings seem to suggest that it is not. 'Dismiss . . . from the mind', she says, this 'exquisite discrimination of human values', and there remains 'the more abstract art which, in the ball-room scene, so varies the emotions and proportions the parts that it is possible to enjoy it, as one enjoys poetry, for itself. . . .' The art that proportions the parts, with this result—is this distinct from that which preserves a scale of values? And what is its relation to the art which, of an episode apparently trivial and commonplace, makes a moment that 'hangs before us, deep, trembling, and serene'?

In a February landscape, a part only of the delight that springs from the sharp yet faint lines, the scarcely suggested colours, which the thin, frosty sunlight gives to the eye, comes of realization that they hold the promise of spring and harvest. (Indeed, there may be no such conscious reckoning made.) Beyond that, there is the delight in understatement, because this, by its very reticence, implies something yet unsaid—stimulating us 'to supply what is not there', and accomplishing this, surely, by the sense that to the thing unsaid, implicit, in understatement there are no such limits as belong to a promise.

But this suggestion is (of course) potent only if scale, proportion, is kept. So long as the things that are said bear a true relation one to another, we can relate them justly to the things that are unsaid.

'If her world is a microcosm,' Saintsbury said, 'the cosmic

quality of it is at least as eminent as the littleness. She does not touch what she did not feel herself called to paint; I am not so sure that she could not have painted what she did not feel herself called to touch.'[1] This is a confidence which springs from the observation of true proportion—from the impression that such proportion within the given limits could not have been preserved by an imagination incapable of transcending those limits.

Thus, Jane Austen's use of understatement, of shallow relief, is seen to be something quite distinct from symbolism. She uses objects sparingly and significantly—Fanny Price's 'works of charity and ingenuity', for example—but not as symbols. Nor does symbolical use of abstractions suit her; I think she ventures it once, in *Mansfield Park* : 'Now I will try and write of something else,' she tells Cassandra, after speaking of her work on *Pride and Prejudice*, '& it shall be a complete change of subject—ordination.'[2] This is an odd way of speaking of the part that Edmund's ordination plays in *Mansfield Park*. It may indicate that she meant ordination to symbolize what was irreconcilable between Edmund and Fanny on the one hand, Mary and Henry Crawford on the other, their discordant scales of values. If so, it is not effectual. Perhaps Sanditon would have developed into some such symbol if the last work had been completed. Would the method have succeeded there? In the view of critics, very likely; so great would be the relief of finding, among Jane Austen's elusive methods, one to which a name can be given. And no name will precisely connote her peculiar use of scale.

Mansfield Park illustrates peculiarly well this suggestive power of truly kept scale. For example, the various preoccupations of the families at Mansfield before the ball gradually resolve themselves into a pattern at the heart of which stands Fanny's concern about the necklace. There is a delicious air of mock-importance—comparable to the mock-heroic air of *The Rape of the Lock*—about the whole affair, beginning with Miss Crawford's diplomacy when she 'argued the case with so much affectionate earnestness

[1] Preface to *Pride and Prejudice*, 1894, p. xv.   [2] *Letters*, p. 298.

through all the heads of William and the cross, and the ball, and herself, as to be finally successful' in persuading Fanny to accept the necklace.[1] It sparkles in the ironic gravity with which the close of this phase in the episode is reported: 'Reflecting and doubting, and feeling that the possession of what she had so much wished for, did not bring much satisfaction, Fanny now walked home again—with a change rather than a diminution of cares since her treading that path before.'[2] And this irony is pointed by the next phase— the sudden turn of fortune when she arrives in her own room, to find Edmund with his offering of the chain, and to be overwhelmed by 'a thousand feelings of pain and pleasure'. 'I feel much more than I can possibly express', she cries; and the mixture of common sense and stupidity in Edmund's answer—'My dear Fanny, you feel these things a great deal too much'[3]—sets all in perspective. And so the episode draws towards its close, with Fanny's ecstasy over Edmund's note—'Two lines more prized had never fallen from the pen of the most distinguished author— never more completely blessed the researches of the fondest biographer'[4]—the meeting on the stairs, and finally the solution of Fanny's small problem, which leaves the characters appropriately grouped.[5] And gradually the radical difference between its mood and that of *The Rape of the Lock* emerges. There, littleness was designed to signify triviality. Here, no such thing. Fanny's emotional response to these small happenings is so strong and true that her author can afford to set it in ironic juxtaposition with its apparent occasion: 'She began to feel' (when she was expecting news of Edmund's engagement to Mary Crawford) 'that she had not yet gone through all the changes of opinion and senti- ment, which the progress of time and variation of circum- stances occasion in this world of changes. The vicissitudes of the human mind had not yet been exhausted by her.'[6]

[1] *Mansfield Park*, p. 258, ch. xxvi.
[2] Ibid., p. 260, ch. xxvi.
[3] Ibid., p. 262, ch. xxvii.
[4] Ibid., p. 265, ch. xxvii.
[5] Compare the way in which the silver knife is used (more slightly) to indicate the uneasy pattern of human relationships at Portsmouth.
[6] *Mansfield Park*, p. 374, ch. xxxvii.

'The visible structure of Jane Austen's stories may be' ...
not flimsy, but slight; the invisible part is not of the
gossamer slightness of Belinda's mind and heart. In *Emma*,
the wrong done to Harriet shows its visible superstructure
in the exquisite comedy of the court-plaster;[1] but its roots
have reached down into Emma's consciousness: 'It was
foolish, it was wrong, to take so active a part in bringing
any two people together. It was adventuring too far,
assuming too much, making light of what ought to be
serious, a trick of what ought to be simple. She was quite
concerned and ashamed, and resolved to do such things no
more.'[2] They are to strike deeper yet, bringing shamed
realization of what she has done, and what she is. Shocked
to discover that—inadvertently, yet by her own fault—she
has led Harriet to fancy herself in love with Mr. Knightley,
she has to face a worse discovery: 'To understand,
thoroughly understand her own heart, was the first endeavour.' Reflection brings unforeseen knowledge of herself: 'She was most sorrowfully indignant; ashamed of every
sensation but the one revealed to her—her affection for Mr.
Knightley. Every other part of her mind was disgusting.'[3]

The world of *The Rape of the Lock* is a bubble world; we
are to suppose that only by bursting out of it could we come
among human beings of normal stature and substance.
Jane Austen's comedies play themselves out in no such
region. Neither are they played in the cloud-cuckoo-land
which Lamb postulates for Restoration comedy. *That* is a
world outside the running of the moral law; its characters
live and move in an element which is their own. 'They
have got out of Christendom' into this element. 'It is
altogether a speculative scene of things, which has no
reference whatever to the world that is.' It is a world in
which effect does not follow cause as in our world—to
enter it is to enjoy 'the escape from life—the oblivion of
consequences'.[4]

---

[1] *Emma*, pp. 337–340, ch. xl.
[2] Ibid, pp. 136, 137, ch. xvi.
[3] Ibid., p. 412, ch. xlvii. Compare the impression made by the shock of self-
knowledge which follows the rudeness to Miss Bates.
[4] *On the Artificial Comedy of the Last Century.*

Miss Welsford's delightful and suggestive book[1] leads me to develop this and distinguish further: to descry, as one among the many worlds of comedy, a region in which the laws of cause and effect are in suspension—momentary suspension, it seems; partial suspension, too, in favour here of the fox, and there of the goose; the machinery of retribution exists—but it just fails to work, *this time*. 'The source of comic delight', she suggests, 'is the pleasing delusion that facts are more flexible than they appear to be.'[2]

Thus modified, the notion of cloud-cuckoo-land will surely account for the source of delight in various kinds of true comedy. But it will not account for Jane Austen's comedy. It requires just such a distortion as, however frankly and deliberately admitted, she will not allow. It is in our familiar element—its pressures, currents, never modified by any such convention—that her people make fools of themselves and one another. Must we, then, set out to find the 'source of comic delight' in her novels? That is a problem more properly left to a philosophic critic. It is too abstract for a mere curious reader. But there is no honest way of evading it. And since she does not stand isolated— since Fielding, for one, is with her outside cloud-cuckoo- land—it must surely be possible to discover, among definitions of comedy already current, one liberal enough to contain within its bounds the particular comic tradition to which, at least so far as treatment of the stuff of observation is concerned, hers belongs.

'It may seem remarkable', Fielding blandly observes, 'that Aristotle, who is so fond and free of Definitions, hath not thought proper to define the Ridiculous, Indeed, where he tells us it is proper to comedy, he hath remarked that villany is not its object: but he hath not, as I remember, positively asserted what is.' And he goes on to offer a definition of his own: 'The only source of the true Ridiculous (as it appears to me) is Affectation.' Presently he qualifies this statement: '. . . Affectation doth not imply an

---

[1] E. Welsford, *The Fool*, 1935.
[2] Op. cit., p. 322. But see the whole conclusion of her book, which cannot be fairly represented in quotation.

absolute Negation of those qualities which are affected:
and therefore, tho', when it proceeds from Hypocrisy, it be
nearly allied to Deceit; yet when it comes from Vanity
only, it partakes of the Nature of Ostentation.'[1] But affectation, even so broadly conceived, is yet too narrow a defining
term: it will not stretch to include all of Fielding's own
comic characters—it will not hold Squire Western. And
what meaning has it in relation to Jane Austen's mature
comedy?—what to Lady Bertram? *Her* comic essence is not
to be explained by a disparity between being and seeming
which comes of pretension or self-deception. There is no
possibility, here, of self-deception—for that needs some
exertion of the faculties inwards; nor of pretension—for
that needs some exertion of the faculties outwards; and the
most notable thing about Lady Bertram's faculties is their
disuse. 'Talking', Cowper says, 'is necessary in a tête-à-tête,
to distinguish the persons of the drama from the chairs they
sit on.'[2] And Lady Bertram signally fails to distinguish
herself from her sofa.

Besides, this term affectation—incongruity between being
and seeming—will serve only for pure comedy of character.
No narrower term than incongruity unqualified will define
the source of delight which is common to our varieties of
narrative and dramatic comedy. This alone will suit equally
well disparity between act and retribution, between being
and seeming—and between Lady Bertram's human form
and vegetable soul.

But though this definition will bear no limiting quali-
fication, it may need a distinction made within itself. Incongruity may, in fact, please in distinct—and seemingly
opposed—ways. The pleasure may arise from contempla-
tion of incongruity, in and for itself—the incongruity of
Malvolio in the posture of a lover. Or it may arise from con-
templation of incongruity in the assurance that its discord
will be resolved—the discord of Viola's cross fortunes in love.

'. . . Our Comedients', Sidney says, 'thinke there is no delight without laughter, which is verie wrong, for though laughter may come with

---

[1] Preface to *Joseph Andrews*.
[2] *Letters*, ed. T. Wright, 1904, i. 49 (letter to Lady Hesketh, 18 October 1765).

delight, yet commeth it not of delight, as though delight should be
the cause of laughter. But well may one thing breed both togither.
Nay rather in themselves, they have as it were a kind of contrarietie:
For delight wee scarcely doo, but in thinges that have a conveniencie
to our selves, or to the generall nature: Laughter almost ever commeth
of thinges most disproportioned to our selves, and nature.'[1]

And surely it is an essential characteristic of romantic
comedy as Shakespeare develops it that Malvolio and Viola
—stubborn disproportion, and disproportion that resolves
itself under our gaze into fair and gracious proportion—
should share its world.

This is not wholly to differ—as I should be very unwilling
to do—from Sir Edmund Chambers, who opens this question of the nature of Shakespearian romantic comedy in his
Survey,[2] and decides that it calls for a distinction to be made
between 'drama of ideas' and 'drama of emotions'.[3] Drama
of ideas he characterizes as the expression of a critical analysis of life, 'in the dry light of reason', unbiased by sympathy;
whereas in the drama of emotions 'the artist is endeavouring
to transfer to the audience not his own judgements, but his
own emotional states, through the medium of their sympathies with the woes and exultations of the characters whom
he fashions for the purpose'.[4] And he will not allow this to
be comedy proper, but prefers to call it tragicomedy. But
I would plead for the use of this term, tragicomedy, only
where an element is introduced which is in its nature alien
to comedy; plead that, though composite, romantic comedy
is formed of elements which are in their nature related to
one another—or how could they fuse, as at the best they do?
—that incongruity may be so presented to the reason as to
satisfy in itself, so presented to the emotions (through
sympathy) as to stir a desire which can be satisfied only by
resolution of its discord.

In order to enjoy this sympathetic satisfaction we must,
of course, accept certain conventions, such (for example) as
that which attaches to marriage in romantic comedy: the
convention that two people are so complementary that their
union by marriage must achieve harmony. *Much Ado* shows

---

[1] *Apologie for Poetrie.*   [2] *Shakespeare, A Survey*, 1925.
[3] Op. cit., '*The Merchant of Venice*', pp. 108, 109.   [4] Ibid., p. 111.

how deep the roots of this convention strike, by its assumption that we shall accept, without demur or afterthought, the marriage of Claudio and Hero as this sort of heavenly accord, which Claudio's *action* cannot untune. And if we are unwilling to accept it here, that is because the action itself belongs to melodrama.[1] Orsino's folly, being proper to comedy, jars less—though the notion of marriage implied in the 'happy ending' of *Twelfth Night* is no less conventional. But each such convention will be made easy of acceptance by an author who does not take kindly to artistic convention of any sort. And Jane Austen is such an author. She even tries to rationalize it. Elizabeth, feeling that she loved Darcy, 'began now to comprehend that he was exactly the man, who, in disposition and talents, would most suit her. His understanding and temper, though unlike her own, would have answered all her wishes. It was an union that must have been to the advantage of both; by her ease and liveliness, his mind might have been softened, his manners improved, and from his judgement, information, and knowledge of the world, she must have received benefit of greater importance.'[2] (So this is how lovers cogitate?)

Here, then, are the chief conditions of the comedy which suits Jane Austen—'from top to toe, from right to left, Longitudinally, Perpendicularly, Diagonally'. It allows things alien to itself to be excluded,[3] but refuses to represent otherwise than faithfully what it includes. It so presents *this* incongruity to the critical faculty that it yields delight of itself; so presents *that* to the sympathetic imagination that the resolution of it yields delight. It does not flatter; yet it allows of good humour.

I have shown that Jane Austen accepts the face of life as

[1] Sir Edmund Chambers explains it in this way: 'the plane of comedy . . . is far nearer to real life than is the plane of melodrama . . .' and 'the things which happen between Claudio and Hero have to stand the test of a much closer comparison with the standard of reality than they were designed to bear' (op. cit., '*Much Ado*', p. 134).

But, if they were to pass this test, should we be satisfied? Surely it is only because they fail to pass it, only because this part of the play remains 'unreal', that it is tolerable; whereas a complication proper to comedy, such as the mistaken identities in *Twelfth Night*, is not dependent upon its unreality for acceptance.

[2] *Pride and Prejudice*, p. 312, ch. l.

[3] Always with the unfortunate exception of the conventionally treated complication of seduction.

more agreeable than the supposedly flattering portrait of it
in fiction—shown, however, that this is not, nor is intended
to be, any great compliment. But while I have also shown
that her comic idea does not extend beyond the region in
which human beings make fools of themselves and of one
another, the assumed province of the satirist, there is nevertheless room within this very region, as it presents itself to
her eyes, for a good-humoured acquiescence which he may
not allow himself. For the professing satirist says that his
target is hypocrisy; and although what he very often means
is inconsistency, yet, since the particular incongruity which
he *professes* to aim at is morally ugly, the ugliest of the possible incongruities between being and seeming, he cannot
condone it. How could he exclaim with Elizabeth Bennet,
'Follies and nonsense, whims and inconsistencies *do* divert
me, I own, and I laugh at them whenever I can'[1]—thankful,
indeed, that the provision of them is never likely to fail—
when the beast that he says he is hunting is one which he
must wish to destroy? 'A satirist', Bradley concludes, 'may
be intellectually pleased by human absurdities and illusions,
but he does not feel them to be good. But to Jane Austen,
so far as they are not seriously harmful, they are altogether
pleasant, because they are both ridiculous and right.'[2] This,
however, is not all. It is not only by its pursuit of hypocrisy
that satire may leave a bitter flavour in comedy. And
Bradley's further suggestion gives us no more than a start-
ing-point. 'Jane Austen, who is said to be Shakespearian,
never reminds us of Shakespeare, I think, in her full-dress
portraits, but she does so in such characters as Miss Bates
and Mrs. Allen.'[3] Wherein this affinity between her fools
and Shakespeare's lies, he leaves us to discover as we
may.

When Sir Andrew Aguecheek ends his challenge 'God
have mercy on one of our souls! He may have mercy on
mine, but my hope is better'—something strange is happening. What is opaque in life has become translucent in art;

[1] *Pride and Prejudice*, p. 57, ch. xi.
[2] A. C. Bradley, *Jane Austen*; *Essays and Studies by Members of the English Association*
(1911), p. 19.
[3] Ibid., p. 21.

but this does not mean that we see through Sir Andrew, as
we see through those characters whom the satirist causes to
expose themselves before us—characters in whom the comic
incongruity is incongruity between being and seeming—
characters such as his counterpart in Ben Jonson's *Silent
Woman*, Sir Amorous La Foole. To create them requires
art indeed, but of a less uncommon sort. Others besides
Jane Austen have made their Eltons, though none quite so
coolly as she. But when daylight shines through Sir Andrew
it is not because we are different from him, superior to him,
that we can see it, but because we are akin—because his
simplicity, though tinctured by his individuality, is nothing
but a drop of human simplicity, and therefore of our simplicity. It is an element in which his thoughts float, encounter-
ing one another with an inconsequence which delights by
being both new and familiar. The tingling shock of pleased
surprise which their collision gives us is enhanced by the
realization that by our success in keeping the denizens of
our minds apart we usually conceal even from ourselves
the fact that they are very ill-assorted company. Sometimes
the impact comes of a floating body, a notion or impression,
blundering against the fixed object, the sunken wreck, of a
habit of thought. 'Well, my dear,' Mr. Woodhouse says to
Emma after Mrs. Elton's first visit, 'considering we never
saw her before, she seems a very pretty sort of young lady.'[1]
Now the comic point of Ben Jonson's Morose is lodged in
the fixed object in his mind, his hatred of disturbance—an
eccentricity which destroys kinship between him and the
wiseacres in the play, and in the audience. The comic
point of Mr. Woodhouse's remark may almost be said, by
contrast, to be lodged in syntax—in the deliciously bland
appearance of logical connexion which it gives to the
encounter between his habit of thought and his impulse
towards polite speech—and over this point a flourish is
set by recollection of Mrs. Weston's manner of humour-
ing him: 'You would not wish to disappoint and mortify
the Coles, I am sure, sir; friendly, good sort of people as
ever lived, and who have been your neighbours these *ten*

[1] *Emma*, p. 279, ch. xxxii.

years.'[1]   This sort of counterfeit connexion had pleased Jane
Austen from her earliest days of burlesque-writing. 'Two
Gentlemen most elegantly attired but weltering in their
blood was what first struck our Eyes.'[2] In her mature work
it is not a mere verbal entertainment; we are made to laugh,
not at a particular idiosyncrasy which may not happen to
be ours, but at the interaction of idiosyncrasy and life.
Indeed, I do not think it too much to say that counterfeit connexion symbolizes this distinctive quality for which
we are examining her comic characters in company with
Shakespeare's: for if the fools of the satirist fail to come to
terms with life, her simpletons (it is the more appropriate
word) and his make terms for themselves. How does this
capacity for sympathy with folly square with Jane Austen's
moral purpose? It squares very well. She has among her
characters some (such as Mrs. Elton) in whom what is
ridiculous is quarry for the satirist, folly that is to be laughed
out of existence. But—and this is what matters—they are
not *distinguished* by their folly; there is not a line drawn
across, with the odious and foolish on one side of it and the
amiable and wise on the other—like the line across *The Rape
of the Lock* that separates Clarissa[3] from Belinda. Along such
a line Miss Bates—with the endearing absurdity of her comment on Mrs. Elton's arrival: 'It is such a happiness when
good people get together—and they always do'[4]—would be
forever straying. Not that there is any sentimental nonsense
about a necessary connexion between goodness of heart and
badness of head—such a notion is firmly snubbed when
Emma, in a fit of generous enthusiasm, propounds it; but
all Jane Austen's characters, the fools with the rest, have the
mental qualities proper to them, to their wisdom or to their
folly.[5] 'What is before me, I see', Miss Bates says—and it is

    [1] Ibid., p. 210, ch. xxv. Compare Mrs. Jennings's description of Delaford: 'To
my fancy, a thousand times prettier than Barton Park, where they are forced to send
three miles for their meat, and have not a neighbour nearer than your mother' (*Sense
and Sensibility*, p. 197, ch. xxx).
    [2] *Love and Freindship*, p. 31; *Minor Works*, p. 99.
    [3] I mean, of course, the Clarissa of the final version, with her 'inspired' lecture on
feminine behaviour.   [4] *Emma*, p. 175, ch. xxi.
    [5] I am sure that John Bailey *simplifies* too firmly when he says that Jane Austen
'definitely, and very strongly, preferred good people to bad, and sensible people
to fools'. *Introductions to Jane Austen* (1931), p. 30.

more than any other character in the story can say, for all the
more intelligent people (even to Mr. Knightley himself) are
peering through mists of prejudice; and if I wanted to know
what happened in Highbury on any particular day I should
go to Miss Bates—just as, if I wanted counsel, I would
rather ask it of Bottom than of any one else in Athens.

This liberty for good humour in comedy suits Jane
Austen even when she is not in a good humour herself,
before she can command the gay serenity of her later years.
I have likened our imaginations to dwelling-places; but I
think that we live in them as caretakers must live in haunted
houses. In the part that is warm and well lit we entertain
our friends; the rest is no place for hospitality. And I am
convinced that Jane Austen regarded her writing as an act
of hospitality. That is the sense in which her novels remained to the last a kind of family entertainment. It is of
relatively small importance that, when she wrote the Chawton novels, she knew that they were to be read by Anna and
Fanny. All her readers were, as a matter of course, her
guests. 'Imbued with the old traditions of her sex . . . she
wrote, as ladies talk, to give pleasure'[1]—to entertain, in
so far as entertainment signifies hospitality. To the artist,
this influence exerted upon the substance of art by an
impulse which is not aesthetic may seem unjustifiable. To
the critic, it must seem surprising in a writer of so delicate
artistic sensibility. But whether or no it is capable of
explanation or justification, it must be taken into account
if her art is to be understood.

(ii) *Handling*

'I cannot . . . conceive,' Henry James says, 'in any novel
worth discussing at all, of a passage of description that is
not in its intention narrative, a passage of dialogue that is
not in its intention descriptive, a touch of truth of any sort
that does not partake of the nature of incident, or an incident that derives its interest from any other source than the
general and only source of the success of a work of art—

[1] Virginia Woolf, *The Common Reader*: 'The Lives of the Obscure', p. 161 (of
Laetitia Pilkington, whom she compares in this respect with Jane Austen).

that of being illustrative.'¹ And, having dealt severely with the critics who like compartments and labels, he asseverates: 'I cannot see what is meant by talking as if there were a part of a novel which is the story and part of it which for mystical reasons is not.'²

This conviction of the integrity of a good novel—this impression that it must be unprofitable to study 'plot' and 'characters' separately—is strongly borne out by a study of Jane Austen's narrative art, and by particular observation of the course of its development. Whether we approach it in the first place by way of her presentation of character, or of her construction of plot, we shall discover the need— more urgent as we draw towards the later novels—of reaching some central vantage-point, from which the 'old-fashioned distinction between the novel of character and the novel of incident' (as Henry James calls it) is seen to be insignificant. For, 'What' (he demands) 'is character but the determination of incident? What is incident but the illustration of character?'³

It is not often that this can be said of those fictitious characters whose internal mechanism is of the simplest kind—characters to which comedy has always been hospitable. They are often curiously intractable—likely, when they are compelled to serve the main interests of the story, to do or suffer injury. If they have been introduced for the sake of suggesting some contrast, they will either give it an unintended turn—throw queer lights on the figure to which they are to act as foil, as Scott's gallant ruffians do on his heroes—or else lose all characteristics but those that serve for this contrast. I think that Isabella Thorpe has been emptied and flattened in this way, despite her bold promise: to Catherine Morland's simplicity she has to oppose sophistication; to her good sense, the shoddiest sort of fashionable sensibility; to her integrity, sly, overreaching cunning. It is all very well done—even to the neatness with which Henry and Eleanor point the contrast:

'Prepare for your sister-in-law, Eleanor,' Henry says,

¹ *Partial Portraits:* 'The Art of Fiction', 1888, pp. 391, 392.
² Ibid., p. 399.   ³ Ibid., p. 392.

when Catherine reports Isabella's supposed engagement to
their brother, 'and such a sister-in-law as you must delight
in!—Open, candid, artless, guileless, with affections strong
but simple, forming no pretentions, and knowing no disguise.'

'"Such a sister-in-law, Henry, I should delight in," said
Eleanor, with a smile.'—None of which talk is intelligible
to Catherine, who unconsciously provides an illustration to
it by her ingenuous comment: 'I never was so deceived in
any one's character in my life before.'[1] But it confines
Isabella to two dimensions.

Alternatively, one of these simply organized comic characters may be compelled to do a hand's turn in forwarding the
action—with disastrous consequences to his own integrity;
of which, I suppose, the most obvious example is Mr.
Micawber turned detective. And some such misfortune
befalls General Tilney. The burlesque pattern of the story
demands a mock villain and Jane Austen creates accordingly
one whom Catherine may suspect but must not see through
—who, while she is spelling out his most unimpeachable
actions in hope of discovering a Montoni, is indeed acting
with a petty duplicity which is apparent to all but her. This
is very well; but his violent act at the climax of the story
sets him nearer to Catherine's image of him than to that
which has been presented to us.

On the other hand, these simply organized characters
may injure the texture of the story by refusing to serve its
ends. The novels of Scott and Dickens are full of comic
characters which perform no service at all—which seem to
have got into them merely because they presented themselves to the novelist's imagination and asked for employment in such engaging terms that he did not know how to
deny them. Scott indeed confesses that he found, when he
attempted to follow a plan, that 'personages were rendered
important or insignificant, not according to their agency in
the original conception . . ., but according to the success,
or otherwise, with which I was able to bring them out'.[2]

---

[1] *Northanger Abbey*, p. 206, ch. xxv.
[2] *Journal*, ed. Douglas, 1890, i. 117 (entry for 12 February 1826).

These unexpected developments may play havoc with the story.

Now one would hardly expect usefulness of Mr. Collins, a creature born of his author's youthful fancy in its most hilarious mood. 'Can he be a sensible man, sir?' Elizabeth asks her father, after hearing him read the letter in which their cousin introduces himself; and Mr. Bennet answers: 'No, my dear; I think not. I have great hopes of finding him quite the reverse.'[1] Indeed, he is a being of some exquisitely non-sensible world, of another element than ours, one to which he is 'native and endued'. Whether he bestows his favour upon Elizabeth, pleased to contemplate the notion of her wit 'tempered with silence', or whether he withdraws it—yet gravely explains that she is not excepted from his good wishes for the health of her family— he does not strain probability, as Sir William Lucas strains it by the simplicity of *his* machinery; he transcends it. And so it is not enough to exclaim, 'No one would speak so'; and one is still too moderate if one protests, 'No one would even think so'; for Mr. Collins is the *quintessence* of a character, in Lamb's sense of the word when he defined quintessence as an apple-pie made all of quinces. He does and says not those things which such a man would say and do, nor even those which he would wish to say and do, but those towards which the whole bias of his nature bends him, and from which no thought of consequences, no faintest sense of their possible impact upon other people, deters him. And is such a creature as this to be put into the shafts and draw a plot? Mr. Elton, his nearest relation, might, and does, perform such a service, for he, with all his comic exuberance, is a being of our familiar element; but can it be exacted of Mr. Collins? It is, and with capital effect. As well as making his own contribution to the story, by the comedy he plays out with Elizabeth and her family and neighbours, he has to draw and hold together Longbourn and Hunsford; to bring Hunsford within range of our imagination awhile before we can be taken there (and incidentally to confirm Elizabeth's ill opinion of every one

---

[1] *Pride and Prejudice*, p. 64, ch. xiii.

connected with Darcy), to draw Elizabeth to Hunsford when the time is ripe, and eventually to send Lady Catherine post-haste to Longbourn on her catastrophic visit. It is worth stopping to notice how unobtrusively this last incident is suggested: Lady Catherine, questioned by Mrs. Bennet, mentions that she saw Mr. and Mrs. Collins 'the night before last'. To Elizabeth, she opens her attack by saying: 'A report of a most alarming nature, reached me two days ago'—the report of her engagement to Darcy.[1] We are left to infer a connexion between these two references; and then, after a sufficient interval for the carriage of a letter, comes Mr. Collins's warning to Elizabeth against 'a precipitate closure with the gentleman's proposals': 'We have reason to imagine that his aunt, lady Catherine de Bourgh, does not look on the match with a friendly eye. . . . After mentioning the likelihood of this marriage to her ladyship last night', he has felt it his duty to offer this warning.[2] Such are the care and ingenuity that Jane Austen expends even on the broadly comic characters of her early invention.

In her later work, however, a subtler (if not a more ingeniously contrived) interaction of these simply organized characters with the development of the story becomes evident. And I think that this growth is to be traced most clearly through a study of a succession of such characters— particularly of those that have some superficial resemblance; for example, of her stupid, middle-aged women.

Mrs. Jennings is the first in this succession; and boldly as she is conceived I think there is some uncertainty as to her part in the story. There is indeed (I suspect) more than one Mrs. Jennings in it. There is the grossly good-humoured vulgarian, in whose company Marianne can find no pleasure, and in whose house Elinor would not willingly have chosen to spend some months. And there is the staunch friend— whose very want of refinement comes to be associated with her resolute adherence to the company of her earlier and less genteel days: a woman who nurses Marianne, and stands up to John Dashwood, and ranges herself with the group of

---

[1] *Pride and Prejudice*, pp. 352, 353, ch. lvi.   [2] Ibid., p. 363, ch. lvii.

characters which opposes an ideal of good sense to Mari-anne's heightened and impracticable sensibility. It is not that these two showings of her are incompatible; the busy matchmaker might well stand by all oppressed lovers, em-bracing indiscriminately the cause of Marianne or of Lucy. But do they convince us that they have been conceived as one by the author? I have spoken of my impression that in *Sense and Sensibility* I perceive Jane Austen working off her own irritability and dejection, writing herself into a good humour. More than mere personal impression this cannot be—unless particular comparison should offer it some slight support. Charlotte Palmer is no sillier than Harriet Smith; and yet, how intolerable we should find it to see and hear as much of Charlotte as we do of Harriet! And would Miss Bates have been endurable if she had been presented in the mood and manner of *Sense and Sensibility*? At all events I believe that, while Mrs. Jennings's services to the plot have been clearly thought out from the begin-ning, there has been an unexpected development of what she means to the story.[1] When Elinor criticizes Marianne for her failure to see in Mrs. Jennings anything but a vulgar busybody,[2] she forgets that she has herself been Mrs. Jennings's severest critic—and I suspect that her author forgot it too, and, half aware later of what had happened, pushed her unruly creature out of sight and allowed no more to be heard of her in the close of the story than might remind us of the Mrs. Jennings of the opening.

The problem which Mrs. Bennet presents is a little differ-ent; she is not the sort of character that is likely to embarrass its creator by uncontrollable vitality—as Mrs. Jennings had just done, and Mrs. Smith was to do later; Mrs. Bennet was 'a woman of mean understanding, little information, and uncertain temper. When she was discontented she fancied herself nervous. The business of her life was to get her

---

[1] I hope that this differentiation may be allowed to indicate the distinction between the succession of events that can be made quite intelligible in a summary, and the train of development which is fully expressed only in the novel itself.

[2] 'Elinor had not needed this to be assured of the injustice to which her sister was often led in her opinion of others, by the irritable refinement of her own mind, and the too great importance placed by her on the delicacies of a strong sensibility, and the graces of a polished manner' (*Sense and Sensibility*, p. 201, ch. xxxi).

daughters married; its solace was visiting and news.'[1] That, summing up for us the impressions of her that we have gained from her first appearance, seems to dispose of Mrs. Bennet, to set her where she must remain throughout the story. But we are to have a good deal of her company, for her post is at the centre of the action; and she must not become a dead weight. Mr. E. M. Forster, when he divides the characters of fiction into 'round' and 'flat', brings his argument to a head in this sentence: 'The test of a round character is whether it is capable of surprising in a convincing way. If it never surprises, it is flat. If it does not convince, it is a flat pretending to be round.'[2] But it seems to me that this analysis does not allow for such a character as Mrs. Bennet, of whose comic essence it is that she should be incapable of any but her habitual, and therefore inapposite, reaction to life in all its variety. She must indeed surprise us—in order to keep our response to her alive—but may surprise us only by the inexhaustible variety of expression devised for her unvarying reaction to circumstance. And it is in devising this variety of form for what is substantially invariable—for a Mrs. Bennet who is to be left as she was found 'occasionally nervous and invariably silly'[3]—that Jane Austen displays her virtuosity, giving her creature the entail on Longbourn, a theme of specious importance, to play her variations upon. We hear of it first when Mr. Collins offers himself as a visitor, and Mr. Bennet reminds his wife that this cousin 'when I am dead, may turn you all out of this house as soon as he pleases'. '"Oh my dear," cried his wife, "I cannot bear to hear that mentioned. Pray do not talk of that odious man. I do think it is the hardest thing in the world, that your estate should be entailed away from your own children; and I am sure if I had been you, I should have tried long ago to do something or other about it."

---

[1] *Pride and Prejudice*, p. 5, ch. i.
[2] *Aspects of the Novel*, p. 106. He admits, however, some flat characters into comedy, provided they give an illusion of intense vitality. Mr. Muir replies to this passage (*The Structure of the Novel*, 1928, ch. vi) with a plea for the flat character as the 'incarnation of habit'—one aspect, that is, of the truth about people; but this does not wholly account for Mrs. Bennet.
[3] *Pride and Prejudice*, p. 385, ch. lxi.

'Jane and Elizabeth attempted to explain to her the nature of an entail. They had often attempted it before, but it was a subject on which Mrs. Bennet was beyond the reach of reason . . .' There we are, in the thick of it, knowing what is to be Mrs. Bennet's inevitable response to this subject, ignorant how its mode will be varied—though the close of this very passage promises something:

'. . . She continued to rail bitterly against the cruelty of settling an estate away from a family of five daughters, in favour of a man whom nobody cared anything about.'[1]

Mr. Collins, on arrival, is offered a sufficiently surprising variation on this theme: '. . . Such things I know are all chance in this world. There is no knowing how estates will go when once they come to be entailed'[2]—and contributes something to it himself by his proposal of marrying one of his cousins in reparation. And when this falls through—and, worse still, he marries some one else—Mrs. Bennet returns to her favourite subject with fresh energy: 'How any one could have the conscience to entail away an estate from one's own daughters I cannot understand; and all for the sake of Mr. Collins too!—Why should *he* have it more than anybody else?'[3]

And yet she still has something in reserve for us: when Elizabeth returns from visiting Mr. and Mrs. Collins her mother asks her whether they do not 'often talk of having Longbourn when your father is dead. . . . Well, if they can be easy with an estate that is not lawfully their own, so much the better. *I* should be ashamed of having one that was only entailed on me.'[4] And so she leaves us with the assurance that, as she had been talking of this subject before the story began, so she will continue after its close, with ever fresh turns of absurdity, happily corresponding with the busy futility of her actions.

Mrs. Allen presents a similar problem, but complicated by her obligations to the burlesque pattern—obligations which are both an embarrassment and a support to most of the minor characters in *Northanger Abbey*. She is to oppose her

[1] Ibid., pp. 61, 62, ch. xiii.   [2] Ibid., p. 65, ch. xiii.
[3] Ibid., p. 130, ch. xxiii.   [4] Ibid., p. 228, ch. xl.

comatose good humour to the hysterical concern of the heroine's guardians in the novel of sentiment;[1] and this duty suits well her unalterable triviality of mind, and her preoccupation with one trifle above the rest—finery; her anxiety about muslins preventing her from feeling the least anxiety on Catherine's account.

'And are Mr. and Mrs. Tilney in Bath?' Catherine asks her, eager for information about Henry's circumstances. 'Yes, I fancy they are,' replies Mrs. Allen easily, 'but I am not quite certain. Upon recollection, however, I have a notion they are both dead; at least the mother is; yes, I am sure Mrs. Tilney is dead, because Mrs. Hughes told me there was a very beautiful set of pearls that Mr. Drummond gave his daughter on her wedding-day and that Miss Tilney has got now, for they were put by for her when her mother died.'[2]

Lady Catherine's part in the story of *Pride and Prejudice* is no less precisely planned, but the fun of it is independent of burlesque; for the execution of this plan is so consistent with the comic essence of her character, that not only her appearances but the very anticipation of them (since she is portentously anticipated) compose themselves into a pattern of comedy. The story is shaped by the original misunderstanding and eventual good understanding between Darcy and Elizabeth; and it is Lady Catherine's office to assist at the first, unwittingly, and at the second against her will: her active interference in their affairs—itself finely in character—is the determining circumstance in their coming to understand one another's feelings and their own. Its effect on Elizabeth is direct and obvious; but what a pleasantly ironic invention it is that Darcy, who has alienated Elizabeth by interfering with her sister's affairs, and is by no means ready to repent his interference, should be roused to indignation and action when Lady Catherine tries to interfere with *his*. Her 'unjustifiable endeavours', as he calls them, to separate him from Elizabeth, send him straight to Longbourn; and so, as Elizabeth remarks: 'Lady Catherine has been of infinite use, which ought to make her happy, for she loves to be of use.'[3] And with that most

[1] Especially in the tradition of *Evelina*.
[2] *Northanger Abbey*, pp. 68, 69, ch. ix.
[3] *Pride and Prejudice*, p. 381, ch. lx.

appropriate valedictory the pattern of her part in the story is completed, as though with a flourish.

But pattern-making of this sort is not, for all its charm, subtle enough to suit the deeper, more elusive implications of the story of *Mansfield Park*. And so the irony of Mrs. Norris's ineffectual busy-ness is more seriously conceived and more subtly presented than that of Mrs. Bennet's. She is the fly on the carriage-wheel, who cries, 'Lord, what a dust I am raising!' She is convinced that her activity alone keeps her world spinning—and yet, from first to last the young Bertrams pass her by heedlessly, as they go their own ways. She is, as it were, the stationary object which enables us to estimate their pace and direction. That is her real relation to poor Maria's wilful marriage and elopement —the marriage which she thought she had arranged, the elopement for which she paid by a broken spirit—and to the follies of Tom and Julia.

It is a measure of the development in Jane Austen's conception of human relationships between *Pride and Prejudice* and *Mansfield Park* that Fanny's youthful consciousness alone will not serve to convey to us all that we must understand; and of the development in her technique that she has learnt how to use so unlikely an instrument as Lady Bertram for this purpose. It is she who makes apparent the truths which all her family ignores or fails to understand— and that, although she never tries to reflect and is incapable of observing: on the morning after the ball 'Lady Bertram was not certain of any body's dress, or any body's place at supper, but her own. "She could not recollect what it was that she had heard about one of the Miss Maddoxes, or what it was that Lady Prescott had noticed in Fanny; she was not sure whether Colonel Harrison had been talking of Mr. Crawford or of William, when he said he was the finest young man in the room; somebody had whispered something to her, she had forgot to ask Sir Thomas what it could be." And these were her longest speeches and clearest communications.'[1] Yet, inert though she may be, she has her proper function to perform, for she acts, in relation to

[1] *Mansfield Park*, pp. 282, 283, ch. xxix.

the other characters and their fortunes, as a delicate instrument, registering the pressure of events according to their real significance.[1] Her very unconsciousness of any attempt at deception exposes the truth. When Mrs. Norris, left a well-provided widow, murmurs resignedly, 'If I can but make both ends meet, that's all I ask for', Lady Bertram answers: 'I hope, sister, things are not so very bad with you neither—considering. Sir Thomas says you will have six hundred a year.' And when Mrs. Norris, more warily, rejoins that she hopes to 'lay by a little at the end of the year', Lady Bertram placidly observes: 'I dare say you will. You always do, don't you?'[2] It is the absence of malice that allows her indolent remarks to penetrate, and let in daylight; just as her failure to play up to a pretence lays it bare. When Tom, intent on his darling project of theatricals, argues with the still reluctant Edmund: '"As to my father's being absent, it is so far from an objection, that I consider it rather as a motive; for the expectation of his return must be a very anxious period to my mother, and if we can be the means of amusing that anxiety, and keeping up her spirits for the next few weeks, I shall think our time very well spent, and so I am sure will he.—It is a *very* anxious period for her." As he said this, each looked towards their mother. Lady Bertram, sunk back in one corner of the sofa, the picture of health, wealth, ease, and tranquillity, was just falling into a gentle doze, while Fanny was getting through the few difficulties of her work for her.'[3]

There is a startlingly direct correspondence between her reaction to events and their emotional reality. Maria's marriage is thus unreal; Lady Bertram 'stood with salts in her hand, expecting to be agitated'.[4] Crawford's love for Fanny may be shallow, but it is not (like the courtship of Maria) a mockery of feeling; and Lady Bertram becomes almost talkative under its animating influence: 'And I will tell you what, Fanny—which is more than I did for

---

[1] 'We measure the extent of the disasters which have fallen upon the family by their effect in overcoming the apathy of Lady Bertram' (Goldwin Smith, *Life of Jane Austen*, 1890, p. 161).
[2] *Mansfield Park*, pp. 29, 30, ch. iii.
[3] Ibid., p. 126, ch. xiii.   [4] Ibid., p. 203, ch. xxi.

Maria—the next time pug has a litter you shall have a puppy.'[1]

The momentous return of Sir Thomas (which has so sadly disappointed Mrs. Norris, by giving her no occasion for officiousness) brings her sister 'nearer agitation than she had been for the last twenty years'.[2] And lastly Fanny's return to Mansfield Park, which is to mean so much, moves her as nothing has moved her before: 'Fanny had scarcely passed the solemn-looking servants, when Lady Bertram came from the drawing room to meet her; came with no indolent step; and, falling on her neck, said, "Dear Fanny! now I shall be comfortable."'[3]

Thus, even those characters in Jane Austen's novels which might be expected to sit very loosely to the story cannot be studied without reference to it—closer reference as her technique develops. And it is worth while to follow for a little way the contrary course, starting from the study of her mode of devising a story, in order to see how inevitably it leads to the same central point.

Certain resemblances and differences between *Sense and Sensibility* and *Pride and Prejudice* illustrate her love and care for nice symmetry in the ground-plan of her stories, and her workmanship in the contrivance of it. 'It may now be proper', wrote the young Jane Austen (whose critical faculty was already playing like summer lightning over all she read), 'to return to the Hero of this Novel . . . of whom I believe I have scarcely ever had occasion to speak . . .'[4] Perhaps she had lately made the acquaintance of one of Sterne's followers, Mackenzie or some other—imitators who succeed in reproducing nothing but his inconsequence.

There is nothing inconsequent about the plan of *Sense and Sensibility*; in fact, it is a little stiff. I suspect that the original form of *Elinor and Marianne* may have something to do with this. It is not easy to see between whom the letters telling the first part of the story could have passed, unless the sisters should have each a confidante;[5] and, if

---

[1] Ibid., p. 333, ch. xxxiii.   [2] Ibid., p. 179, ch. xix.
[3] Ibid., p. 447, ch. xlvi.   [4] *Jack and Alice* (*Volume the First*), p. 44; *Minor Works*, pp. 24, 25.
[5] More than one of Marianne's speeches, especially in the earlier chapters, might without alteration be read as passages from letters—for example: her soliloquy on

they had, then these characters, since they have disappeared
without leaving a trace, must have been little more than
dummies, significant only in virtue of their position—like
Charlotte Lutterell and Mrs. Marlowe in *Lesley Castle*, Mrs.
Johnson and Lady de Courcy in *Lady Susan*. It is worth
noticing here that *those* two stories had been set in motion
with the help of confidantes, and then proceeded indepen-
dently; the contrivance of *Elinor and Marianne* may well
have been of this sort. Such a pair of confidantes, in
character so contrasting with one another and agreeing
with their correspondents, would point the central contrast
in the story between two temperaments and ways of life,
and would moreover give opportunity for descriptions of
the same episode from opposed points of view—as in *Lady
Susan*; a device of which the tart flavour would suit Jane
Austen's mood in 1795. Surely some trace of it remains in
the double account of the disclosure of Lucy's engagement?

Whatever the cause, there they all stand, formally grouped
as for a dance: Marianne and her mother (supported as they
imagine by Willoughby) challenging Elinor; while behind
Elinor are ranged not merely Edward and Colonel Brandon
with their sad moderation, but also the good-humoured
worldling, Mrs. Jennings, whose crude raillery comes at
length to seem almost like frank common sense, set over
against Marianne's excessive sensitiveness and reticence.
And this antithetic pattern appears to have imposed itself
on all the characters, giving us those capriciously contrasted
pairs, the Middletons and the Palmers.

This symmetry is emphasized by the way in which the
similarity in the fortunes of Elinor and Marianne points
the central opposition, between their tempers and opinions.
When Marianne wonders at Elinor's coolness in love, and
Elinor soberly reasons with her own heart, something is
being offered us for subsequent comparison: we are to
observe, later, the nature of Marianne's reaction to a similar
situation. And the parallel is ingeniously kept before us by
means of its reflection in their minds: Marianne's disap-

p. 27, ch. v, her praise of dead leaves on pp. 87, 88, ch. xvi, and of picturesque landscape on p. 97, ch. xviii.

proval of Edward's unforthcoming manner 'ended, as every feeling must end with her, by carrying back her thoughts to Willoughby, whose manners formed a contrast sufficiently striking to those of his brother elect'[1]—while Elinor could not reflect upon her sister's situation without comparing it with her own: 'In her earnest meditations on the contents of the letter [from Willoughby to Marianne], on the depravity of that mind which could dictate it, and, probably, on the very different mind of a very different person, who had no other connection whatever with the affair than what her heart gave him with every thing that passed, Elinor forgot the immediate distress of her sister . . .'[2] Her consciousness of the resemblance between her own situation and Marianne's is kept awake by the realization that it can be apparent to none but herself; there is no one to share her dry amusement at the thought that Mrs. Jennings's odd remedy for the pains of love 'might be as reasonably tried on herself as on her sister'.[3]

This, however, is not the only symmetrical correspondence in the story; Marianne's fortunes follow a curve which brings her back, as in some figure of a dance, to her original position, but facing the opposite way:

'Marianne Dashwood was born to an extraordinary fate. She was born to discover the falsehood of her own opinions, and to counteract, by her conduct, her most favourite maxims. She was born to overcome an affection formed so late in life as at seventeen, and with no sentiment superior to strong esteem and lively friendship, voluntarily to give her hand to another!—and *that* other, a man who had suffered no less than herself under the event of a former attachment, whom, two years before, she had considered too old to be married,—and who still sought the constitutional safe-guard of a flannel waistcoat!'[4]

The curve is completed with a light, quick hand; Marianne's original opinion of her lover is recalled by a single brief pleasantry; there is no awkward attempt at explanation. Was Jane Austen's ear caught for an instant by the tones of a voice out of her own youth? 'A second attachment is seldom attended with any serious consequences; against

---

[1] *Sense and Sensibility*, p. 87, ch. xvi.   [2] Ibid., p. 184, ch. xxix.
[3] Ibid., p. 198, ch. xxx. This, surely, makes her persistence in the comparison natural enough.
[4] Ibid., p. 378, ch. l.

that therefore I have nothing to say. Preserve yourself
from a first Love & you need not fear a second.'[1]

Pride and Prejudice is no less deliberately shaped; its
pattern shows an equal delight in the symmetry of correspondence and antithesis; but there is a notable difference
in the contrivance. This pattern is formed by diverging
and converging lines, by the movement of two people who
are impelled apart until they reach a climax of mutual
hostility, and thereafter bend their courses towards mutual
understanding and amity. It is a pattern very common in
fiction, but by no means easy to describe plausibly.

Of the two courses, Jane Austen traces but one by means
of a continuous line; that line, however, is firm and fluent.
Elizabeth's chief impetus is due to Wickham; but there is
hardly a character in the story who contributes no momen-
tum to it, nor any pressure from without to which she does
not respond characteristically. Her misunderstanding of
Darcy is thus much less simple, much less like the given
condition of an invented problem, than Marianne's misunderstanding of Willoughby, or of Elinor. Her initial
impulse towards this misunderstanding comes, of course,
from Darcy himself, in that piece of flamboyant rudeness[2]
which I suspect of being a little out of keeping; but from
this point on all follows plausibly. Darcy's more characteristic reference to his own implacability[3] prepares her to
believe just what she is going to hear of him so soon as
Wickham addresses her. And how insinuating that address
is! There had been a suspicion of burlesque about Willoughby's mode of entrance into the story—something that
recalls the ironic apology for the absence of the hero in the
opening of *Northanger Abbey*; chance has disposed it too
smoothly to his advantage. Wickham owes no more to
chance than that first silent encounter with Darcy that stirs
Elizabeth's wakeful curiosity; it is his adroitness that trans-
forms curiosity into sympathetic indignation. What provincial young lady, brought up among the small mysteries
and intrigues of Mrs. Bennet's world, would not be flattered

---

[1] *Jack and Alice* (*Volume the First*), pp. 27, 28; *Minor Works*, p. 16.
[2] *Pride and Prejudice*, pp. 11, 12, ch. iii.   [3] Ibid., p. 58, ch. xi.

into sympathy by his relation of his own story[1] (so nicely corresponding with that of many heroes in popular fiction), or would criticize him for telling or herself for listening to such a private history? Or what young lady of Elizabeth's self-assurance would suspect that she was not to remain its only hearer? Henceforward his adversaries—and even indifferent spectators—play into his hands: Miss Bingley's insolent interference rouses Elizabeth's pride and clouds her judgement; Charlotte Lucas causes her to mistake her own prejudice for generous sentiment;[2] Mr. Collins, by associating Darcy in her mind with the idol of his worship, strengthens every ill impression; Lady Catherine herself, by answering to Wickham's description, confirms part of his story, and by her proprietary praise of Darcy[3] fixes some of its implications; and Colonel Fitzwilliam, by his indiscreet half-confidence, ensures that Elizabeth shall see Darcy's action towards her sister in the harshest light.

Meanwhile, Darcy's ill opinion of the Bennets has been growing, under the influence of these very people and events, until the climax of the ungracious proposal and refusal is reached. And yet, in the centre of this disturbance, forces have begun to stir, and, almost imperceptibly, to allay it. And this entails a change of course which is very difficult to contrive. The initial impulse must not seem to have spent itself—that would leave a fatal impression of lassitude. There must be deflexion; and this, for Jane Austen, means cause and opportunity to reconsider character and action. (Not conduct alone; she has little use for those casual encounters in ambiguous circumstances which are the staple of Fanny Burney's misunderstandings between lovers.[4]) Even while they are drawing yet farther apart,

---

[1] He is ready with a creditable reason for making a confidence of it (p. 80, ch. xvi).
[2] p. 90, ch. xviii.
[3] To Elizabeth she 'talked of his coming with the greatest satisfaction, spoke of him in terms of the highest admiration, and seemed almost angry to find that he had already been frequently seen by Miss Lucas and herself' (p. 170, ch. xxx).
[4] 'Where . . . ,' she says, 'though the conduct is mistaken, the feelings are not, it may not be very material' (*Emma*, p. 431, ch. xlix). She mocks the conventional misunderstanding in *Northanger Abbey*, when Catherine sees Henry talking to a young woman 'whom [she] immediately guessed to be his sister; thus unthinkingly throwing away a fair opportunity of considering him lost to her for ever, by being married already' (p. 53, ch. viii).

Elizabeth and Darcy have begun to feel unfamiliar doubts; sure as each still is of his and her own critical judgement, both have come to question the standards of their own social worlds. Her mother's behaviour at Netherfield on two uncomfortable occasions disturbs Elizabeth in such a way as to suggest that she had not been embarrassed by it before; and Charlotte Lucas's conduct shocks her. Presently, Colonel Fitzwilliam's manners give her a standard by which to judge Wickham's. In the meantime Darcy has been unwillingly learning to criticize the manners of his world as it is represented by Miss Bingley, and—touching him more smartly—by Lady Catherine.

‘ "I have told Miss Bennet several times, that she will never play really well, unless she practises more; and though Mrs. Collins has no instrument, she is very welcome, as I have often told her, to come to Rosings every day, and play on the piano forte in Mrs. Jenkinson's room. She would be in nobody's way, you know, in that part of the house." Mr. Darcy looked a little ashamed of his aunt's ill breeding, and made no answer.'[1]

And so, even when the climax of mutual exasperation is reached, Elizabeth's criticism of Darcy meets some response in his consciousness, his statement of his objections to her family means something to her; and the way is open for each to consider anew the actions and character of the other. What Darcy has done is now shown afresh in his letter; this I do not find quite plausible. The manner is right, but not the matter: so much, and such, information would hardly be volunteered by a proud and reserved man—unless under pressure from his author, anxious to get on with the story. And perhaps it may be the same pressure that hastens Elizabeth's complete acceptance of its witness; for there is no time to lose; she must have revised her whole impression of him before her visit to Pemberley—revised it confidently enough to be able to indicate as much clearly to Wickham, for our benefit:[2] 'I think', she says enigmatically in answer to his searching questions, 'Mr. Darcy improves on

[1] p. 173, ch. viii.
[2] But not, unfortunately, for Scott's. He may be suspected of skipping when he says that Elizabeth 'does not perceive that she has done a very foolish thing [in refusing Darcy] until she accidentally visits a very handsome seat and grounds belonging to her admirer' (review of *Emma*, pp. 194, 195).

acquaintance.' This disturbs and provokes him to further
inquiry: '"For I dare not hope," he continued in a lower
and more serious tone, "that he is improved in essentials."
"Oh, no!" said Elizabeth. "In essentials, I believe, he is
very much what he ever was"'—and she develops this
proposition to Wickham's discomfort.[1]

The Pemberley visit is to supplement this revised impression of Darcy with evidence as to character: Mrs. Reynolds
is a useful piece of machinery—but I do not think that the
more exacting Jane Austen of the later novels would have
been content with her. It is more to the purpose that here
Darcy and Elizabeth see one another for the first time in
favourable—even flattering—circumstances: he at his best
on his own estate (a piece of nice observation), and she
among congenial companions. Lydia's disgrace has still to
come—to give him opportunity for proving that he has
taken her strictures to heart, to show her how much she
values those hopes of a better understanding which it seems
bound to frustrate. And Lady Catherine will involuntarily
give the last turn to the plot by her interference. But these
are needed to bring about rather the marriage than the better
understanding. *That* had sprung from the very nature of
the misunderstanding, from the interaction of character and
circumstance. There had been, for example, something of
wilfulness, even of playfulness, in Elizabeth's mood from
the first, to promise eventual reaction: 'I dare say you will
find him very agreeable', Charlotte Lucas assures her, when
she is to dance with Darcy; and she replies: 'Heaven
forbid!—*That* would be the greatest misfortune of all!—
To find a man agreeable whom one is determined to hate!—
Do not wish me such an evil.'[2]

Exactness of symmetry such as this carries with it one
danger. The novelist's subtlety of apprehension may be
numbed by this other faculty of his for imposing order on
what he apprehends. His apprehension of human relationships, for example, may fail to develop or, if it develops, fail
to find due expression because he is impelled to simplify
these relationships in his story in the interests of its pattern.

---

[1] *Pride and Prejudice*, p. 234, ch. xli.   [2] Ibid., p. 90, ch. xviii.

To a contemporary it might perhaps seem, when *Pride and Prejudice* appeared, that such a misfortune was about to overtake Jane Austen.[1] *Mansfield Park* shows that it did not. In the earlier novels, all those indefinable sympathies and antipathies which, like filaments, connect people whom kinship or fortune associates, occasionally threaten to be resolved into likes and dislikes, or even reduced to the simpler terms of approval and disapproval. These sympathies and antipathies have been adroitly complicated by misunderstandings; but such misunderstanding of the character and conduct of other people is simple compared with the Bertrams' and Crawfords' misunderstanding of the nature of their relationships, one to another and each to himself. For *Mansfield Park* is a comedy, with grave implications, of human interdependence numbly unrealized or wilfully ignored until too late. And as Lady Bertram's unreflective response to events serves to register their pressure, so the perverse reaction of each of the family to the thrusts and strains of human relationships is used in making us understand their force.

Lady Bertram, in her simplicity, is (as I have suggested) less deceived than any of her sons and daughters; though, well as she knows herself to be dependent on others, she hardly recognizes the feline character of this dependence— on any one who will make her comfortable—nor her real indifference as to which niece performs this service. Tom and Julia have to learn, belatedly and unhappily, the insecurity of their fancied independence. Mrs. Norris and Maria, in their self-assurance, are farthest from realization of the truth—Mrs. Norris's favourite phrase 'between ourselves', with its suggestion of conspiracy and wire-pulling, being pitiably at variance with her ignorance and impotence. Maria is most disastrously mistaken: she discounts passion,[2] convinces the most careful observer in her own family that 'her feelings are not strong',[3] and enters on the relationship

---

[1] Not having seen a recent dramatization of it, he would not realize how much farther its human relationships could be simplified.

[2] J. A.'s treatment of this miscalculation and its outcome is the best answer to Charlotte Brontë's charge: 'She has no acquaintance with the passions.'

[3] p. 116, ch. xii.

of marriage in a mood whose frigid ugliness is communicated to us by the device of relinquishing all mention of the engagement to those unfeeling people, the conventional sentimentalists. 'The general lookers-on of the neighbourhood . . . had, for many weeks past, felt the expediency of Mr. Rushworth's marrying Miss Bertram.'[1] And when this expectation is fulfilled, Mrs. Norris and old Mrs. Rushworth, with her 'stately simper', sit nodding and smiling over the couple in an ecstasy of false sentiment. 'It is quite delightful, ma'am, to see young people so properly happy, so well suited, and so much the thing!'[2] Mrs. Norris remarks complacently; and the intonation of irony in her author's voice anticipates her treatment of the wedding, when her abhorrence of human relationships controlled by unfeeling calculation will almost make her forget her habitual reticence, and present herself as a condemning spirit:

'It was a very proper wedding. The bride was elegantly dressed—the two bridemaids were duly inferior—her father gave her away—her mother stood with salts in her hand, expecting to be agitated—her aunt tried to cry—and the service was impressively read by Dr. Grant. Nothing could be objected to when it came under the discussion of the neighbourhood, except that the carriage which conveyed the bride and bridegroom and Julia from the church door to Sotherton, was the same chaise which Mr. Rushworth had used for a twelvemonth before. In every thing else the etiquette of the day might stand the strictest investigation.'[3]

The actual pattern of human relations at Mansfield is visible only to the reader, to whom alone it is allowed to occupy Fanny's observation-post, and, with perception quickened by her sensibility, but with more critical detachment, to gather and relate impressions derived from the motions of all the characters; to appreciate, moreover, the irony of this very situation. For to the rest of the characters it would be incomprehensible: to the Bertrams and Crawfords alike Fanny is the only *dependant* at Mansfield—they have not insight to perceive any but material need; how should they realize that she, having reached through

painfully acquired self-knowledge independence beyond
their imagining, often understands their feelings more clearly
than they do themselves? 'Fanny saw and pitied much of
this in Julia; but there was no outward fellowship between
them. Julia made no communication, and Fanny took no
liberties. They were two solitary sufferers, or connected
only by Fanny's consciousness.'[1] *Solitary*—the very word
is echoed when Fanny returns to Mansfield and finds her
aunts and Tom numbed by calamity; they had been together, she returned as though from exile; but her isolation
had not been more entire than theirs: 'They had been all
solitary, helpless, and forlorn alike.'[2] It is Fanny alone who,
her sense of the reality of human interdependence sharpened
by her own sense of need, can 'connect them by her consciousness'. Even Edmund has his share of the family
obtuseness as to human relations—so that to Fanny his
very kindness has often been more painful than the harsh
usage of her other cousins. 'Your uncle thinks you very
pretty, dear Fanny', he tells her. '. . . Anybody but myself
would have made something more of it, and any body but
you would resent that you had not been thought very pretty
before; but the truth is, that your uncle never did admire
you till now—and now he does. Your complexion is so
improved!—and you have gained so much countenance!—
and your figure—Nay, Fanny, do not turn away about it—
it is but an uncle.'[3] (His own habit of turning towards her
whenever he wished to receive or impart confidences should
have revealed to him their mutual need.)

'Forethought', Trollope says, 'is the elbow grease which
a novelist requires. . . . To think of a story is much harder
work than to write it.'[4] Particularly hard, I should guess, if
the story is of such an ordered complexity as are all Jane
Austen's novels; hardest of all, if its substance is of the kind
which composes her Chawton novels—of which one might
almost say, that it would bleed if violence were done it.
The forethought that she needs, and uses, for them could

---

[1] p. 163, ch. xvii.
[2] p. 448, ch. xlvii.
[3] pp. 197, 198, ch. xxi.
[4] *Thackeray* (E. M. L.), 1879, pp. 122, 123.

fairly be praised in the terms that Thackeray applies to
Tom Jones, when he calls it

'the most astonishing production of human ingenuity. There is not an
incident ever so trifling, but advances the story, grows out of former
incidents, and is connected with the whole. Such a literary *providence*,
if we may use such a word, is not to be seen in any other work of
fiction . . . the history of Tom Jones connects the very first page with
the very last, and it is marvellous to think how the author could have
built and carried all this structure in his brain, as he must have done,
before he began to put it to paper.'[1]

This practice of forethought is so evidently important an
element in Jane Austen's art that it should be worth while
to ascertain its value and significance for her. This will not
be simple. The little that her letters tell us must, as usual, be
interpreted with the help of her practice itself.

Mere inconsequence irritates her, of course. She complains of *Fitz-Albini* that the story is 'told in a strange,
unconnected way. There are many characters introduced,
apparently merely to be delineated.'[2] The introduction of
parenthetical stories she has always found a little stiff and
absurd—'Will you favour us', asks one heroine of another
in an early burlesque, 'with your Life & adventures?'[3]
And this sense of absurdity has not diminished when she
drafts the *Plan of a Novel*. I should surmise that she was
particularly critical of any abuse of this licence for parenthesis in the novel because the dangerous prestige which
had been given to it by Fielding and Goldsmith[4] was being
renewed by Scott. 'You and I', she tells her nephew
Edward, when his novel is on the stocks, 'must try to get
hold of one or two [of Henry Austen's sermons], & put
them into our Novels;—it would be a fine help to a volume;

---

[1] *The Times*, Wednesday, 2 September 1840 (reprinted in *Stray Papers*, 1901,
p. 108)—review of an edition of Fielding's works with memoir by T. Roscoe. This
praise of Fielding's plot-architecture is not repeated in Thackeray's account of him
in his *English Humourists*. Compare with it the passage in the 'Introductory Epistle'
to *The Fortunes of Nigel*, in which Scott describes an ideally planned novel, and
concludes that *Tom Jones* must be its only exemplar.

[2] *Letters*, p. 32.   [3] *Jack and Alice* (*Volume the First*); p. 35, *Minor Works*, p. 20.

[4] 'Some . . . apology may be judged necessary for introducing a Legendary Tale
but slightly connected with the principal story. . . . The example of the inimitable
Goldsmith, and many later writers, who have successfully interspersed poetry with
prose in works of this nature, excited a wish to gratify the publick taste by similar
variety' (Jane West, *A Gossip's Story* (1797), Introduction).

& we could make our Heroine read it aloud of a Sunday
Evening, just as well as Isabella Wardour in the Antiquary,
is made to read the History of the Hartz Demon in the ruins
of St. Ruth. . . .'¹ She has, it is true, two of these parenthetical tales herself; but Willoughby's belongs to the
original form of *Sense and Sensibility*, to the novel-in-letters,
where—since the whole is built of the several contributions
of the characters—it is appropriate; and Mrs. Smith's will
have to be examined presently.² Elsewhere—for example, in
the story of Jane Fairfax and Frank Churchill—it is worth
noticing how carefully and skilfully she avoids this device.

Improvisation, on the other hand, she seems to condemn
only where it can be detected—to judge by this advice to
Anna: 'St. Julian's History was quite a surprise to me;
You had not very long known it yourself I suspect—. . . .
Had not you better give some hint of . . . [it] . . . in the
beginning of the story?'³ There survives, however, no
positive recommendation of 'literary providence' among
these letters to Anna; and, where it is referred to, it does
not obtain the warmest praise she has to give.

'Your Aunt C. does not like desultory novels,' she tells Anna, '& is
rather fearful yours will be too much so, that there will be too frequent
a change from one set of people to another, & that circumstances will be
sometimes introduced of apparent consequence, which will lead to
nothing.—It will not be so great an objection to *me*, if it does. I allow
much more Latitude than she does—& think Nature and Spirit cover
many sins of a wandering story—and People in general do not care so
much about it—for your comfort.'⁴

On this score, then, she ranges herself rather with 'people
in general' than with Cassandra. This is the only passage
among her letters which shows her in such a position. It
seems to tally, however, with the intention of two allusions.
In *Northanger Abbey*, which keeps, despite revision, something of the air of family entertainment,⁵ there is an aside
which sounds like mock defiance of familiar censorship:
to an account of the man whom Eleanor Tilney married,
'I have only to add', she says, '—(aware that the rules of

---

¹ *Letters*, p. 468.   ² See pp. 192–194.
³ *Letters*, p. 421.   ⁴ Ibid., pp. 395, 396.
⁵ For example, in such private jokes as 'a very respectable man, though his name
was Richard' (p. 13, ch. i).

composition forbid the introduction of a character not connected with my fable)[1]—that this was the very gentleman whose negligent servant left behind him that collection of washing-bills, resulting from a long visit at Northanger, by which my heroine was involved in one of her most alarming adventures.'[2] This might, indeed, be a reply to any theorist, encountered in person or in print, but for its correspondence with that letter in which Jane teases Cassandra by threatening to follow fashion and diversify *Pride and Prejudice* by the introduction of 'something unconnected with the story', and ends impudently : 'I doubt your quite agreeing with me here. I know your starched notions.'[3]

These starched notions, then, she will not apparently allow to be essential; and yet they steadily govern her practice. The value which she deliberately assigns to forethought does not seem to tally with the pains she spends on it.

Now, I believe it to be a truth of wide application, but too seldom taken into account, that certain literary accomplishments are of value primarily to the writer, and only through their effect on him to the reader. Trollope, who stubbornly denied the very existence of artistic problems for the novelist, who flouted his admirers by representing himself as a mere retailer of fiction, differing from the grocer and draper only in that they sell by the pound or yard, he by the page—Trollope himself had to allow that the artist has to decide whether 'in fact he sells shoddy for broadcloth', and that he 'may have a difficulty which will not occur to the seller of cloth, in settling within himself what is good work and what is bad,—when labour enough has been given, and when the task has been scamped'.[4] This is indeed a teasing doubt, which I seem to hear again (though conditioned by personal differences) in the many passages in Kipling's stories that glorify those crafts, and those ways of life, in which a certain price is to be paid for a certain

[1] This 'rule' is observed in the frugal and legitimate use of Mrs. Younge in *Pride and Prejudice*.

[2] *Northanger Abbey*, p. 251, ch. xxxi.

[3] *Letters*, pp. 299, 300.   [4] *Autobiography* (1883), p. 144.

mistake, and in his exaltation of the incorruptible, unforgiving opponents—natural forces or machinery—against
which men in such circumstances pit themselves. This is
the artist's envy of the artificer. And to a novelist in particular every other workman must seem, by comparison with
himself, a very Robinson Crusoe, able to test the sea-
worthiness of the vessel he has made. Two distinct kinds of
accomplishment may, however, present themselves to him,
as test or challenge by whose means he can reassure himself;
and both (I think) are implied in that passage in Kipling's
autobiography which describes the great novel he was to
have written:

'. . . I dreamed for many years of building a veritable three-decker
out of chosen and long-stored timber—teak, green-heart, and ten-
year-old oak knees—each curve melting deliciously into the next that the
sea might nowhere meet resistance or weakness; the whole suggesting
motion even when, her great sails for the moment furled, she lay in some
needed haven—a vessel ballasted on ingots of pure research and knowledge, roomy, fitted with delicate cabinet-work below-decks, painted,
carved, gilt and wreathed the length of her, from her blazing stern-
galleries outlined by bronzy palm-trunks, to her rampant figure-head
—an East-Indiaman worthy to lie alongside *The Cloister and the Hearth*.'[1]

Surely that simile (for all its strangeness, and the odd
comparison in the close) clearly implies that, for his own
satisfaction and reassurance, Kipling would endeavour to
achieve a certain kind of symmetry and of factual verisimilitude—an accomplishment which (I believe) signified
to him a certain challenge met. Symmetry, both for him
and for Jane Austen, would be most obviously represented
by that exact and frugal articulation of parts, one with
another and every one with the whole, which I have already
illustrated, and also by precision of contrast and correspondence, such as 'chimes and cries tinke i' the close, divinely'.

For her, these correspondences will usually be ironic:
for example, there is the pattern made in *Pride and Prejudice*
by the argument on persuadability at Netherfield, by
Elizabeth's assertion that she will not risk her happiness on
the chance of being asked a second time in marriage, by
Mr. Bennet's recommendation of Wickham as a creditable

[1] *Something of Myself* (1937), p. 228.

jilt—and the answer to all these challenges; in *Emma* by the opinions of the characters set over against the facts which they are bound to learn. There are few of Emma's own estimates of the people in her little world—from her recommendation of Harriet as a suitable wife for Mr. Knightley[1] to her choice of Frank Churchill as confidant for her fancies about Jane and Mr. Dixon—which do not wake their own ironic echoes. On the very day of her humiliating discovery of the real Mr. Elton she has been rejecting John Knightley's warning, and 'amusing herself in the consideration of the blunders which often arise from a partial knowledge of circumstances, of the mistakes which people of high pretensions to judgment are for ever falling into'.[2] And even Mr. Knightley, for all his good sense, is not proof against this puckish magic, and must surely remember with vexation his former wish: 'I should like to see Emma in love, and in some doubt of a return; it would do her good.'[3]

Factual verisimilitude for Kipling meant command of outlandish facts such as it pleased him to collect arduously for *Captains Courageous*. What it meant for Jane Austen can be variously illustrated. Here and there in her criticism of Anna's novel, amidst the pervading care for 'nature', for consistent faithfulness to observed truth, she offers to correct this or that detail of fact. 'I have scratched out Sir Tho: from walking with the other Men to the Stables &c the very day after his breaking his arm—for though I find your Papa *did* walk out immediately after *his* arm was set, I think it can be so little usual as to *appear* unnatural in a book . . . Lyme will not do. Lyme is towards 40 miles distant from Dawlish & would not be talked of there.—I have put Starcross indeed. If you prefer *Exeter*, that must always be safe.'[4] Here and there in her references to her own novels she discloses the same careful habit: 'I learn from Sir J. Carr that there is no Government House at Gibraltar. I must alter it to the Commissioner's.'[5]

Care, of this sort, we might have inferred from the smooth

---

[1] *Emma*, p. 64.   [2] Ibid., p. 112, ch. xiii.
[3] Ibid., p. 41, ch. vi.   [4] *Letters*, p. 394.
[5] Ibid., p. 292. Sir John Carr is her informant through his *Descriptive Travels*; see Index V to the *Letters*.

surface of her work,[1] and from what has been discovered as to her method—for I can see no reason for doubting the conclusions of Dr. Chapman and Sir Frank MacKinnon: that, using the almanac of the current or a recent year, she constructed time-schemes for her novels,[2] nor Sir Frank MacKinnon's further supposition that she used road-books for similar topographical schemes. 'As she had an almanac for her dates,' he says, 'so, I have little doubt, Jane Austen used Paterson's or Carey's road-books for the travels of her heroes and heroines',[3] and he shows, in an examination of the novels severally, how regularly the distances tally with the time spent in covering them. I cannot believe that this custom was for her merely what Stevenson called 'a precaution', a means of avoiding 'some of the grossest possible blunders'.[4] Rather it has the air of a device by which the artist may ease, if not satisfy, his desire for a problem more definite than any that the practice of his art affords, simply in the exercise of skill and pains. It may be significant— but, from such casual evidence, we cannot be certain—that, while she surely used a road-book in correcting Anna's novel—'They must be *two* days going from Dawlish to Bath; They are nearly 100 miles apart'[5]—she does not apparently recommend the use of one to her. This I guess to have been her private game, or known only to Cassandra. Her nephew and nieces make no mention of it.

Surely a satisfying sense, as of a challenge fairly met, must come from making the facts of your imaginary world rhyme(as it were) both with those of the actual world and with one another—correspond with those by simple resemblance, with these by ironic likeness in difference. To have done either is to have solved a stubborn problem; to do both together is more than the solving of two such problems. For their demands are not easily reconciled. In the familiar world which (by her very observance of factual

---

[1] An orchard in blossom at midsummer (*Emma*, p. 360, ch. xlii) stands out as the one error detected.

[2] See appendix (to each novel except *Sense and Sensibility*) on Chronology.

[3] 'Topography and Travel in Jane Austen's Novels' in *The Murder in the Temple and other Holiday Tasks*, 1935, p. 86.

[4] 'My First Book' in *The Art of Writing*, p. 130 (I doubt whether it was merely this for him).   [5] *Letters*, p. 395.

verisimilitude) Jane Austen invites us to compare with hers events do not often 'chime and cry tink in the close'.

More and more clearly her art seems to present itself as one that derives from a capacity for due consideration of claims which may conflict, an art of reconciliation, of harmony.

It is this due consideration of the claims of plot and character, of symmetry and verisimilitude, that makes possible the subtle integrity of the Chawton novels.

II. THE NARRATOR AND HIS READER

(i) *The means of communication*

There is another sort of harmony to be achieved by a writer besides harmony among the elements of his work: agreement—not in opinion, but in direction of exertion—between himself and his reader. His aim, Vernon Lee argues, in her essay on Style, is to convey his meaning to the reader 'with the least possible difference between the effect produced and that intended, and also with the least possible wear and tear of the Reader's capacity and goodwill. . . .' She develops this notion figuratively: the writer

'must, as it were, drive the Reader to a certain goal along a certain road of his choice; and the Reader . . . , like a horse, . . . has to be always kept awake, and kept extra awake whenever any new turn is coming, so that much of the craft of writing consists in preventing the Reader from anticipating wrongly on the sense of the Writer, going off on details in wrong directions, lagging behind or getting lost in a maze of streets. . . . People catch naturally at what is most familiar to them, as a horse turns naturally down the streets he knows; and considerable attention on the part of the literary coachman is required to forestall such effects of habit.'[1]

This figure will no doubt serve for the writer intent on exposition or persuasion: a reader, brought to the conclusion of an argument by a capable writer, has something in common with a horse responding to a good driver. But for the story-teller this is only half of the problem. For him it is necessary to control attention—without allowing his reader to suspect him of such activity, until the illusion he

[1] Vernon Lee, 'On Style' in *The Handling of Words* (1923), pp. 40, 41, 42.

designs has been formed. The essayist may at least say himself what he wishes said. But the story-teller must compel his story to say it for him—because, if he does not, it will leave him to say it over its corpse. Once the illusion has been created, however, his reader may be, as it were, half-horse, half-man; may like to *feel* himself well handled, to *understand* the skill with which his attention and energy have been directed. This double response makes the pleasure of re-reading work of so fine a texture as Jane Austen's, where so much is missed by so brief a failure of attention. (But if we speak too volubly of this pleasure we may seem to be playing a private game, and so make enemies, not for ourselves—which would not matter—but for her.)

Now the story-teller's problem may be peculiar; but so is the power at his disposal. His relation to the reader may sometimes forbid direct communication; but he is able to communicate with him indirectly, by means of the consciousness of his characters. To use it profitably he must seem to efface himself. And an important development in Jane Austen's art is that of the technique of self-effacement.

This technique is shown most simply, but most sharply, in those cases where she wishes not merely to convey, but also to lay so-and-so much emphasis (weighed, as usual, to a scruple) on some small piece of information—that is, to direct our attention. The first necessity is, of course, to find the right place for it. Fielding, when he came to write *Amelia*—tired, and perhaps impatient with the elaborate mechanism of narration that he had invented—no longer exerted himself for this, but was content to inform the reader of Mrs. James's passion for Booth so long after the incident which it should have explained that he could not disguise the awkwardness of the arrangement but had to excuse it by a languid pleasantry: 'This will account for some passages, which may have a little surprised the reader in the former chapters of this history, as we were not then at leisure to communicate to them a hint of this kind; it was, indeed, on Mr. Booth's account that she had been at the trouble of changing her dress at the masquerade.'[1] Jane

[1] Bk. xii, ch. i.

Austen sets about a like task with her usual method and tact: in his first letter to Fanny at Portsmouth Edmund mentions that the Grants are to leave Mansfield for a while. Thus, information is conveyed to us unobtrusively—in the shape of such a trifle of family news as might while still fresh find place in a letter. This unobtrusiveness, however, may allow us to overlook it, and therefore Edmund, out of its very insignificance for himself, makes a rueful joke: '. . . Your aunt seems to feel out of luck that such an article of Mansfield news should fall to my pen instead of her's.'[1] And, lest this should not be enough, the author herself, in her established character of amused commentator on manners in general, takes up his theme:

'Every body at all addicted to letter writing, without having much to say, which will include a large proportion of the female world at least, must feel with Lady Bertram, that she was out of luck in having such a capital piece of Mansfield news, as the certainty of the Grants going to Bath, occur at a time when she could make no advantage of it, and will admit that it must have been very mortifying to her to see it fall to the share of her thankless son, and treated as concisely as possible at the end of a long letter, instead of having it to spread over the largest part of a page of her own.'[2]

And so we pass on easily to the description of Lady Bertram's style in letter-writing—well prepared, without realizing it, for Mary Crawford's remarkably indiscreet application to Fanny for information as to Tom's chance of recovery, and the reason for it: 'Had the Grants been at home, I would not have troubled you.'[3]

A more complex example of this kind of tact is afforded by *Emma*, in the mode of presenting a particular train of events, so that we may realize exactly all their intricate interplay of character and circumstance, their comic pattern pricked on a ground of everyday life, without ever suspecting that our attention is being manipulated. And since their 'visible structure' is so light and fine that *Emma* has been called (even by Jane Austen's fellow novelists[4]) a novel without a plot, it may be worth while to illustrate this mode

---

[1] *Mansfield Park*, p. 424, ch. xliv.
[2] Ibid., p. 425, ch. xliv.
[3] Ibid., p. 434, ch. xlv.
[4] Scott, Susan Ferrier, Mr. E. M. Forster.

of presentation by tracing them throughout the course of
the quarrel between Jane Fairfax and Frank Churchill. In
such a situation as these two have framed, her caution and
his recklessness are bound to strain their relationship. His
reference at Hartfield to a piece of local gossip (which has
reached him through one of her letters)—a blunder carelessly
made and mischievously enjoyed—prompts Miss Bates's
admission that her household has been the source of information, and her unlucky comment: 'I will not positively
answer for my having never dropt a hint, because I know I
do sometimes pop out a thing before I am aware. I am a
talker, you know; I am rather a talker; and now and then I
have let a thing escape me which I should not. I am not
like Jane; I wish I were. I will answer for it *she* never
betrayed the least thing in the world.'[1] This is too much
for Frank, and it provokes him to tease Jane in the alpha-
bet game—inexcusably, but he might have obtained pardon
for it the next time he came to Highbury if he had not, by
the very plausible coincidence of Mrs. Churchill's 'nervous
seizure', arrived at the wrong moment—too late to find Jane
at Donwell, where, in the security of a large party, she would
have spoken to him, soon enough to meet her on the road,
where she would not, and where her refusal would exasper-
ate him into further offences. For the outcome of that
meeting is his outrageous flirtation with Emma at the
morrow's 'exploring party', which makes itself intelligible
to Jane in the cruel reference to engagements hastily formed
and soon regretted—'How many a man has committed himself on a short acquaintance, and rued it all the rest of his
life!'[2] Her guarded reply should warn him that he must
seek a reconciliation at once or it will be too late; but he is
a poor listener to words and no listener at all to silences,
and so he keeps his petulance warm with a final burst of
Byronic enthusiasm for foreign travel and, like Emma herself on this very occasion, departs with his fault unacknow-
ledged and unpardoned. But, unlike Emma, he wilfully
forgoes further opportunity: leaving Highbury, he allows
Jane to learn, through the talk of servants, not only that he

[1] *Emma*, p. 346, ch. xli.   [2] Ibid., p. 372, ch. xliii.

is gone but also that no vagary of Mrs. Churchill's health has
been the occasion—and so to nerve herself to signify that
their engagement is at an end, by writing to him and by
closing with Mrs. Elton's proposal. Here, in particular,
the workmanship is of cobweb lightness and fineness, and
yet firm. Emma, visiting Miss Bates the next morning, to
convey her sense of her own need for pardon, is met by the
news of the closure with Mrs. Elton and, being contrite
enough to persist in her polite inquiries as to the circumstances, elicits for us the complete sequence of events:
Jane's decision, announced on the previous evening at the
rectory, has been not merely sudden, but directly opposed
to her mood of 'the day before yesterday, the very morning
we were at Donwell'.[1]

' "I was so astonished when she first told me what she had been saying
to Mrs. Elton, and when Mrs. Elton at the same moment came congratulating me upon it! It was before tea—stay—no, it could not be
before tea, because we were just going to cards—and yet it was before
tea, because I remember thinking—Oh! no, now I recollect, now I have
it; something happened before tea, but not that. Mr. Elton was called
out of the room before tea, old John Abdy's son wanted to speak with
him. Poor old John, I have a great regard for him; he was clerk to my
poor father twenty-seven years; and now, poor old man, he is bed-
ridden, and very poorly with the rheumatic gout in his joints—I must
go and see him today; and so will Jane, I am sure, if she gets out at all.
And poor John's son came to talk to Mr. Elton about relief from the
parish: he is very well to do himself, you know, being head man at the
Crown, ostler, and every thing of that sort, but still he cannot keep his
father without some help; and so, when Mr. Elton came back, he told
us what John ostler had been telling him, and then it came out about the
chaise having been sent to Randall's to take Mr. Frank Churchill to
Richmond. That was what happened before tea. It was after tea that
Jane spoke to Mrs. Elton." '

'Miss Bates would hardly give Emma time to say how perfectly new
this circumstance was to her; but as without supposing it possible that
she could be ignorant of any of the particulars of Mr. Frank Churchill's
going, she proceeded to give them all, it was of no consequence.'[2]

And they include the reassuring note from his uncle as to
his aunt's health.

There it all is: the sequence of small events—whose
order is so significant yet to Emma so meaningless that she

---

[1] Ibid., p. 380, ch. xliv.   [2] Ibid., pp. 382, 383, ch. xliv.

suffers the recital only as an act of penance—suspended in
the limpid confusion of Miss Bates's talk, and by this
means brought into the closest possible relation with the
course of everyday life at Highbury by which they are
conditioned. We seem to draw them from their source by
our own exertions, without the least interference by the
author.

Tactful direction of the reader's attention to particular
circumstances is, however, among the simplest of the tasks
imposed on the narrator by their peculiar relationship, made
possible by a wise use of the characters in the story as a
means of communication between them. *Sense of place*,
for example, can be communicated in this way. Sense of
place is important in Jane Austen's novels—not sentiment
of place, which, judged by romantic standards, she wants
altogether. Passages describing the visible world are, as I
have said, rare in her novels, and those few are related to
the needs of the story: Mrs. Jennings's description of Dela-
ford describes Mrs. Jennings; Fanny Price's methodical
observation of the country between Mansfield and Sotherton is of value for what it tells us of Fanny; the picture of
Donwell (to which Mr. Read objects) is a picture of what
Emma sees, with appraising rather than observant eye.[1]
There is seldom much concrete particularization in these
passages. 'You describe a sweet place,' she writes to Anna,
'but your descriptions are often more minute than will be
liked. You give too many particulars of right hand & left.'[2]
But there is another possible significance in sense of place.
Jane Austen's foremost concern is with what Mr. Logan
Pearsall Smith calls 'the moral atmosphere of places, the
tones, that is, of collective feeling, the moral climates which
are produced by, and surround, different groups of people,
and fill, as with a body of dense and saturated air, the places
where they live'.[3] 'In Jane Austen's earlier novels,' he
continues, 'there is little or no diversity of moral climates;
but the rich effect of *Mansfield Park* is largely due to the
masterly contrast of the peace and quiet air of that mansion,

---

[1] See *English Prose Style*, pp. 118, 119.
[2] *Letters*, p. 401.   [3] *Reperusals and Recollections* (1936), p. 369.

with the very different weather which pervades Fanny's home in Portsmouth. In *Emma*, the air of Highbury is so dense that Jane Austen seems to have felt no contrast of climate was needed to enhance its rich effect; but *Persuasion* is rich in the chiaroscuro of these contrasts—the atmosphere of Kellynch, then that of Uppercross, and then the elegant air of Bath.'[1] This is suggestive, but so brief that it may be allowable to develop it a little; besides, it is not quite just to some of the earlier novels. The burlesque intention of *Northanger Abbey* requires that Catherine should find the Abbey featureless and unmeaning, because its moral climate is made not, as she supposes, by its history, but by its present owner—and he, once he ceases to be a Montoni in her eyes, becomes for her featureless and unmeaning. And the theme of *Pride and Prejudice* demands that, while there should be contrast between the moral climates of Meryton on the one hand and Rosings and Pemberley on the other, Elizabeth should not be so responsive to either as to be wholly subdued to it—that she should stand a little aloof from Meryton, should be unimpressed by Rosings, and studiously detached at Pemberley. There is no denying, however, Jane Austen's far greater power over atmosphere of place in the Chawton novels. The value of the contrast between Mansfield and Portsmouth catches the attention even of the casual reader; and, as Mr. Logan Pearsall Smith implies, Highbury is so presented as to satisfy by itself all need of variety. The social world of *Emma*, more complex than the family world of *Mansfield Park*, is constantly present to our imagination even before it becomes visible to our mind's eye; a faint but steady hum of talk seems to come from it: 'Mr. Frank Churchill was one of the boasts of Highbury, and a lively curiosity to see him prevailed, though the compliment was so little returned that he had never been there in his life. His coming to visit his father had been often talked of but never achieved.'[2] And when Highbury takes visible shape we understand why there is no need for Emma to leave it; where definition is so sharp and scale so exactly kept the contrasts which it offers within itself are

[1] Ibid., p. 370.   [2] *Emma*, p. 17, ch. ii.

sufficient. There is range enough between the 'busiest part
of Highbury' where Emma could watch 'the butcher with
his tray, a tidy old woman travelling homewards from shop
with her full basket, two curs quarrelling over a dirty bone,
and a string of dawdling children round the baker's little
bow-window eyeing the gingerbread'[1]—and the Martins'
farm where she leaves Harriet 'at the end of the broad,
neat gravel-walk, which led between espalier apple-trees to
the front door'.[2] The very disposition of the story demands
that it should stand alone, insular—should seem to warn us
that, if we were to grow discontented with these confines
and stray beyond them, we might find ourselves at Maple
Grove.

In Jane Austen's treatment of *place* in *Sanditon* Mr. E. M.
Forster sees something without precedent. While he finds
the fragment, as to 'character-drawing, incident and wit',
a mere echo of her earlier work, he detects elsewhere the
beginning of an experiment. 'Topography comes to the
front, and is screwed much deeper than usual into the story.'[3]
Something of this new direction of interest he attributes to
the influence of Burns, Scott, and Wordsworth; and he concludes: 'Sanditon gives out an atmosphere, and also exists
as a geographic and economic force.'[4]

Sanditon is certainly a force, an agent, perhaps one
might even say a character, in the story. Emphasis is
deliberately laid upon it from the first. 'Everybody has
heard of Sanditon', Mr. Parker protests; and, sitting by the
road-side, he embarks on the first puff of it that the Heywoods have ever listened to; not, however, *his* first—that is
evident from the smoothness with which it runs from his
tongue: 'Such a place as Sanditon Sir, I may say was wanted,
was called for.—Nature had marked it out—had spoken in
most intelligible Characters.'[5] Nor can it be his last. We
have the impression that he was still murmuring, 'No Mud
—no Weeds—no slimey rocks——' as he was carried into

[1] *Emma*, p. 233, ch. xxvii.   [2] Ibid., p. 186, ch. xxiii.
[3] *Abinger Harvest* (1936), 'Jane Austen', p. 150 (he quotes in illustration the
passage describing Sanditon as Charlotte saw it from her window on arrival).
[4] Ibid., p. 151.
[5] *Sanditon*, p. 14; *Minor Works*, p. 369.

the house, and continued for the fortnight that he remained there. At least, when we next hear him speaking, on the journey home, he has returned to his favourite subject.

No, there is no doubt of the importance of Sanditon— but, 'a geographic and economic force'? The Parkers were to lose money over it, we may be sure; but if this was really to touch the lives of the people in the story, then Jane Austen had changed very much since *Sense and Sensibility*, and I see no other evidence for this change. A geographic force? Sanditon counts for something in the story, in virtue of its being Sanditon and not another place—not Eastbourne, not Brinshore—but does it count in this way more than Lyme does in *Persuasion*? It appears as though it must be going to count for more people—to show several facets, like the date of Sir Thomas Bertram's return in *Mansfield Park*. But I am not sure that it was going to make, as a place, such a deep impression on any one in the story as Lyme does on Anne. Indeed, I feel sure of only one thing—that we have not enough to judge by. *Sanditon* was making, as John Bailey points out,[1] a very slow start: it may have been something of an experiment; it was certainly written in the languor of ill health; besides, it is a rough draft, and would probably have undergone, with other revision, some pruning; at all events, its twelve chapters give us no certain clue to the way in which it was going to develop. And therefore I think that the last phase of Jane Austen's treatment of *place* is best studied in *Persuasion*. There I see it 'screwed deep into the story'; for the story of *Persuasion* can be described not solely as the reconciliation of Anne and Wentworth, but also as the bursting open, for Anne, of the prison that Sir Walter and Elizabeth have made of Kellynch—the expansion of her world. This is represented by Jane Austen (with her unfailing choice of the right tool for her own aptitude and purpose) not by analysis but by a peculiar nicety of planning. The introductions of the several characters are so contrived that they contribute to this impression of an expanding world.

In *Emma*, all characters of any consequence (except Mrs.

[1] *Introductions to Jane Austen* (1931), p. 135.

Elton) had been presented to us at the beginning, whether in person or by report. In *Persuasion*, the opening shows us the Kellynch party significantly grouped: Sir Walter and Miss Elliot side by side; Lady Russell, drawn towards Anne by her likeness to her mother, constant as the family friend who is called in at times of difficulty, to talk of plans with all the family, to think how they will affect Anne; and, under Lady Russell's disapproving eye, Mrs. Clay. They seem immovable; but presently the Crofts begin to be heard of, and a fresher air stirs—faintly at first, but, when they actually appear, irresistibly, for light as it is it has crossed the Atlantic.

'"What a great traveller you must have been, ma'am!" said Mrs. Musgrove to Mrs. Croft.

'"Pretty well, ma'am, in the fifteen years of my marriage; though many women have done more. I have crossed the Atlantic four times, and have been once to the East Indies, and back again; and only once, besides being in different places about home—Cork, and Lisbon, and Gibraltar. But I never went beyond the Streights—and never was in the West Indies. We do not call Bermuda or Bahama, you know, the West Indies."

'Mrs. Musgrove had not a word to say in dissent; she could not accuse herself of having ever called them any thing in the whole course of her life.'[1]

Meanwhile we have been allowed to suppose that even familiar Uppercross had some sort of freshness for Anne, after Kellynch, and so have received an impression of it through her reflective observation. She analyses impression and sensation as no earlier heroine in Jane Austen's novels had done:

'She acknowledged it to be very fitting, that every little social commonwealth should dictate its own matters of discourse; and hoped, ere long, to become a not unworthy member of the one she was now transplanted into.—With the prospect of spending at least two months at Uppercross, it was highly incumbent on her to clothe her imagination, her memory, and all her ideas in as much of Uppercross as possible.'[2]

Uppercross is presented more pictorially than any house in the earlier novels.

'To the Great House accordingly they went, to sit the full half hour in the old-fashioned square parlour, with a small carpet and shining floor, to which the present daughters of the house were gradually giving the proper air of confusion by a grand piano forte and a harp,

---

[1] *Persuasion*, p. 70, ch. viii.   [2] Ibid., p. 43, ch. vi.

flower-stands, and little tables placed in every direction. . . . The Musgroves, like their houses, were in a state of alteration, perhaps of improvement. The father and mother were in the old English style, and
the young people in the new.'[1]

This group, in its setting of family portraits, seems moreover
to reflect a new interest in the social organism; but whether
this means that Jane Austen's mood has changed, or that
she now has a heroine old enough to be interested in such
matters, cannot be determined. I think, however, that some
of the qualities which Mr. Forster detects for the first time
in *Sanditon* are already present in *Persuasion*—less obvious
because it is finished work.

The 'family-piece' at Uppercross looks as firmly settled
as that at Kellynch; but, where the Crofts are, stagnation is
impossible. They draw into this circle Frederick Wentworth; and he, with the talk of ships that naturally springs
up between the Admiral and himself, sets all the Musgroves fluttering. Presently he makes them understand
that this brave new world is not so remote but that they may
catch a glimpse of it, for his friends the Harvilles—of whom
he has spoken, and who, like the Crofts and himself, are
eagerly anticipated and make a distinct impression as soon
as ever they are mentioned—are found to be settled for
the winter at Lyme. And so the expedition to Lyme is
undertaken—Lyme which would have been memorable
even if Louisa had not chosen the Cobb for her escapade—
memorable to Anne for her poignant impressions of the
Harvilles' home, and for the *romantic* beauty and strangeness of the place—memorable to us because it is the first
time that Jane Austen has used this adjective sympathetically.
The description of the shore is, in spite of its impersonal
manner, surely intended to present it as Anne saw it, but
her author does not dissociate herself from her,[2] as she would
do from Marianne; there is eagerness in the very unusual
stumbling awkwardness of its sentences.

Lyme, however, seems likely to dwindle into a mere
'agreeable impression'. Anne must return to her father and

---

[1] Ibid., p. 40, ch. v.
[2] She shows us, indeed, more of Lyme than the visitors from Uppercross could
have seen; but I doubt whether she intended to do this, or knew she had done it.

sister—'ashamed to have it known, how much more she was thinking of Lyme, and Louisa Musgrove, and all her acquaintance there; how much more interesting to her was the home and the friendship of the Harvilles and Captain Benwick, than her own father's house in Camden-place, or her own sister's intimacy with Mrs. Clay'.[1] But Bath does not prove so strait a confinement as she has feared. She learns from Nurse Rooke, through Mrs. Smith, that not all of it is so dull as Camden Place; for they are denizens of that shabby-genteel world which remarks, not too gravely, what the genteel world is about; and as their quick tongues run over its affairs Camden Place itself comes to seem less formidable. This is not Anne's only—nor her most exhilarating—discovery: as soon as the Crofts arrive in Bath she sees the place afresh—thronged with congenial company. She falls into the habit of watching these two as they walk about:

'They brought with them their country habit of being almost always together. . . . Knowing their feelings as she did, it was a most attractive picture of happiness to her. She always watched them as long as she could; delighted to fancy she understood what they might be talking of, as they walked along in happy independence, or equally delighted to see the Admiral's hearty shake of the hand when he encountered an old friend, and observe their eagerness of conversation when occasionally forming into a little knot of the navy, Mrs. Croft looking as intelligent and keen as any of the officers around her.'[2]

This is the world to which, as she had felt at Lyme, she should herself belong—and which indeed is presently to receive her; the confines of the world she leaves being brought again to mind by our last sight of Sir Walter, brooding over the Baronetage, in his very posture of the opening scene.

Jane Austen had from the first possessed a sense as keen as a dramatist's of the importance of a proper introduction for every character—both as to the moment chosen and the manner. Mere smartness she could already command in her early days of burlesque-writing:

'My dear CHARLOTTE
' You could not have applied for information concerning the report of Sir George Lesleys Marriage, to any one better able to give it you than

---

[1] *Persuasion*, p. 124, ch. xiii.   [2] Ibid., p. 168, ch. xviii.

I am. Sir George is certainly married; I was myself present at the Ceremony, which you will not be surprised at when I subscribe myself
your

Affectionate

Susan Lesley.'[1]

From this she advances, through the mock-heroic entry of
the hero into *Sense and Sensibility*, to the lighter, brisker use
of anti-climax in *Pride and Prejudice*—first, for the Netherfield party at the ball, and then for the family of de Burgh:
' "And is this all?" cried Elizabeth. "I expected at least that
the pigs were got into the garden, and here is nothing but
Lady Catherine and her daughter!" '[2]

It is not until *Persuasion* that the entry of a new character
is charged with more than comic significance—that it can
imply *our* entry into a new human world; not until Jane
Austen has conceived a heroine endowed with such sensitiveness as Anne's to these distinctions between one 'moral
climate' and another, capable of the wish 'that other Elliots
could have her advantage in seeing how unknown, or
unconsidered there [at Uppercross], were the affairs which
at Kellynch-hall were treated as of such general publicity
and pervading interest'.[3]

Sense of time is at least as important as sense of place,
and probably harder to communicate. Mr. Lubbock refers
disparagingly to 'the order of story-tellers who imagine
that time may be expressed by the mere statement of its
length';[4] and certainly for the novelist the representation
of time is a problem which, in virtue both of its difficulty
and its importance, lies very near the centre of his art. In
this kind of fiction,[5] the narrator must convey a sense of
two sorts of time—the time of clocks and almanacs and the
time (so to speak) of human pulses. According to calendar-
time (if I may use some such convenient nick-name) Tuesday follows Monday at the same pace that Monday followed
Sunday, and they differ from one another no more than
days of the week should—they are not of different colours,

---

[1] *Love and Freindship*, p. 53; *Minor Works*, p. 116.   [2] *Pride and Prejudice*, p. 158.
[3] *Persuasion*, p. 42, ch. vi.
[4] *The Craft of Fiction* (1921), p. 228.
[5] That is, the *kind* of the novel, as distinct from the kind of allegory, or of fantasy.

do not smell different. According to what I must call personal time (since it is not identical for any two people) Monday may bustle after Sunday, Tuesday lag after Monday, and if they are surveyed in retrospect Wednesday may seem no farther away than Thursday. A story conducted by the time of clocks and calendars alone would be a story not of human beings but of **mechanical** toys. Such may be a satirist's intention; the clock that governs the day of Crabbe's prude 'clicks from prayer to prayer, from meal to meal'; but this impression must not be conveyed, unless designedly. Yet these irregularities of 'personal time' proper to a story of human beings are only perceptible as deviations from the norm of clock-time—derive their value, as do the variations in verse, from the presence of a pattern.

Jane Austen's two great predecessors, whom she found established as models for English novelists, had discovered each his own solution for this problem, one proper to his genius and to the conventions of narrative art that he had formed. Richardson, with his skill in adjustment of means to end, had created, by his progression from letter to letter (and, in the journals, from entry to entry), that 'close, hot, day-dreamy continuity' which Coleridge noticed :[1] and where a strong enough sense of continuous time has been achieved the imagination can dispense with reminders of clock-time's regular beat against the emotional rhythm of the characters' lives. Fielding's method is nearer akin to the dramatist's, but skilfully fitted for service to narrative art: he presents scenes of which the pace approximates, as nearly as the conventions of the stage demand, to clock-time, and links them one to another by his custom of addressing the reader in the intervals; thus pledging his credit for the continued existence of his characters, but varying the pace of that existence. This device is proper only where the narrator is ready to appear in person; there-

[1] *Coleridge's Miscellaneous Criticism*, ed. T. M. Raysor, 1936, p. 303 (notes on *Tom Jones*, from *Literary Remains*). The phrase seems to have struck Thackeray as apt; he quotes it in his *English Humourists*.

Fanny Burney is lost when she departs from the novel-in-letters, and the method with which Richardson had endowed it.

fore Jane Austen occasionally avails herself of it in *North-anger Abbey*—that is, in those parts where she allows her own voice to be heard interpreting the burlesque inten-tion.[1]

'Monday, Tuesday, Wednesday, Thursday, Friday and Saturday have now passed in review before the reader', she says (towards the beginning of the visit to Bath, and before Henry has begun to perceive Catherine's foible and play upon it); 'the events of each day, its hopes and fears, mortifications and pleasures have been separately stated, and the pangs of Sunday only now remain to be described, and close the week.'[2] And at the end she reappears in person, professing a doubt whether the anxiety of Catherine and Henry can touch the readers, 'who will see in the tell-tale compression of the pages before them, that we are all hastening together to perfect felicity'.[3] But a very different method is needed, and found, for her other novels.

There was, indeed, no model of general usefulness avail-able for English novelists. The need of one is illustrated by the ingenuous clumsiness of the lesser people, such as Mrs. Inchbald, who, though a workmanlike story-teller in other respects, often mismanages her representation of time. Up to the opening of Chapter XXIV in *A Simple Story*[4] (for example), she advances at her most leisurely pace, but this opening itself contains a summary account of a few weeks, and within it the crisis of the story. Again, the first chapter of *Nature and Art*[5] is composed of a passage of dialogue (between two brothers travelling to London) which is closed by the words: 'In conversation such as this they pursued their journey. . . .' And upon this follows Chapter II: 'After three weeks passed in London, a year followed.' This is the sort of amateurishness that the young Jane Austen had ridiculed in *Volume the First*:

'At the end of 3 days Captain Roger and Rebecca were united and

---

[1] Before she surrenders this office to Henry Tilney, and after she resumes it.
[2] *Northanger Abbey*, p. 97, ch. xiii.
[3] Ibid., p. 250, ch. xxxi.
[4] 1791. It may be worth noticing that her technique was probably learnt from the stage; if so, she had not found out how to modify it.
[5] 1796.

immediately after the Ceremony set off in the Stage Waggon for the Captains seat in Buckinghamshire.

'The parents of Elfrida, alltho' they earnestly wished to see her married to Frederic before they died, yet knowing the delicate frame of her mind could ill bear the least exertion & rightly judging that naming her wedding day would be too great a one, forebore to press her on the subject.

'Weeks & Fortnights flew away without gaining the least ground; the Cloathes grew out of fashion & at length Capt: Roger & his Lady arrived, to pay a visit to their Mother & introduce to her their beautifull Daughter of eighteen.'[1]

Changes of pace are, of course, inevitable in any story which comprehends time beyond the strictest dramatic 'unity', and they are besides potentially valuable; but they are liable to remind us of the narrator's agency. Time must indeed be *made to pass*, by him, but we must not become aware of his presence without particular warrant for it. A narrator who is supposed to be inside the story may remark its passage, as Ellen Dean does in *Wuthering Heights*, may fix Isabella's death 'some thirteen years after the decease of Catherine, when Linton was twelve, or a little more', or may observe: 'That Friday made the last of our fine days, for a month.'[2] For memory keeps only this and that event, but connects them by belief in a continuous existence, marshalled by the seasons, of the one who remembers. But what business has the impersonal narrator with anything so personal as memory? He has to present the two sorts of time—the steady passage of the one, the irregular gait of the other—without letting us suppose that it is in his consciousness that they play against one another.

In *Sense and Sensibility*, Jane Austen had contrived to give some such impression of double time by contrasting the beat (as it were) of Elinor's normal with Marianne's feverish pulse, by making us realize the senselessness for Marianne of Elinor's sensible plea: 'Wait only till to-morrow.'[3] But this method seems to me to be timidly assayed; I do not think it suited her so well as that which she began to use in

---

[1] *Frederic and Elfrida* (*Volume the First*), pp. 17, 18; *Minor Works*, pp. 10, 11.

[2] Ch. xvii. I think that Mr. Muir overlooks the significance of the personal narrator when he comments on this use of dates in *Wuthering Heights* (*The Structure of the Novel* (1928), p. 101).

[3] *Sense and Sensibility*, p. 177, ch. xxviii.

Pride and Prejudice.[1] There, working on a time-scheme, she regulates pace by references to what may be called a Long-bourn calendar. The first six chapters present occasions evidently related in direct succession, but not dated. Then a carefully planned passage in the opening of Chapter VII suggests the pace at which events usually follow one another in the Longbourn world: the Miss Bennets are 'usually tempted' to visit Meryton 'three or four times a week, to pay their duty to their aunt and to a milliner's shop just over the way'. A seemingly casual indication of the time of year follows: 'At present, indeed, they were well supplied both with news and happiness by the recent arrival of a militia regiment in the neighbourhood; it was to remain the whole winter. . . .' And to this succeeds an unobtrusive suggestion that the narrative is settling down to a con-venient gait: 'Every day added something to their know-ledge of the officers' names and connections.'[2]

The conditions of *Mansfield Park* are more exacting: it is important that we should hold in imagination a composite impression of Fanny, as child and woman, and therefore she must be first presented to us some years before the crisis of the story. This imposes a double problem: there will be at least one sharp change of pace—from the rapid passage through Fanny's youth to the slow, and ever slower, movement of the days of intrigue and quarrel about *Lovers' Vows*. This change corresponds with a change in the rhythm of Fanny's own life—the dull, peaceful years sliding by unremarked, and then the uneasy days jerked, like a much knotted cord, through her hands. But that is a rhythm that can only be conveyed to us directly by a highly developed character, and the Fanny of those early years is not, and cannot suddenly become, such a character. Jane Austen solves this double problem by a carefully designed succession of references to dates which are signifi-cant for more than one of the family at Mansfield. She had already used simple anticipation of day or month to control

the pace of *Pride and Prejudice* : 'With no greater events than
these in the Longbourn family, and otherwise diversified
by little beyond the walks to Meryton, sometimes dirty and
sometimes cold, did January and February pass away.
March was to take Elizabeth to Hunsford.'[1] In *Mansfield
Park*, however, she creates anticipation which is shared
among several characters but wears a different aspect for
each. The first knot in the cord has been the arrival of the
Grants at Mansfield, an event connected with the 'losses on
his West Indian Estate' which take Sir Thomas Bertram
abroad. He leaves England 'with the probability of being
nearly a twelvemonth absent'.[2] Fanny, preoccupied with
expectation of William's leave, feels nothing but the natural
and proper wish for his safe return. Mrs. Norris takes it
upon herself to be anxious. To Maria and Julia, their
father's home-coming has a significance unsuspected by her,
and outside Fanny's comprehension.

'November was the black month fixed for his return. . . . Maria was
more to be pitied than Julia, for to her the father brought a husband,
and the return of the friend most solicitous for her happiness, would
unite her to the lover, on whom she had chosen that happiness should
depend. It was a gloomy prospect, and all that she could do was to
throw a mist over it, and hope when the mist cleared away, she should
see something else. It would hardly be *early* in November, there were
generally delays, a bad passage or *something*. . . . It would probably be
the middle of November at least; the middle of November was three
months off. Three months comprised thirteen weeks. Much might
happen in thirteen weeks.'[3]

The interval lessens, and an indication of it appears even on
the parsonage calendar : 'Every thing seems to depend upon
Sir Thomas's return', Mary Crawford says to her sister. In
their talk, however, it appears that another date besides is
coming to be urgently anticipated; the skein of cross-pur-
poses is to be disentangled 'as soon as the play is all over'[4]
—and gradually we become aware of a connexion between
these two events, an anxiety that they shall arrive in a certain
order. The pace is changing; the passage of time is recorded no longer in weeks but in days; without a jolt we are

[1] *Pride and Prejudice*, p. 151, ch. xxvii.   [2] *Mansfield Park*, p. 32, ch. iii.
[3] Ibid., p. 107, ch. xi.   [4] Ibid., p. 162, ch. xvii.

set down at one particular day, in the middle of its bustle of
expectation; and, suddenly but not awkwardly, that expectation is heightened by a single sentence which stands out
from the buzz of talk: '"I believe," said Fanny to her aunt
Bertram, "there will be three acts rehearsed to-morrow
evening, and that will give you an opportunity of seeing all
the actors at once."'[1] There is a sharp definition about
that 'to-morrow evening': all the characters seem to be
looking in one direction, at a particular point—and it is
not the point which is supposed to be occupying their
thoughts and wishes. This distinction is accentuated by
Mary Crawford's casual remark on the morrow morning:
'Could Sir Thomas look in upon us just now, he would
bless himself, for we are rehearsing all over the house.'[2]
Fanny, compelled to witness one of these rehearsals, between Mary and Edmund, reflects cheerlessly that she will
have to endure its repetition that very evening. The
evening brings this tensely expected rehearsal. It brings,
also, Sir Thomas Bertram.

After this first climax, the advance towards the second is
comparatively straightforward. Fanny is now no longer a
child, and her single consciousness will serve to communicate as much as we are meant to understand of the progress
of events, and, as the story begins to draw itself taut again,
to give it continuity with variation of pace, by her eager
anticipation first of William's visit, then (at Portsmouth) of
a letter from Edmund, or failing this from Mary Crawford.
'The postman's knock within the neighbourhood was beginning to bring its daily terrors.'[3]

I have not observed anything quite like this use of anticipation in previous English fiction. Now, of course, it is a
commonplace; but with development it has come to resemble one of those flowers that have attracted the nursery-
man's busy attention—that have increased in size, and
variety of colour; that are to be bought everywhere and at
all times of year; that have, indeed, everything to recommend them, except their original distinctive grace.

---

[1] Ibid., p. 167, ch. xviii.   [2] Ibid., p. 169, ch. xviii.
[3] Ibid., p. 398, ch. xl.

In *Mansfield Park*, then, we are presented with 'calendar-time' of the world as we know it and 'personal time' of human beings as we know them. And by the interplay of these two rather than by any visible agent the pace of the story seems to be firmly controlled. This control, moreover, makes possible bold and subtle variations, which themselves are useful in regulating emphasis—a gradually diminished pace, for example, giving the impression of continuous attention, and therefore of something of moment impending. (Charlotte Brontë has an acute sense of the value of this continuous attention and, in *Jane Eyre* and *Villette*, uses dreams to prevent a night's blank interval in the experience of her heroine before a crisis.) These variations of pace are valuable also on account of the variety of texture that they can give. It may be worth noticing that, if the pace of direct narrative is taken as the normal pace of a story, then passages of dialogue are likely to vary from it by seeming slower, and passages of reflection (on the part of the characters) most adaptable, and potentially slowest. Therefore alternation between one and another of these three will give variety of texture in this, as well as in the more obvious, way. It will need to be all the more carefully handled for this reason. There is, I think, a slight jerk in the transition from the story of the elder Mrs. Dashwood's fortunes to the celebrated discussion of her prospects between her stepson and his wife; but this may be allowable in the opening. In *Pride and Prejudice*, with its many outstanding passages of dialogue, which resemble in their completeness scenes of a play, this difficulty often besets the narrator and is narrowly evaded. *Emma* contains more dialogue, but it is more skilfully modulated into narrative and reflection.

It seems to me that Jane Austen becomes increasingly sensitive to this need for variety of pace, both for the sake of emphasis and for its own sake; and I conjecture that it was this sensitiveness (even more cogent than the personal motive which I have already mentioned) which impelled her to rewrite the end of *Persuasion*. As she originally drafted it, Chapter IX (of the second volume),[1] which is

[1] Ch. xxi of modern editions.

occupied with Mrs. Smith's disclosures, was directly followed by the encounter between Anne and Wentworth at
the Admiral's house. Thus nothing separated two long
and important passages of dialogue but the small piece of
narrative machinery required to carry Anne from Westgate
Buildings to Gay Street; and the peculiar pace of the crisis
of the story had been anticipated throughout a chapter.
Moreover, these two passages of dialogue are noticeably
similar: in each, a tentative beginning, broken talk at cross-
purposes conditioned by a misunderstanding as to the
relationship between Anne and Mr. Elliot, is succeeded by
a rush of talk releasing pent-up feeling so soon as this very
misunderstanding precipitates a better understanding. Yet
there is no suggestion of ironical correspondence intended;
nor is the similarity masked (as it might have been) by
concentration of the interest on Mr. Elliot in the first scene
—Mrs. Smith attracts it all to herself. Therefore it may
fairly be assumed that Jane Austen did not in fact notice the
similarity until she had reached the end—and suffered the
reaction of disappointment and dissatisfaction (perceptible
to her friends) which impelled her to rewrite this part.
Further, I conjecture, but more tentatively, that one of these
two passages must, as we now have it, be an afterthought.
Jane Austen's habitual forethought would hardly have
allowed her to make such a mistake in her plan for the novel
as a whole; it was in the course of executing this plan that
she succumbed to the state of fatigue in which mistakes are
made. I think, moreover, that it was Mrs. Smith who
developed beyond her author's original calculations. '*Mrs.
Smith's* history was quite a surprise to *me*,' Anna might have
retorted. 'You had not very long known it yourself, I suspect. . . . Had not you better give some hint of it in the
beginning of the story?' Mr. Elliot had been well prepared
for; Mrs. Smith had omitted even to leave her washing-bills
in an earlier chapter. I am ready to suppose some such
explanation as this: Jane Austen, in her original plan,
reckoned on no more than a communication from a minor
character for the machinery of exposing Mr. Elliot; but
Mrs. Smith developed under her hand into the admirable

creature she is. When she discovered the consequence of this development, Jane Austen was faced with the necessity of destroying one of these similar scenes—and chose to keep this lively piece of improvisation. The other—the scene at the Admiral's house—went (as I have suggested) against the grain of her habitual preference for respecting her lovers' privacy;[1] it also set the Admiral (whose delicate consideration for her feelings had warmed Anne's heart at Kellynch) in a situation which forced upon him the sly drollery of a figure of farce. I think there are indications that she was dissatisfied with his part in this scene even while she was writing it; the close of it had been drafted in these words: 'Capt. W.— had taken care to meet the Adm[1] as he returned into the house, to satisfy & to endeavour to silence him . . .'—but 'endeavour to silence' has been erased; '. . . the delicacy of the Admiral's good nature', she continues, 'kept him from saying another word on the subject to Anne.'[2] Surely she is uneasily aware that Admiral Croft has not acted with his usual delicacy in this scene?

One more detail supports me in my conjecture that the episode of Mrs. Smith, as we have it, may be improvisation; it is not neatly joined *at the end* to the rest of the narrative: Anne is intent on passing on her information to Lady Russell; she defers the occasion—and we are left in expectation of an episode of which, in fact, no more is said; when Lady Russell is next mentioned, she is in the act of 'relinquishing Mr. Elliot'.

The constant characteristic, at all events, of Jane Austen's representation of time is this: that it is rooted in her (gradually mastered) technique for using the consciousness of her characters as a means of communication with the reader.

It is worth noticing in this that eclectic habit of mind which governs every activity of her artistic faculties. So far as the outcome of these activities shows, she may never have given a thought—never have turned even with a fleet-

---

[1] 'I shall not dwell minutely on this Part of my Hero's Life', Sarah Fielding says, 'as I have too much Regard for my Readers to make them *third Persons to Lovers*.' *David Simple* (1744), bk. iv, ch. viii. I think that Jane Austen would have agreed with her unreservedly.

[2] *Two Chapters of Persuasion*, p. 26; see notes.

ing impulse of curiosity—towards the vagaries of human consciousness for their own sake—unless, perhaps, towards that one of them to which her own habits of mind drew her, its response to *reading*. For all we know, of course—so habitual is her reticence—she may have been keenly excited by these vagaries. But the evidence goes no farther than to show that she was at pains to understand just so much of them as she needed for the purpose to which she meant to put them.

This *consciousness* of fictitious characters is, of course, a variable medium. Indeed, to some writers the consciousness of their unreflective characters is of very little service. I have shown how, in a fictitious world where scale is exactly kept, action, however trivial, may be used significantly; how much is signified by Lady Bertram's 'putting away her work, moving Pug from her side, and giving all her attention and all the rest of her sofa to her husband', on his return.[1] I have shown, too, something of the mastery of idiom in dialogue by means of which Jane Austen makes the talk of her people communicate to us more than they are aware of themselves. 'Mr. Parker's Character & History were soon unfolded. All that he understood of himself, he readily told, for he was very openhearted;—& where he might be himself in the dark, his conversation was still giving information, to such of the Heywoods as could observe.'[2] When it is important that we should get the essence of his information, it may be distilled for us; his account of Sanditon, for example, comes to us as Charlotte Heywood, listening to him, sifted it out and arranged it in her shrewd, clear head. With such various ingenuity may the consciousness of the characters be used as a means of communication between story-teller and reader.

This is not the only function which the characters are able to perform. Wisely directed, they may, by their very positions, help him to mask the artificial isolation of the action of his story. Such isolation is, of course, inevitable. Perhaps it may best be described figuratively. The action of a story which is set in the familiar world of human inter-

---

[1] *Mansfield Park*, p. 179, ch. xix.   [2] *Sanditon*, p. 20; *Minor Works*, p. 371.

course is like a stone dropped into a pool—the narrator can show circles spreading outwards from that point—can even show how these encounter wind-flaws that were disturbing the surface before the stone entered the water; but—what is to happen when these spreading circles reach the brink? If they do this within our sight we receive the impression of water encircled by land—of the element we are regarding surrounded by another element—of human life surrounded by another kind of life. This may be well enough in medieval romance, whose human world is bounded by another and alien element. But it will hardly do for the daylight world of Jane Austen's novels, whose subject is 'three or four families in a country village'—not on Robinson Crusoe's island.

A novelist of a philosophical turn of mind may, I suppose, meet this difficulty by explicitly making his characters representatives of their species. It is more commonly dealt with, among English novelists, by means of a pervading impression of abundance, even of fertility—an impression which can best be conveyed by saying: They make us feel sure that, were a catastrophe to sweep away all of their characters but a pair, the world would be peopled again. Scott, Dickens, Thackeray, Trollope, all give this impression.[1] I do not know whether it is mere coincidence that these are all men, and that Mrs. Woolf achieves this sense of multiplicity by a way of her own, one that suggests multiplication by reflection from innumerable admirably arranged mirrors. At all events, that more familiar impression of abundance does not belong to Jane Austen's novels; and because her world is never in danger of being 'strangled by its waste fertility' it has been called sterile.[2] But this is to confuse difference of degree with difference of kind; she develops her own way of keeping the brink of the pool out of sight. It is a method analogous with that of pictorial perspective for persuading us that, if *these* objects are clearly visible because they are near, and *those* hard to see because they are far, then there

---

[1] I do not mean to imply that they create it deliberately, in order to solve this difficulty; rather it seems with them to be instinctive, a condition of their genius.

[2] e.g. H. W. Garrod, 'Jane Austen: A Depreciation'.

may well be others that are invisible because they are farther. By presenting her people in perspective, as none but a writer with an exact sense of scale can do, Jane Austen indicates recession, and so gives the impression of a limitless human world beyond her visible scene. Herein lies the value of many minor characters who contribute nothing to the impetus of the story.

The value of one group among these characters springs to the eye after a reading of Lady Balfour's essay on the servants in the novels.[1] What sort of density would Sir Thomas Bertram have if it were not for his 'friend Christopher Jackson'? So little that he would be in danger of evaporating when out of our sight; whereas we see him come and go, between his plantations and Lady Bertram's dressing-room, without the smallest fear of such an accident. In order to realize the importance of another such character, William Larkins, to his master, we have only to compare Mr. Knightley with Mr. Darcy. When Darcy leaves Elizabeth's (and our) presence, he has nowhere to go. (Most of those critics who generalize about Jane Austen's men have Darcy in mind; that is why a general account of them is usually unfavourable.) When Mr. Knightley escapes from the Hartfield drawing-room, it is to confer with William Larkins: William, whom we never see, but whose opinions on the disposal of his master's apples and his master's attention—'he had been walking away from William Larkins the whole morning, to have his thoughts to himself'[2]— establish him, solid and immovable, just beyond our range of vision. (He seems even to lend solidity to those fields and hedges and ditches that George and John Knightley talk about when they come together; Jane Austen's people generally have more to lend to landscape than to borrow from it.) Just within our range of vision, moreover, are set a number of silent characters: there is, for example, Mrs. Goddard, whose school rather than herself is described to us; who is 'almost always at the service of an invitation from

<hr />

[1] 'The Servants in Jane Austen', *Cornhill*, December 1929—an essay which delightfully discriminates these minor but not-to-be-spared characters.
[2] *Emma*, p. 449, ch. li.

Hartfield', to enjoy the food Emma provides—if Mr. Wood-house will let her eat it; who does nothing distinctive, and says nothing at all—but is individualized by a single delicate stroke: Harriet Smith, who thinks she can never wish to leave Hartfield and the flattering attentions she receives there, is thankful to go back to Mrs. Goddard when she feels ill. But there is no reckoning these figures in the distance and middle distance—whole families 'too numerous to mention' of Perrys, Coles, and Hayters, and Mrs. Long's obligingly plain nieces—characters who have no share in the story yet could not be spared. For Jane Austen communicates with us not only by means of the consciousness of her people—though that must always be her chief medium—but also by means of their aspect, even when they are seen as no more than the distant trees and hedgerows of her human landscape.

(ii) *The relationship established*

Landscape must owe something to the eye of the beholder. 'No novel, alas,' Anne Douglas Sedgwick writes in 1919, 'and I can't think how I shall, until there's some shape in the world.'[1] There was 'shape in the world' in which Jane Austen wrote—the firm contours of a society which to our eyes appears taut in resistance to threatened or impending change; but none of her contemporaries has her power to make us discern it. The lesser people can give us no assurance of an intelligible order in the arrangement of the room in which they sit—and Scott is looking out of the window. His eye does not focus on what is immediate—and they cannot see it in perspective.

Perspective implies a seeing eye, whether the narrator's or another, a point of view established; as Scott suggests when he argues that 'there is a distance as well as a foreground in narrative, as in natural perspective, and the scale of objects necessarily decreases as they are withdrawn from the vicinity of him who reports them'[2]—reports them if he

---

[1] *Anne Douglas Sedgwick, A Portrait*, letters chosen and edited by Basil de Selincourt, 1936, p. 195.

[2] 'Memoirs of Jonathan Swift', in *Miscellaneous Works*, 1827, ii. 491.

is an eyewitness (or supposed eyewitness—Scott is talking of Gulliver), and, even though he hold no such office, may yet be required to see them in perspective.

'The whole intricate question of method, in the craft of fiction,' Mr. Lubbock says, 'I take to be governed by the question of the point of view—the question of the relation in which the narrator stands to the story'[1]—a question which acquires new interest and complexity for everybody who reads his book, and indeed at every fresh rereading of it, so potent are its suggestions. They may not be accepted, but they must be met by any one who now analyses the art of the novel. What matters, Mr. E. M. Forster replies, is not so much the solution of this problem of the point of view as 'the power of the writer to bounce the reader into accepting what he says'.[2] But he is not to be propitiated when the point of view is altered in *Villette*.[3] And C. E. Montague, though he comes to the conclusion that 'in some moods one may find oneself thinking that the curious state of absorption and semi-belief (never literal belief), which we call illusion in a reader's mind, may be actually favoured by a certain easy-going way of the writer's, an unguarded-looking habit, an unprofessional seeming lack of technical apparatus'[4] in his dealing with the point of view, is never-theless sensible of the advantages of that nice management of it which Mr. Lubbock demands. It seems to me that his opponents are obliged to acknowledge the wastefulness of the methods he condemns, and that his most valuable con-tribution is indeed his fine sense of the means to conserve power, his refusal to praise spendthrift genius not because it is genius but because it is spendthrift; but it may be that this very bias of his critical practice makes him lay too much emphasis on *not being found out*, too little on positive power of persuasion.

Whether or no a study of Jane Austen's art must lead to such perplexing problems as those Mr. Lubbock discusses, it can surely be approached by way of some that are much

[1] P. Lubbock, *The Craft of Fiction* (1921), p. 251.
[2] *Aspects of the Novel* (1927), p. 107.
[3] Ibid., pp. 124, 125.
[4] *A Writer's Notes on his Trade* (1930), p. 49.

simpler. There is, for example, a means to understanding of her management of the point of view in those characters to whom she assigns a share of the task of interpreting people and events to us. This is, according to Mr. Forster, a favourite type with her—'the well-scoured channel through which comment most readily flows'[1]—a type which he finds successfully embodied in Elinor Dashwood, Fanny Price, and Anne Elliot, but with small promise of success in Charlotte Heywood. As to Charlotte, we cannot be sure what her function in the story was to be, knowing so little as we do of Clara Brereton's; perhaps these two, differing in temperament, were to divide the office of interpreter between them, and so give us a composite impression. The various uses that Jane Austen had made of this capability in her several heroines encourages conjecture; indeed, they cannot all be dismissed with a single epithet. To Elinor Dashwood the metaphor of a well-scoured channel for the author's own comments may be appropriate; for although she is uncertainly handled, and we are not given the means of deciding whether her change of feeling towards Mrs. Jennings signifies the clearing of her own vision or the softening of her author's mood, nor whether her *sense* was intended to leave her, so often as it does, at fault in reckoning likelihood, yet passages evidently designed to convey the *moral* of the story are cast into the form of her observations and reflections,[2] and for the expression of them she has been lent her author's cool dry wit.

As for Elizabeth Bennet, our chief reason for accepting her point of view as a reflection of her author's is the impression that she bears of sympathy between them—an impression of which almost every reader would be sensible, even if it had not the explicit confirmation of Jane Austen's letters. Yet, as she is presented to us in *Pride and Prejudice*, she is but a partial and sometimes perverse observer.

Fanny Price's case is different again. While the Elizabeth of *First Impressions* had been her author's contemporary,

---

[1] E. M. Forster, *Abinger Harvest* (1936), p. 149.
[2] e.g. the observations on Willoughby's conduct (pp. 331, ch. xliv, and p. 352, ch. xlvii).

Fanny is separated from hers by a generation; and this distance is kept. Entering the story as a child, Fanny *grows into* her office of observer and interpreter of the action. Her cousins and their new friends the Crawfords encounter and size one another up. 'And Fanny, what was *she* doing and thinking all this while? and what was *her* opinion of the new-comers? Few young ladies of eighteen could be less called on to speak their opinion than Fanny.'[1] She learns, it is true, to form an opinion—diffident but independent: '. . . she could never see Mr. Crawford with either sister without observation, and seldom without wonder or censure . . .';[2] gains, too, some insight into the springs of action, discerns Mary Crawford trying 'to be more ambitious than her heart would allow'.[3] And yet to the end she is bewildered (as a child may be) by many of the actions which she observes so clearly—by what is irrational, for example, in the attachment of Edmund and Mary Crawford: 'His objections, the scruples of his integrity' (she reflected), 'seemed all done away—nobody could tell how; and the doubts and hesitations of her ambition were equally got over—and equally without apparent reason. It could only be imputed to increasing attachment.'[4] And against Maria's passion she closes her consciousness. From the author who knows, and from us who are made acquainted with, much that she cannot or will not understand, Fanny is bound to keep this distance, to remain youth sympathetically observed, not youth re-lived. Besides, she evidently bears no resemblance to her author. Nevertheless on the moral issues of the story they share a point of view.

Thus Fanny's judgement, so far as it goes, is to be accepted as juster than that of any previous heroine—and sharply contrasted with Emma's. For it is Emma's part not merely to see everything that comes to her notice upside-down, but also, by her easy flow of worldly wisdom—'A man', she tells Mr. Knightley, as though speaking out of a lifetime's experience, 'always imagines a woman to be ready

---

[1] *Mansfield Park*, p. 48, ch. v.
[2] Ibid., p. 115, ch. xii.
[3] Ibid., p. 417, ch. xliii.
[4] Ibid., p. 367, ch. xxxvii.

for anybody who asks her'[1]—to give her author opportunity for ironical indication of her own views.

The fact is, of course, that while the mind of any of Jane Austen's heroines may be a means of communicating her opinions to us, the mode of communication may be complicated in any of several ways—irony being her favourite.

Moreover, she seems to have no habitual objection to direct intercourse with us. Apart from the explanatory openings of most of the novels, the notes of explanation which sometimes follow the introduction of a new character, and the moral analysis of the action in the close—in all of which we may hear her voice—she allows herself a general observation here and there. More often than not it is the satirist in her who speaks, though the tone may vary from the critical dissidence of *Sense and Sensibility*—'On every formal visit a child ought to be of the party, by way of provision for discourse'[2]—to the humorous acquiescence of *Persuasion*—'Husbands and wives generally understand when opposition will be vain.'[3] Sometimes it is a passage of sustained irony, such as the praise of ignorance as a womanly charm[4]—on which Miss Mona Wilson delightfully comments: 'The words are the words of Dr. Gregory, but it is the Wolf speaking, not Grandmamma.'[5] These interjections may be more common in the earlier novels, before she has learnt how to translate her critical impressions of society into their proper language; likewise her grave, matter-of-fact explanations of character and motive are to be found most often in this same early work, before she can count on her serious dialogue to carry its fair share. But she never relinquishes this method. *Sanditon* indeed suggests that she was apt to use it freely in a first draft, and her latest finished work shows that, even when she had assigned much of the responsibility for communication to her characters, she was content that some should rest with her.

Point of view, in fact, may mean position rather than

[1] *Emma*, p. 60, ch. viii.   [2] *Sense and Sensibility*, p. 31, ch. vi.
[3] *Persuasion*, p. 55, ch. vii.
[4] *Northanger Abbey*, pp. 110, 111, ch. xiv.
[5] *Jane Austen and Some Contemporaries* (1938), p. 35—referring to Dr. Gregory's *A Father's Legacy*.

vision; and whatever means of communication Jane Austen may choose, and however she may use it, she habitually establishes the heroine's *position* as the *point of view* for the story. I do not think this generalization need be modified by recognition of the rare occasions on which she allows us to be present in the heroine's absence, for (with one or two curious exceptions which must be considered presently) we learn by this means nothing that the heroine's *position* prevents her from knowing. For example, we hear Mrs. Weston and Mr. Knightley talking about Emma, but the opinions they exchange are opinions which neither conceals from Emma. Our point of vantage is still hers, whatever may be the difference in vision. Here lies, I believe, at least a partial explanation of Jane Austen's relinquishment of the novel-in-letters: in that form, however constant the vision (the moral and emotional point of view) may remain, the position (the point of vantage from which people and happenings are descried) must shift for every correspondent, as it shifts in *Lady Susan*.

I have tried to distinguish hitherto between the direct and indirect advantage of certain niceties of practice available to the novelist—between those that communicate their benefits immediately to the reader, and those that reach him through the satisfaction that the writer finds in them. The indirect advantage is evident here: the sense of stability suiting the particular writer. There is besides one plain direct advantage. Constancy of position suits a story in which there is a secret to be kept: such a plot as that of *Emma*, consisting in a series of happenings which, once their cause is revealed, appear in their true significance as intimations of what has not been seen; a story whose pattern is a secret kept until the end. *Persuasion* offers a less obvious, perhaps a more interesting, illustration. Its principal pattern is formed by the change in Wentworth's feelings towards Anne; and of the progress of this change we are allowed to judge only from a train of incidents which comes under her observation.

The point of vantage which we are to share with Anne is precisely indicated in the opening of the story; there we are made acquainted with the range of her field of vision. We realize that we are in possession of knowledge which is denied to the other characters in the book; few of them are aware that Wentworth's life has impinged upon hers, and of those few none knows her present feelings; but we know what their first strength was, and that it is not diminished. We can perceive, too, how poor is the visibility from her solitary observation-post, in the earlier weeks at least of the autumn in which the story opens; besides chance allusions, in talk which she may never encourage, must not even seem to understand, she has 'only navy lists and newspapers for her authority' as to his fortunes, and 'no reason to believe him married'.[1] They encounter, but his formal manner, outcome of resentment, withholds from Anne the means of estimating his feelings.

At this point comes the first, and more important, of the exceptions to Jane Austen's maintenance of the consistent point of view in this novel: not only does she tell us in her own voice something of those feelings, but she goes on to present Wentworth in intimate, if not quite candid, talk of them with his sister. This I can only suppose to be an oversight; for it is altogether different from the right to interpret manner which Jane Austen habitually reserves to herself. The episode is comparable only to those scenes in Mansfield parsonage which disclose to us, but not to Fanny, knowledge of Crawford's intentions towards her; and it jars more than they, because the opening of *Persuasion* has suggested no such composite impression as had that of *Mansfield Park*. I surmise that Jane Austen had always been liable to fall back upon various means of explanation in momentary failures of confidence,[2] and that here, in a novel which had not had time to become a 'gradual performance', she had not yet noticed the inappropriateness of this one. It may be convenient to point out here the other, and lesser, oversight of this kind, the gossip about Anne and Mr.

----

[1] *Persuasion*, p. 30, ch. iv.

[2] She felt, it seems, some anxiety that Henry Crawford should be rightly understood by the reader. 'Henry is going on with "Mansfield Park"', she writes to Cassandra. 'He admires H. Crawford: I mean properly, as a clever, pleasant man' (*Letters*, pp. 377, 378).

Elliot to which Captain Wentworth has to listen when Anne
has left him and his companions behind her in the shop.[1]
Except in these two passages, Anne's point of view is
steadily maintained : we share her alternating moods of confidence and diffidence as to her power to read Wentworth's
manner and actions; with her, we sometimes overhear words
of his that seem to bear a meaning beyond that addressed
to the immediate listener;[2] or hear his friends' account of his
intentions, wondering how much it is worth. We share, too,
her gift for drawing people out, and so learn from Captain
Harville of a strain of tenderness in Frederick Wentworth
of which the Musgroves know nothing. Then these two
are separated again, and Anne must make what she can of
such news as comes her way, often unable to interpret it for
want of the clue for which she may not ask—her position
defined for us by her encounter with the Admiral, the teasing incompleteness of his news of Louisa's engagement to
Benwick, and her fruitless inquiries as to its effect on
Wentworth :

' "It did certainly seem, last autumn,' " she says, ' "as if there were an
attachment between him and Louisa Musgrove; but I hope it may be
understood to have worn out on each side equally, and without violence. I hope his letter does not breathe the spirit of an ill-used man."
    ' "Not at all, not at all; there is not an oath or a murmur from begin-
ning to end. . . . He very handsomely hopes they will be happy together, and there is nothing very unforgiving in that, I think."
    'Anne did not receive the perfect conviction which the Admiral meant
to convey, but it would have been useless to press the enquiry further.'[3]

Again she and Wentworth are together; but his manner
has become ambiguous. Now it seems that she wants but
opportunity to read it : 'If she could only have a few
minutes conversation with him again, she fancied she should
be satisfied.'[4] Now she is puzzled by its implications,
deliberate but seemingly inconsistent. And so this subterraneous pattern is kept fairly out of sight until the climax
when, by Wentworth's confession to Anne of that gradual
change in his feelings towards her which he has but now

[1] *Persuasion*, p. 177, ch. xix.
[2] Ibid., p. 88, ch. x.
[3] Ibid., pp. 172, 173, ch. xviii.   [4] Ibid., p. 180, ch. xix.

fully realized himself, it is united with the visible train of
events to make a single composition.

Why is it that the secondary pattern of subterraneous
progress and visible incident, that formed by the intrigue
of Mr. Elliot and Mrs. Clay, is so much less satisfactory?
Early enough in the story we are let into the secret of Anne's
suspicions: 'With a great deal of quiet observation, and a
knowledge, which she often wished less, of her father's
character, she was sensible that results the most serious to
his family from the intimacy, were more than possible.'[1] But
Lady Russell barely prevents us from forgetting the matter
until Sir Walter and Mrs. Clay are within sight again and
some languidly invented conversation can bring it once
more to our notice; and with no more than this, and some
instances of Mrs. Clay's intimacy with Elizabeth, to prepare
us, we are plunged into Mrs. Smith's news of the 'general
idea among Sir Walter's acquaintance, of her meaning to be
Lady Elliot',[2] on which our understanding of Mr. Elliot's
character is to depend. In support of this, Mrs. Clay has to
perform a tedious little act of duplicity before Anne's eyes;
and then she and her accomplice are left at a loose end until
the author *tidies them up* by informing us, in her own voice—
and in tones of that voice which remind me of the end of
Lady Susan—that Sir Walter would have been willing to
buy, at the price of a socially disgraceful marriage, flattery
which he had been getting for nothing, while Mr. Elliot
was prepared to pay for the removal of this danger by
the sacrifice of his carefully acquired respectability—and we
realize that we have never, in effect, had anything but her
word for the whole affair.

How has Jane Austen come to let us suppose that she has
forgotten, or neglected, to invent enough of those incidents
that should intimate it to us? It may fairly be argued that
Anne was not interested in it—but that obstacle could have
been circumvented either by heightening her concern, or by
the use of another consciousness besides hers as a means of
communication; either device being well within Jane Austen's
power. Surely the real explanation must be that, for a reason

---

[1] *Persuasion*, p. 34, ch. v.   [2] Ibid., p. 206, ch. xxi.

I have already suggested,[1] she was not interested in the intrigue herself.

The stream of those incidents which illustrate the other pattern in *Persuasion*, that in which her real interest lies, has never failed. This, however, is not its only virtue. The plot of *Tom Jones* (and of *Amelia*, too, although it is not so clear an illustration) had been of this double make, part visible, part to be guessed at: the revelation of the circumstances of Jones's birth—or, indeed, of Amelia's situation among persecuting suitors—had eventually allowed us to perceive the significance and interrelations of happenings which we had hitherto been able only to observe. There had been no dearth of inventive activity. Fielding indeed delights in the exacting demands which this kind of narration makes on him—demand for invention of illustrative incident as well as of invisible train of development. This is how he concludes a passage which has revealed the hidden causes of those parts of the action we have been allowed to see: 'These were several Matters, of which we thought necessary our Reader should be informed; for, besides that it conduces greatly to a perfect Understanding of all History, there is no Exercise of the Mind of a sensible Reader more pleasant than the tracing the several small and almost imperceptible Links in every Chain of Events by which all the great Actions of the World are produced.'[2] And again: 'We shall endeavour to satisfy an Enquiry which may arise in our most favourite Readers, (for so are the most curious) . . .'.[3] But even if he had set himself the task of concealing this activity of his it is hard to see how, given his method of narration, it could have been accomplished; how he would have made us forget that he is, at his own will and pleasure, alternately vouchsafing and withholding information. For that is indeed how he separates his invisible and his visible stories, bringing this and this fact to our view to serve as illustrative incident, keeping that and that fact from sight, as though in a game, and—as in a game—pretending to complain that we are slack adversaries: those readers who misinterpret one of his characters 'make a very bad and ungrateful

[1] p. 81.   [2] *Amelia*, bk. xii, ch. i.   [3] Ibid., bk. xii, ch. v.

Use of that Knowledge which we have communicated to them'.[1] Yet the incidents which illustrate the principal train of development in *Persuasion* never give the impression of having been arbitrarily selected by the narrator; rather the choice seems to have been imposed by a necessity which binds her equally with us, that very necessity which must result from the establishing of a fixed point of view; for by sharing Anne's position we are of course precluded from seeing more than those incomplete indications of the progress of events which are visible to her.

I have used this simple problem—the value of a constant point of view to a story in which there is a secret to be kept—as a means of winding into a more difficult one— the connexion between the point of view and the relationship of story-teller to reader; this way of approach promising to direct attention towards the importance of that relationship, which (I believe) lies at the core of narrative art.

It is a relationship with which Mr. Lubbock concerns himself; but by his urgent anxiety as to the story-teller's credentials (which can surely be but the sum of his powers of persuasion) he seems to divert attention from a simpler and, as it were, earlier condition of this relationship. The problem, as Henry James has taught readers of his critical prefaces to see it, can be indicated by this bald question: Here, the narrator may say, is the world in which the story happens; here is the world in which you live; and where am I? For he can never evaporate, never occupy the dramatist's position. Is he to take his stand beside the reader? Given certain conditions—for example, a past age as setting for his story—he can thus put himself at a distance from his subject, and yet, by the device of Chaucerian reference to *old books*, *authority*, *my author*, establish his right to interpret it to us, much as a man with field-glasses might report distant happenings. (Scott occupies this position every time he refers to oral tradition or to documentary witness; but he cannot keep still enough to let the illusion settle.) Failing these conditions, is he to take his stand in the world of the

---

[1] *Tom Jones*, bk. iii, ch. v.

story? Given the reader's acquiescence in certain conventions—the conventions proper to fictitious autobiography,
correspondence, journal—he may make good his right to
speak to us from this world. And indeed the necessary
concessions are easily made. 'How many improprieties,'
Lamb says, 'perfect solecisms in letter-writing, do we put
up with in "Clarissa" and other books [in the epistolary
form], for the sake of the delight which that form upon the
whole gives us.'[1] The delight springs from the illusion that
we are doing the business ourselves, *making* the story out
of the raw materials which compose it. The solecisms can
hardly diminish this delight unless the writer is tempted by
consciousness of them to practise such mystification as
must strain his relations with the reader while drawing
attention to what it is meant to hide.

'I have no objection but to the preface,' Johnson writes to Richardson when *Sir Charles Grandison* appears, 'in which you first mention
the letters as fallen by some chance into your hands, and afterwards
mention your health as such, that you almost despaired of going
through your plan. If you were to require my opinion which part
should be changed, I should be inclined to the suppression of that part
which seems to disclaim the composition. What is modesty, if it departs
from truth? Of what use is the disguise by which nothing is concealed?'[2]

The serious disadvantages which Mr. Lubbock finds in
the 'fixed position' of the narrator who, speaking in the
first person, addresses us *from* the world of the story are
such as must surely attach themselves to a fixed position in
either world: the limited range—'the reader . . . may be
said to watch a reflection of the facts in a mirror of which
the edge is nowhere in doubt'; the set interval of time,
'between the narrator and the events of which he speaks, . . .
across which the past must appear in a more or less distant
perspective'.[3] For him, the remedy is to be found in that
sort of subtle compromise which we associate with Henry
James's theory and practice—'That magnificent and masterly

---

[1] *On the Tragedies of Shakespeare.*
[2] *Letters*, ed. G. Birkbeck Hill, number 49 (letter of 26 September 1753).
[3] *The Craft of Fiction*, p. 257. In *Esmond*, Thackeray annihilates this time-interval
by a gentle oscillation between time remembered and time re-lived which suits his
meditative hero.

indirectness,' as James himself calls it, 'which means the *only* dramatic straightness and intensity'.[1] By this means, Mr. Lubbock says, the story-teller may enjoy the advantages of the established position (within the world of the story), while transcending its limitations.

'For now, while the point of view is still fixed in space, still assigned to the man in the book, it is free in *time.* . . . All the variety obtainable by a shifting relation to the story in time is thus in the author's hand; the safe serenity of a far retrospect, the promising or threatening urgency of the present, every gradation between the two, can be drawn into the whole effect of the book, and all of it without any change of the seeing eye. . . .'[2]

Moreover, by this means

'the author has the chance of using a much greater latitude than he need appear to use. The seeing eye is with somebody in the book, but its vision is reinforced; the picture contains more, becomes richer and fuller, because it is the author's as well as his creature's, both at once. Nobody notices, but in fact there are now two brains behind that eye; and one of them is the author's, who adopts and shares the *position* of his creature, and at the same time supplements his wit.'[3]

Thus, in sum, the story is 'passed through a fashioned and constituted mind'.[4]

Does this *go far enough back*? This preoccupation with the need for the story to seem to play itself out—without the author's seeming to intervene, yet with the benefits of that intervention—surely it concentrates attention on a point short of that at which the story-teller's powers are first and crucially tested?—overlooks, indeed, the singularity of his position? One thing he has to accomplish which the dramatist need not attempt: to obtain command of the most private possession that we have—the theatre of our imagination in which his action must be played out. For this no more than for the condition Mr. Lubbock diagnoses is there any sovereign prescription. To gain admission to a fastidious imagination, one worth entering, the narrator will have to draw upon every persuasive art that he has. His aim, however, will be single and clear: to engage his reader's

[1] *Letters*, ed. P. Lubbock (1920), i. 330 (letter of July 1899 to Mrs. Humphry Ward).
[2] *The Craft of Fiction*, pp. 257, 258.
[3] Ibid., p. 258.   [4] Ibid., p. 271.

imaginative co-operation. How is this active relationship—
between a deviser of entertainment for the theatre of the
imagination and the owner of any such theatre—to be
achieved?

The older novelist often directed his force towards the
readers' emotions, meaning to obtain of them sympathetic
response to the experience of his characters. This may have
a misleading appearance. If I were to ask of some one—an
unreflective person, but one willing to meet a question
squarely and take pains to answer it—what prompts sympathy in everyday human intercourse, he would probably
reply: 'Well, you must like the person you are to sympathize
with, I suppose'—and it is to be hoped that we should not
here entangle ourselves in the connexion between liking
and approbation—'or you must be sorry for him; perhaps
it makes a difference if you know a good deal about him'—
and then he would subside into silence, baffled by realization
of the mysterious character of those filaments which connect
human beings. Now, the older novelists compared with
their successors (and, I dare say, any English compared with
almost any French novelist) appear something like my
imaginary interlocutor: they systematically, and as it were
under our noses, catch hold of, and pull on, those threads
of sympathy which I have supposed him to be able to name;
it is only intuitively, and almost imperceptibly, that they
draw on those mysterious filaments which he might be able
to recognize but certainly could not describe.

Thus Richardson, in his methodical, business-like way,
sets about the task of obtaining one sort of sympathy for
Sir Charles Grandison: 'Mr. Richardson has been so good as
to call on us twice', Miss Talbot writes to Mrs. Carter in
December of 1750. 'Pray send me in mere hints your idea of
the good and agreeable man, whom everybody wants him
to draw, but he must resolutely refuse to fight a duel—how
then must he shew (without romantic adventures, or a red
coat which must not be neither) his fighting bravery?'[1]
(We are not the first generation to resent this procedure.

[2] *A Series of Letters between Mrs. Carter and Miss Talbot, 1741–1770*, ed. Montagu
Pennington, 1809, i. 370.

Lady Mary Wortley Montagu, after a stubborn resistance to another of Richardson's claims, has to own: 'I was such an old fool as to weep over Clarissa Harlowe, like any milkmaid of sixteen over the ballad of the Lady's Fall.'[1]) But is Richardson's endeavour so simple as, in his own eyes and his readers', it appears? When he tells Pamela's story, he deliberately winds in, as on a reel, our compassion for her, spending unprofitable pains to ensure that the line shall not be kinked by disapprobation. Yet all the while he draws, with intuitive dexterity, on a more tenuous but a tougher filament: on our sense of her spirit as a flame in danger of extinction. (It does not matter that his symbol for that spirit is an illiberal conceit of her chastity.) So that it may fairly be said that life threatened with extinction is here the imperious attraction to our sympathy. Nevertheless, sheer abundance of life may elsewhere command it—such abundance as banishes from our minds the very thought of extinction. These two are indeed complementary; no narrower term than *sympathy with life* (crude and insufficient as it is) serving to indicate what is common to the various effectual claims to be made upon our imaginative sympathy. Now, because the relation between these claims eludes definition, the proper end of imaginative participation in the hopes and fears, in every degree of concern, of fictitious characters is apt to be misconstrued. For the writer of bad fiction who commands sympathetic response cunningly aims at one or other of two sensitive spots in the reader: he stimulates and gratifies either his[2] desire to identify with himself a character who demands compassion, and so to indulge in self-pity; or his desire to identify an agreeable character with himself or with the mate whom his wishes and fancies offer him, and so to indulge in some kind of self-love. But it ought to be remembered that the difficulty of an undertaking may lie, not in its magnitude, but in the narrow margin it allows between success and failure—for example, in its dependence upon means which, according as

[1] *Letters*, ed. Lord Wharncliffe and W. Moy Thomas, 1861, ii. 232.
[2] Although in the following passage I use the masculine form of the pronoun for brevity, 'he or she' is to be understood throughout.

they are employed, will produce very good or very ill results; and I suppose that any evocation of an emotional response will have something of the double property of that curious herb in Friar Laurence's basket which

> being smelt, with that part cheers each part;
> Being tasted, slays all senses with the heart.

Certainly the novelist's draft upon imaginative sympathy, when it is presented in the name of affection or compassion, has this twofold possibility of outcome. The power generated may be used in an active, a creative, partnership between story-teller and reader; or it may dissipate itself in day-dreaming.

It is, of course, absurd that abuse should bring discredit upon use; and yet so little attention is paid to the distinction between them that we are at present confronted with the dreary play between the reader who 'doesn't understand art, but knows what he likes' and can only repeat numbly 'I want to read about pleasant people',[1] and the hard-boiled novelist who, supported by the critic of similar consistency, supposes that by refusing this one request he is escaping from sentimentality; a supposition which is not only erroneous but irrelevant; the issue being further obscured by an element of social as well as intellectual snobbery in the temper of those who fondly suppose themselves to be anti-sentimentalists: Lady Mary might have forgiven the success of the assault on her emotions if it had not made her feel like a milkmaid. Occasionally the critic goes farther and, offering to analyse the ordinary reader's request, explains that we only desire that of which we have little or no experience.[2] (Thus, if I admit to a preference for stories of civil people, the amateur psychologist is entitled to form the darkest conjectures as to the company I keep.)

Is Jane Austen's reaction to this problem so simple as it appears? Like other early novelists, she makes no secret of her concern as to the sympathy with her characters that may be drawn from the reader by the simplest means.

---

[1] He used, of course, to be supported by the critics: see, for example, Saintsbury's *Consideration of Thackeray*; but unfortunately they never gave their reasons.

[2] Q. D. Leavis, *Fiction and the Reading Public* (1932).

'She . . . took', her nephew says, 'a kind of parental interest in the beings whom she had created':[1] and she wished her readers to share her feelings towards them. References to them in her letters, and her manner of recording her friends' opinions of them, make this clear. 'I must confess that I think her as delightful a creature as ever appeared in print,' she says of her own Elizabeth Bennet, 'and how I shall be able to tolerate those who do not like *her* at least I do not know.'[2] That is her frankest expression of this feeling, but I think it may fairly be taken as representative. She evidently expects us to entertain for her heroines the semblance of those feelings that we experience in actual human inter-course. As to Emma's welcome, she was anxious—not without reason, for a snob and a busybody does not promise well. Therefore she takes particular pains to let us realize from the beginning how far Emma's situation is accountable for her folly: her father's idiosyncrasies confine her to the society of her inferiors—inferior especially in ability, though it is the inferiority in rank that she would notice—and force her besides to play up to his belief in her superiority; and in his presence she must direct the very current of the talk, if he is not to be made uncomfortable by the asperities of John Knightley or the exuberance of Frank Churchill. Thus her managing ways are first seen as the wrong side of her protective care for him. If this design had failed, if we were still unable or disinclined to sympathize with Emma, should we feel the sharp pangs of shame that strike through us when she is rude to Miss Bates?

Fanny Price has had to encounter as cold looks as any that their author expected for Emma. Even Bradley says: 'I pity, approve, respect, admire her, but I neither desire her company nor am greatly concerned about her destiny, and she makes me impatient at moments when I doubt if she was meant to.'[3] He knows, he complains, what is asked of him; but he cannot respond. But surely he mistook Jane Austen's intention here? For her other heroines she means

---

[1] *Memoir*, p. 157.
[2] *Letters*, p. 297. For her record of her friends' opinions, see *Life* and *Plan of a Novel and other Notes*, ed. R. W. Chapman.
[3] *Jane Austen*, p. 28.

us to feel as we feel for friends and lovers; but for Fanny as
for a creature less well furnished for offence and defence
than those with which it is compelled to live. Among the
Bertrams she is like a mortal among giants. That is why,
contrary to her author's general rule,[1] we are allowed first
to make her acquaintance when she is a child; why we are
more than once reminded of her childhood afterwards. 'We
used to jump about together many a time, did not we?'
William asks her, 'when the hand-organ was in the street?'[2]
It is tenderness as towards a child that is implied in
Jane Austen's use of a phrase exceptional with her—'my
Fanny'.

Sympathy compounded of liking and compassion in varying proportions evidently seemed to Jane Austen the most
natural incentive to imaginative interest in a character.
That is how her own Charlotte Heywood (no sentimentalist)
responds to the pitiable account of Clara Brereton, in Mr.
Parker's talk of Sanditon : 'The interest of his story increased
very much with the introduction of such a Character.
Charlotte listened with more than amusement now;—it was
solicitude & Enjoyment, as she heard her described to be
lovely, amiable, gentle, unassuming, conducting herself
uniformly with great good sense, & evidently gaining by
her innate worth on the affections of her Patroness.—
Beauty, Sweetness, Poverty & Dependance . . .',[3] these are
the claims upon imaginative sympathy which Charlotte
Heywood—'a very sober-minded young Lady, sufficiently
well-read in Novels to supply her Imagination with amusement, but not at all unreasonably influenced by them'[4]—
is ready to admit; and which, I believe, Jane Austen would
herself have acknowledged. She could hardly have recognized that inclination in herself towards what I have called
sympathy with life in its abundance—an inclination that
has been overlooked by the many readers who apprehend
only her sympathy with life that is in danger of extinction,
with Fanny Price's spirit or Anne Elliot's hope. Chaucer

[1] 'Till the heroine grows up', she tells Anna, 'the fun must be imperfect' (*Letters*,
p. 401).
[2] *Mansfield Park*, p. 250, ch. xxv.
[3] *Sanditon*, pp. 38, 39; *Minor Works*, p. 378.   [4] Ibid., p. 76; *Minor Works*, pp. 391,
392.

would have understood better than they do the gusto in Mrs. Norris's malice or Mr. Collins's folly.

Sympathy, then, of more kinds than are apparent, is Jane Austen's means to obtaining her reader's imaginative co-operation. But does she realize how easily it may overflow without the writer's leave into the channels which bad fiction has worn for it in the imaginations of too many readers?

The greatest of those novelists who draw freely and deliberately on our sympathies seem almost afraid to make any wholly sympathetic character without mixing a little absurdity among its amiable and even heroic qualities; Fielding, Scott, Dickens, Thackeray afford such obvious illustrations that it is needless to particularize, and Jane Austen is no exception. Even the most sedate of her heroines—that one who, having little of her own satiric gift, was 'almost too good' for her—is obliged to smile at herself sometimes; while her favourite among them can be deliciously absurd: Elizabeth Bennet, listening to Wickham's fine professions, 'honoured him for such feelings, and thought him handsomer than ever as he expressed them'.[1] But perhaps a minor character who is not of necessity involved in the comic pattern of the story may be a more persuasive example. William Price is as near to a romantic hero as any person in her novels, and the romantic feeling that his author is supposed to want glows in his relationship with Fanny; and yet there is the breath and spirit of comedy in this very relationship—in her emotions on seeing him in his new uniform, in his castle-building on her behalf, his

'schemes for an action with some superior force, which (supposing the first lieutenant out of the way—and William was not very merciful to the first lieutenant) was to give himself the next step as soon as possible, or speculations upon prize money, which was to be generously distributed at home, with only the reservation of enough to make the little cottage comfortable, in which he and Fanny were to pass all their middle and latter life together.'[2]

But this is like an instinctive movement to trim the boat;

[1] *Pride and Prejudice*, p. 80, ch. xvi.
[2] *Mansfield Park*, p. 375, ch. xxxviii.

and of course it is not really needed. For Jane Austen, indeed, as for her fellow novelists, the true preservative against the risk of imaginative sympathy abused must always be the very *substance* of the characters in the story. Hazlitt suggests the clue in an essay, 'Why the Heroes of Romance are Insipid': he opens with the conceit that, since they are to be represented as irresistible, the prudent writer will not risk making his readers familiar with them; why not let them 'rely on their names and the author's good word'?[1]

'Mrs. Radcliffe's heroes and lovers are perfect in their kind; nobody can find any fault with them, for nobody knows any thing about them. . . . Theodore, Valancourt,—what delightful names! and there is nothing else to distinguish them by. Perhaps, however, this indefiniteness is an advantage. We add expression to the inanimate outline, and fill up the blank with all that is amiable, interesting, and romantic.'[2]

Jane Austen's own satire had glanced lightly off this foible, in *Northanger Abbey*: Eleanor Tilney's husband was 'to a precision the most charming young man in the world. Any further definition of his merits must be unnecessary; the most charming young man in the world is instantly before the imagination of us all.'[3]

It is this nebulous, this *spongy* substance of the characters of second-rate fiction that gives licence for abuse, and the firmness of substance of the characters of great fiction that denies it.[4] By what perverse and stubborn ingenuity could any reader identify himself with a being of such 'solidity of specification' (to use Henry James's phrase[5]) as a truly made fictitious character? And yet, who has not, at some time, felt the impulse towards willing absorption, into some Valancourt or his Emily? Jane Austen at least knew what

[1] *Works*, ed. P. P. Howe, xvii. 246 (from the *New Monthly Magazine*, November 1827).
[2] Ibid., p. 251.
[3] *Northanger Abbey*, p. 251, ch. xxxi.
[4] This discrimination between good and bad fiction must seem harsh and un-gracious, and yet I cannot convince myself that it is unnecessary; for it is this two-fold capacity of the novel that has kept all fiction so long in disrepute, and must continue to confuse criticism until it is distinguished. A further valuable distinction might be that between romance and novel.
[5] *The Art of Fiction*, p. 390.

it was like—and the awakening from the day-dream. 'Dearest Miss Morland, what ideas have you been admitting?'

The great novelists have, of course, each his own variety of means to the achievement of this firmness of substance in his work; and, the sounder that work, the less opportunity will it give to the critic for studying any one of these means in isolation, and the more unprofitable will the use of such terms as plot, characterization, setting, and the rest (sometimes thoughtlessly borrowed from dramatic criticism) seem to him. What he has to analyse will hardly suffer definition by a narrower term than the novelist's art.

I have tried to show of what elements Jane Austen's own art is composed: a close and genial relationship with the familiar, daylight world, a Johnsonian belief in the value of 'those parallel Circumstances, and kindred Images to which we readily conform our Minds',[1] and a scrupulous fidelity to the evidence at her disposal; mastery, moreover, of her chosen methods of representation, wise use of all the resources she can command, of her own powers and her reader's capacity for response.

It may be worth adding that there is another sort of sympathy, besides this sympathy with the creatures of his imagination, on which the story-teller can draw—on which, indeed, the English novelist is apt to draw very freely—in order to persuade the reader to enter into partnership: I mean, sympathy with himself as creator. The critic acknowledges its outcome in terms of intellectual co-operation. From the moment that the novelist's subject is announced, Mr. Lubbock says,

'his privilege is shared. . . . From point to point we follow the writer, always looking back to the subject itself in order to understand the logic of the course he pursues. We find that we are creating a design . . . or again there is a flaw and a break in the development . . . and the critical question, strictly so called, begins. Is this proceeding of the author the right one, the best for the subject? Is it possible to conceive and to name a better? The hours of the author's labour are lived again by the reader, the pleasure of creation is renewed.'[2]

This is the sympathy of a fellow craftsman; and, as Henry James says, it has its drawbacks:

'I'm a wretched person to *read* a novel—I begin so quickly and con-

---

[1] *Rambler*, 60.   [2] *The Craft of Fiction*, pp. 23, 24.

comitantly, *for myself*, to write it rather—even before I know clearly
what it's about! The novel I can *only* read, I can't read at all !'[1]

Besides, it is not to his fellows but to the Common Reader
that the novelist must first address himself. And the faculty
which, in the Common Reader, responds to this very invitation is that faculty by virtue of which *he* is akin to the
story-teller—the *story-making* power of his imagination. This
it is to which Fielding appeals in his passages of direct
intercourse with the reader—so establishing a tradition in
English fiction which puzzled and offended Henry James
and is condemned out of hand by most modern critics. But
I think that it is not the practice itself—rather, some error
in the use of it—which has brought it into discredit. The
invitation may be given in a way which allows us to become
too sharply aware of the personal element in this relationship with the writer. This is what numbs response even to
Fielding's persuasive introduction of Sophia—to Scott's,
and Thackeray's, and Trollope's friendly invitation. For
although we are probably most of us better fitted by habits
of thought and feeling for sympathy with a person than for
that sympathy with a 'fashioned and constituted mind'
which Mr. Lubbock recommends, yet the stronger the
impression of this personal presence the less chance there
can be of the action seeming to *play itself out* in that theatre
of the imagination which personal sympathy has helped to
persuade us to open.

What distinguishes Jane Austen's manner of inviting us
to share in the act of creation but a greater delicacy of
intimation? Her invitation is not conveyed directly at any
given moment—when it might be summarily refused. It is
implicit in all her dealings with us, in what Raleigh called
'a certain subtle literary politeness that is charm itself',[2] above
all in her mood of hospitality. 'The truth is,' Katherine
Mansfield writes, 'that every true admirer of the novels
cherishes the happy thought that he alone—reading between
the lines—has become the secret friend of their author.'[3]

---

[1] *Letters*, ed. P. Lubbock, i. 334 (letter of 26 July 1899 to Mrs. Humphry Ward).
[2] *The English Novel* (1894), p. 264.
[3] *Novels and Novelists*, p. 302.

How has it come about that we feel so towards this most reserved of writers? That very reticence may suggest a partial explanation: '. . . the personality of the author,' Henry James says, '. . . however enchanting, is a thing for the reader only, and not for the author himself . . . to count in at all.'[1]

[1] *Letters*, ed. P. Lubbock, p. 335 (letter of 26 July 1899 to Mrs. Humphry Ward).

INDEX